A Cowboy of the Pecos

Patrick Dearen

LONE
STAR
BOOKS

Guilford, Connecticut
Helena, Montana

LONE
STAR
BOOKS

An imprint of Globe Pequot

Distributed by NATIONAL BOOK NETWORK

Copyright © 2017 by Patrick Dearen

Map: Alena Joy Pearce © Rowman & Littlefield

British Library Cataloguing-in-Publication Information available

Library of Congress Cataloging-in-Publication Data

ISBN 978-1-4930-2416-2 (paperback)
ISBN 978-1-4930-2417-9 (e-book)

∞™ The paper used in this publication meets the minimum requirements of American National Standard for Information Sciences—Permanence of Paper for Printed Library Materials, ANSI/NISO Z39.48-1992.

CONTENTS

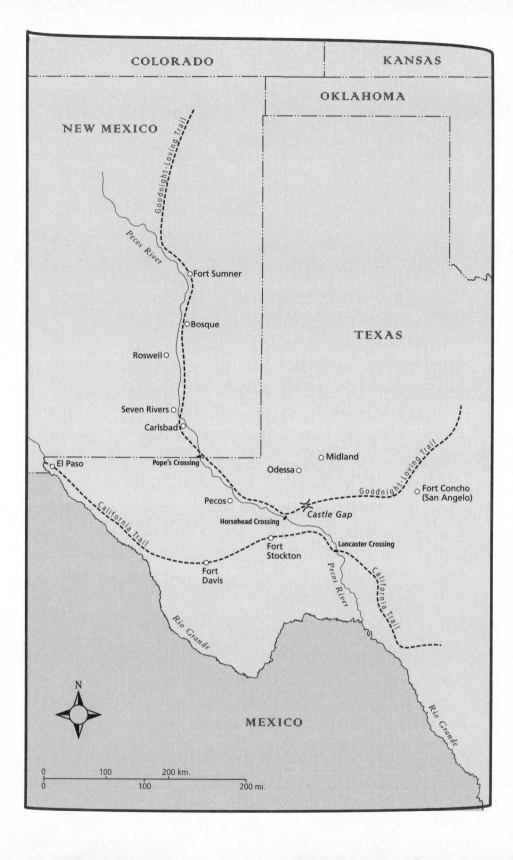

If in the old days a man said of another, "He is a cowboy of the Pecos," that might mean many things.
J. FRANK DOBIE, *A VAQUERO OF THE BRUSH COUNTRY*

CHAPTER ONE

The Cowboy's Paradise

HE RODE HELL-BENT-FOR-LEATHER ALONG A SOUTHWEST RIVER LIK-
ened to hell and entered the myth of the West.

He was a cowboy of the Pecos.

With skills tailored to the river's unique demands and with character honed by a no-man's-land in which "pecos" also meant *murder*[1] and
"pecos swap," *theft*,[2] he was a breed of cowhand unlike any other. F. S.
Millard, a Pecos cowboy of the 1880s, recalled one cowhand reckoning
that "the Pecos boys were the most expert cowboys in the world" and
another one adding, "Yes, with the *ex* left off."[3]

They were indeed maybe the "best damned cowboy[s]"[4] who ever sat
a horse, men who rode wild broncs by day and even wilder ones over a
plate of beans by night. But no Pecos hand ever had need to brag of his
skill in working cattle; either he rode out into a midnight storm mutter-
ing, "If I couldn't hold this damned herd alone, may I go to hell,"[5] or he
rolled up his bedroll and went home to mama.

It was a confidence that many would carry into the sunsets of their
lives.

"If we could turn back fifty years now [from the 1950s]," reflected
septuagenarian Julius D. Henderson, a Pecos hand of the late 1890s, "we
could show those drugstore cowboys how it was done."[6]

They lived like coyotes, said the old-timers, out of a chuck wagon or
a cow camp and never "made a kick,"[7] unless someone cut them out a
string of "dogs" to ride—that is, sorry old beaten-out horses. And "quittin'
time" wasn't determined by a pocket watch or the rise or fall of the sun;

Julius D. Henderson circa the late 1960s. COURTESY OF
ODESSA AMERICAN, AND PERMIAN HISTORICAL ARCHIVES, UNIVERSITY
OF TEXAS OF THE PERMIAN BASIN, ODESSA, TEXAS

they worked, as one old-time hand put it, from *you can till you can't*.[8] "All anybody asks of a man in the Pecos is a good day's work and to keep his privacy," wrote a young cowhand with a Texas cattle outfit at Pope's Crossing in 1867.[9]

All in all, it was "one devil of a life out there—hard but good," observed L. B. "Bill" Eddins, who cowboyed on the Pecos in the 1910s and 1920s.[10]

The Pecos seemed uniquely suited to nurturing the lifestyle of a cowboy, a fact not lost on newspapers of the nineteenth century. The *San Angelo* (Texas) *Standard,* in the fall of 1886, even went so far as to proclaim the valley of the Pecos "the cowboy's paradise."[11] Nevertheless, no cowhand ever smiled when he pulled rein at the river's bank.

"The Pecos—the graveyard of the cowman's hopes . . . I hated it!" lamented Charles Goodnight, who first drove cattle along its bank in 1866.[12]

It was a river cursed with a vengeance by all, and few cowhands would have disputed the buffalo hunters' claim that, "when a bad man dies, he goes either to hell or the Pecos."[13]

Its headwaters, 11,750 feet high in the Sangre de Cristo range in northern New Mexico, would have looked more like Heaven to a Texas cowboy, however. Cradled by pristine peaks rising 13,000 feet, the singing stream cascades down through columbine-spangled meadows and alpine-green forests before emptying into the lowlands and setting a course to the southeast. Striking Texas as the lone river in an arid empire three hundred miles wide, it slithers on through forbidding desert flats, carves a mighty rockwalled canyon, and intersects the Rio Grande and Mexican border near Langtry, Texas, 926 river miles from the Sangre de Cristos.[14]

Along much of its Texas stretch today, the Pecos is only a polluted trickle, squeezing through a jungle of salt cedars that choke banks sloughed and neglected. The modern motorist crossing it by bridge is more likely to greet it with a yawn than with visceral emotion. But were he to read the history buried deep in its banks, he would find the sweat and blood of cowhands who knew this ghost as the most formidable and treacherous river in the West.

3

The sharp bank of the Pecos in 1890, as captured by a pinhole camera, likely. COURTESY OF SOUTHEASTERN NEW MEXICO HISTORICAL SOCIETY, CARLSBAD, NEW MEXICO

"Just two things that cowboys were afraid of—the Pecos River and rattlesnakes," wrote James Hinkle, a Pecos cowboy of the 1880s.[15]

Generally four to fifteen feet deep[16] and forty to sixty feet wide in the flats,[17] it flowed without a murmur but swift as a war horse between treeless banks as perpendicular as the walls of an edifice. "An animal may wander along the banks half a day," said one traveler, "without finding a point where he may drink."[18] In fact, in the hundreds of miles between the New Mexico line and the Rio Grande, a cowboy could cross the Pecos only at a handful of sites—primarily, Pope's Crossing, one crow-flight mile south of New Mexico; Emigrant Crossing, fifty-nine miles on downstream; Horsehead Crossing, Spanish Dam Crossing, and Pontoon Bridge in the mid-Texas stretch; and Lancaster Crossing, sixty-five miles above the river's mouth.[19]

Cattle watering in the Pecos before salt cedar infestation, circa 1890. COURTESY OF SOUTHEASTERN NEW MEXICO HISTORICAL SOCIETY, CARLSBAD, NEW MEXICO

Seldom less than half-bank full, the Pecos was so turbid with red sediment that, said one cowboy, a bucket of its water would yield an inch of sand[20]—a condition which led to the formation of quicksand below the unscalable walls. So tenacious was this mire, went one yarn, that whenever a forty-niner crossed a wagon and bogged an ox, efforts to pull it out succeeded only in putting another bend in the river.[21]

Judging by the "unmatchable sinuosity"[22] of this waterway, cursed by one cowpuncher as the "crookedest river in the world,"[23] more oxen must have succumbed to the Pecos sands than ever reached the California gold fields. Consider the experience of cowhand F. S. Millard: "We used to go in a-swimming. We would jump in the river [depositing their garments at that point], go about half a mile downstream, and come out at our clothes."[24]

Cattle drover Pete Narbo found the river's horseshoe bends less obliging. Sighting a stray steer across the river and shooting it for meat, he swam his horse to the far bank only to find the carcass still across-river; he and the steer had been on the same side.[25]

Absent of a telltale valley except in its lower reaches, and without bordering vegetation in frontier times except for rushes below its banks,[26] the river might drop at the breast of a cold-jawing horse before its rider even realized a stream was near. Presenting an appearance far removed from the traditional concept of a waterway, the Pecos was as likely to be thought of in terms of a canal as it was a river.[27]

Frequently, however, even the barrier walls couldn't contain its currents, which unexpectedly would flee across the flats until a mile-wide lake glistened in the desert. Often salty and laden with impurities, the waters would recede to leave overflow ponds which not only served as breeding grounds for mosquitoes,[28] but held concentrations of brine and alkali deadly to stock.

Nor was the vegetation which covered the flood plain less forgiving. Drawing sustenance from the alkaline ground, plants such as goldenrod invited cattle and horses to graze, only to take a toll in carcasses or "alkalied" animals.

Snaking under a relentless sun through a barren land with "the curse of thirst upon it," as U.S. Army Captain W. H. C. Whiting observed in 1849,[29] the Pecos was, first and foremost, a study in nature's sovereignty. "I lost my brand new hat . . . when trying to cross the river just last week when brim full and the wind blowing every which way," a cowhand wrote home from Pope's Crossing in 1867. "You just can't believe how the wind blows out here. It has so much room to get started in."[30]

Nevertheless, cattlemen seeking open range for their herds saw promise in the Pecos and the "luxuriant growth of nutritious grasses" beyond its flood plain.[31] "The hills and plains east and west of it," noted a correspondent of the San Antonio Daily Express in 1877, "furnish a stock range almost unlimited in extent and of the best quality for cattle, horses, sheep, and goats."[32]

But even as cattle found sustenance, the scrub mesquite, catclaw, lechuguilla, and cacti proved inhospitable to any cowhand not astride a horse. "Every thing that grows," lamented *The* (Clarksville, Texas) *Standard* of July 20, 1861, "has a thorn on the end of the leaves, or spears of grass so sharp they will stick you."[33]

This then was the river and land known as the Pecos, which loomed a vast wilderness known only to Indians afoot from 9000 B.C. until the coming of the Spaniards in the sixteenth century. In 1583 Spaniard Antonio de Espejo, bearing downstream from Cicuye pueblo near its headwaters, planted the first seeds of cowboying on the river. Reaching present Texas, members of the Espejo expedition traveled the riverbank by mule and horse, the first saddle stock ever introduced to this region where, as in the rest of the New World, the horse was not indigenous.[34]

Were it not for that animal, there could never have been a cowboy. "A cowboy without a horse," observed Billy Rankin, a Pecos cowhand of the 1920s, "is just like a one-legged man at a butt-kicking."[35]

When future New Mexico governor Don Juan de Oñate imported 7,000 horses to the Southwest in 1598, native Indians quickly absorbed the animal into their cultures. By the latter 1600s, the Apaches and Comanches were horse peoples, and by the middle of the eighteenth century, the Comanches had seized the Southern Plains, established rancherias on the Arkansas and Red Rivers, and marked the Pecos as the southwestern boundary of Comancheria. For the next 125 years, while Mescalero Apaches raided from western strongholds in the Guadalupe and Sacramento Mountains, Comanches pushed down by fall to cross at Horsehead Crossing and plunder deep into Mexico.[36]

No cowboy of the Pecos ever envied the free haircuts meted out by these warriors, whom he hated and feared even while sometimes respecting their courage. "I have often heard it said that Indians were sneaking cowards and would not fight," said cattle drover G. F. Banowsky, survivor of two Indian battles on the Pecos in the 1870s. "In my dealings with them, I found it the other way about. I never knew them to decline a battle in the open with the white man, when they had anything like as good guns; nor do I believe that anybody else ever did [know them to decline]."[37]

Even as Spain's rule over the Pecos ended in 1821, and on through fifteen years under the flag of Mexico and a near decade of Republic of

Texas dominion that ended when Texas joined the United States,[38] the Pecos largely was shunned by white men, who settled no closer than hundreds of miles to the east. Then came a gold strike near Sutter's Mill, California, in January 1848, stirring the imaginations of men and women throughout the nation.[39]

Soon, the Pecos witnessed the approach of not only emigrants, but their herds of work oxen, beeves, and breeding stock. A caravan setting out from Fredericksburg, Texas, in early 1849, for example, had "numerous herds of cattle," reported a Houston newspaper of the day.[40] And riding in the dust raised by the hooves were "herdsmen"—the first cowboys of the Pecos—pointing the way into myth and history for all the cowhands who would follow.

NOTES

Unless otherwise indicated, all towns, counties, and map quadrangles throughout notes are in Texas.

1. Paul Patterson, videotaped interview with author, Crane, 29 April 1991; and J. Frank Dobie, *A Vaquero of the Brush Country* (New York: Grosset and Dunlap Publishers, reprint, n.d.), 274.
2. Ramon F. Adams, *Western Words: A Dictionary of the American West* (Norman: University of Oklahoma Press, rev. edition, 1968), 223.
3. F. S. Millard, *A Cowpuncher of the Pecos* (J. Marvin Hunter, n.d.), 36. Throughout the text, I have edited Millard's comments for spelling and punctuation.
4. From an old song, as quoted by 1880s cowhand Ed Burnett, manuscript statement, J. Evetts Haley Collection (hereinafter, Haley Collection), Nita Stewart Haley Memorial Library (hereinafter, Haley Library), Midland.
5. Burnett, manuscript statement.
6. Julius Drew Henderson, "The Life of an Oldtimer," manuscript, Special Collections, Library, University of Texas of the Permian Basin, Odessa, book four, 9. In this manuscript, divided into "books," book one is preceded by a numbered section which hereinafter I will refer to as the prologue.
7. A cowhand's way of saying "complained."
8. Will Durham, taped interview with author, Sterling County, 25 February 1989. Durham began cowboying as a mere boy before the turn of the twentieth century.
9. Jake to Dear Ones, letter dated April 1867 and evidently published in its entirety in: Marj Carpenter, "Letter from 1867 Reveals Early Pecos River Deeds," *The Pecos Independent and Enterprise*, 17 May 1962.
10. L. B. "Bill" Eddins, taped interview with author, Kermit, 5 September 1989.
11. R. W. Landrum, "A Trip to the Pacific Coast," letter to editor dated 4 October 1886, *San Angelo Standard*, 16 October 1886, 1, col. 6.

12. J. Evetts Haley (hereinafter, Haley), *Charles Goodnight: Cowman and Plainsman* (Norman: University of Oklahoma Press, 10th Printing, 1987), 134.

13. Dobie, *Vaquero*, 274.

14. The river's length, presumably including all bends, is from Delmar Hayter, "The Crookedest River in the World: A Social and Economic Development of the Pecos River Valley from 1878 to 1950," (dissertation, 1988), 11, Southwest Collection, Texas Tech University, Lubbock, Texas.

15. James F. Hinkle, *Early Days of a Cowboy on the Pecos* (Santa Fe: Stagecoach Press, reprint, 1965), 44. Hinkle punched cattle on the Pecos in southern New Mexico.

16. "Journal of scout of detachment, Company M, 9th Cavalry, commanded by Second Lieutenant Thomas Davenport, 9th Cavalry; from Fort Stockton, Texas to Pecos Falls ... pursuant to special order ... dated March 16, 1874," journal of marches, scouts, and expeditions, Fort Stockton, microfilm, Fort Stockton Public Library, Fort Stockton (hereinafter, Fort Stockton); Captain George Gamble, Ninth Cavalry, to Lieutenant J. S. Loud, post adjutant, Fort Stockton, 4 October 1867, letters received, Fort Stockton; and *San Antonio Daily Express*, 25 May 1877.

17. Extracts from a letter of Major C. M. Tunnel, paymaster, Fort Concho, 21 October 1869, in E. D. Judd, paymaster's office, Fifth Military District, to Brevet Colonel H. Clay Wood, assistant adjutant (hereinafter, AA) general, 11 November 1869, letters and telegrams received, Fort Stockton; and *San Antonio Daily Express*, 25 May 1877.

18. Colonel Nathaniel Alston Taylor, *The Coming Empire or Two Thousand Miles in Texas on Horseback* (Dallas: Turner Company, reprint, 1936, originally published 1877), 296, 301.

19. I have given these distances in air miles, but elsewhere I have sometimes elected to give distance in trail miles. Neither accurately reflects river miles. For a study of these crossings, see Patrick Dearen, *Crossing Rio Pecos* (Fort Worth: Texas Christian University Press, 1996), 1–122.

20. Millard, *Cowpuncher*, 36.

21. Bill Oden, "Cowboy Standards of 50 Years Ago," manuscript, Haley Library, Midland. Oden cowboyed on the Pecos in the 1880s.

22. Taylor, *Coming Empire*, 300.

23. Millard, *Cowpuncher*, 36.

24. Ibid.

25. Charles Goodnight, interview with Haley, Clarendon, 12 September 1928, Haley Library, Midland.

26. John Russell Bartlett, *Personal Narrative of Explorations and Incidents in Texas, New Mexico, California, Sonora and Chihuahua, 1850–1853*, Vol. 1 (Chicago: The Rio Grande Press, Inc., 1965, originally published in 1854), 93.

27. Davenport, journal of scout, pursuant to special order dated 16 March 1874, journal of marches, scouts, and expeditions, Fort Stockton.

28. Ruth Shackleford diary as contained in Kenneth L. Holmes, ed., *Covered Wagon Women: Diaries and Letters from the Western Trails 1840–1890*, Vol. 9, 1864–1868 (Spokane: Arthur H. Clark Company, 1990), 191.

29. Journal of William H. C. Whiting in Ralph P. Bieber, ed., *Exploring Southwestern Trails 1846–1854* (Glendale: Arthur H. Clark Company, 1938), 259.

30. Carpenter, "Letter from 1867."

31. "Tom Green County, Its Rivers and Springs, Its Soil and Timber, Graphically Described by an Actual Settler," *San Angelo Standard*, 4 October 1884.

32. H. C. K., *San Antonio Dairy Express*, 25 May 1877, Clayton Wheat Williams Collection, Haley Library, Midland.

33. *The Standard* (Clarksville), 20 July 1861, transcript, Haley Collection, Haley Library, Midland.

34. Narrative of Espejo in Herbert Eugene Bolton, *Spanish Exploration in the Southwest* (New York: Barnes and Noble, Inc., reprint, 1952), 189–190. Cicuye was near present Pecos, New Mexico.

35. Billy Rankin, taped interview with author, Rankin, 9 August 1989.

36. W. W. Newcomb Jr., *The Indians of Texas* (Austin: University of Texas Press, 1961; reprint 1969), 86–88, 107–109, 114, 156–157, 161 (map), 233; Ernest Wallace and E. Adamson Hoebel, *The Comanches: Lords of the South Plains* (Norman: University of Oklahoma Press, 1986), 12, 38, 39, 288, 289; and O. W. Williams, *Pioneer Surveyor-Frontier Lawyer: The Personal Narrative of O. W. Williams, 1877–1902*, ed. by S.D. Myres (El Paso: Texas Western College Press, 1966), 278.

37. W S. Adair, "Texas Pioneer Tells of Fights with Indians," *Dallas Morning News*, 8 June 1930.

38. "A History of Texas," *Texas Almanac 1970–71* (A. H. Belo Corporation, 1969), 79, 83, 87.

39. Mabelle Eppard Martin, "California Emigrant Roads through Texas," *The Southwestern Historical Quarterly* (hereinafter SHQ) 28, No.4 (April 1925), 287, 290–291.

40. *Telegraph* (Houston), 8 March 1849, as quoted in Haley, ed., "A Log of the Texas-California Cattle Trail, 1854," SHQ 35, No. 3 (January 1932), 209.

CHAPTER TWO

The California Cattle Trail

THE CATTLE HERDS OF THE FORTY-NINERS MARKED THREE TRAILS TO the Pecos with their bleaching bones: the Upper Road, which struck out from Central Texas, crossed at Horsehead Crossing,[1] and turned upstream to veer west near the New Mexico line; the Emigrant Road, which bore southwest from North Texas to cross at Emigrant Crossing[2] and merge with the Upper Road; and the Lower Road, which extended west from San Antonio and crossed at Lancaster Crossing.[3]

The Lower Road provided passage through Comancheria from the cattle country of South Texas, a fact which destined it alone to be remembered as the California Cattle Trail. Even as wagon train herds trailed west along the other routes, "cow-hunters," as early roundup hands were known, scoured the South Texas brush for longhorns to point down its ruts. Cattle were plentiful in Texas—many of its 1,430,174 head[4] ran free and unbranded—and in a region without railroads, markets were rare. Where gold glittered on the horizon, there had to be miners anxious for beef. And even though their California camps lay 1,500 miles distant, the hardy longhorn could carry itself every step of the way.

"As trail cattle their equal has never been known and never will be," cowman Charles Goodnight observed. "Their hoofs are superior to those of any other cattle. . . . No animal of the cow kind will . . . take care of itself under all conditions as will the longhorns. They can go farther without water and endure more suffering than others."[5]

On the California Trail, the longhorn would need those attributes and more. From end to end, wrote range historian J. Evetts Haley, it was a trail of "dangers and uncertainties—long dry drives that set cattle mad with thirst and drew saddle horses to 'skin and bones'; alkaline lakes that poisoned and killed thirsting herds; *malpais* ridges that cut hoofs to the quick and set the riders afoot; and the eternal threat of loss to white and Indian thieves."[6]

Blazed as far as El Paso by Captain W. H. C. Whiting in 1849,[7] the trail bore west from San Antonio, skirted the site of present Del Rio, and turned north up the Devils River, which coursed through a rugged desert fit for no one but its namesake. From the river's head, the trail veered northwest to a vital water source—Howard's Well or Springs—and on over an arid plateau that suddenly dropped five hundred feet into the valley of the Pecos. Four miles past the site of later Fort Lancaster, the trail struck the Pecos at Lancaster Crossing, adjacent to modern Sheffield. Turning upriver between castellated bluffs and passing Pecos Spring, it traced the riverbank for thirty-five miles before leaving the Pecos approximately four and one-half miles west of the present Highway 349 bridge. By the time a longhorn reached El Paso, it already had survived 673 miles of hell since leaving San Antonio.[8]

Few points along that route were more treacherous than Lancaster Crossing. James G. Bell, who accompanied the John James herd west in 1854, described it as "turbulent and rapid," with banks "high and dangerous for cattle; depth from 5 to 10 feet."[9]

The Pecos, no matter the location or era, always proved challenging anytime cowhands turned cattle into its waters. A major concern was ensuring that a herd entered the river exactly where a ford's sloping banks allowed access and egress. "You can have all kinds of hell," noted Billy Rankin, who crossed herds in the late 1920s and early 1930s. "If you've got very many head, you need somebody on the [downstream] side . . . to keep them fought back. . . . You get below it and that's just steep bank."[10]

Rankin, who leased a forty-one-section ranch near Horsehead Crossing in 1928, had firsthand knowledge of just how unmanageable the banks were for an animal drifting downstream in the water. "The river wasn't fenced, and stray mares would get over on me," he related. "I've jumped them off in the river to [force] them back across. I've had them

Olin Smith at Lancaster Crossing in 1993. COURTESY OF THE AUTHOR

go half a mile down there before they'd all get out, 'cause the current throws you against the high wall of the crooked river."[11]

Even if cowboys succeeded in turning a herd straight into a crossing, the animals didn't always take to water.

"You have to swim 'em," said Bill Eddins, who frequently crossed herds not far below the New Mexico line in the 1910s and 1920s. "You'd take a few head to start with, cut them off and get them down [to the water].... Put good men down there to herd them across and hold them on the other side right down next to the water. Then bring *another* bunch in, and they'll see those across the river and they'll go to 'em."[12]

Cowboys employed other methods, as well, to lure cattle into the river. Rankin considered it a good practice to have "one man lead an extra saddle horse as a scout for the cattle to follow."[13] Young Bell trained a steer for just such a task in the early 1900s, and used the animal repeatedly in crossing white-face cattle above the city of Pecos.[14]

Frequently, however, trail herds were so crazed with thirst by the time they neared the Pecos that they needed little encouragement.

"We'd always find a place where it was sloping down to the river, an old wagon road, and usually these old cows or steers . . . would run into it, dry for water," recalled Hudson "Bud" Mayes, who crossed herds on two regional drives in the 1920s. "We'd just keep a-pushing them on and they'd just keep a-going, trying to get a drink, across the river."[15]

Not only was crossing the Pecos challenging, but it was life-threatening. Saddle horses, for example, sometimes were prone to turn on their sides and float downstream rather than swim across—a serious matter considering the river's barrier walls.[16] Even on the best horse, a good cowboy knew to slip his boots free of the stirrups, pull them up behind the saddle, and give the animal its head.[17] Even then, a skittish horse might panic and drown its rider.

Nathaniel A. Taylor, at Horsehead Crossing in 1876, came close to just such a catastrophe. "I took my horse to the river, spurring him gently," he wrote. "He smelt the water, trembled and snorted. He reared back to the right and left several times . . . but at last . . . he stuck out his left fore foot into the water, cautiously, as if feeling for bottom. But not finding any, he lost his balance and tumbled headlong into the current. We sank under the surface, and for a moment everything

Cowhand J. Evetts Haley and mount in the Pecos in the early 1920s. COURTESY OF J. EVETTS HALEY COLLECTION, N. S. HALEY MEMORIAL LIBRARY, MIDLAND, TEXAS

was confusion. I believed we rolled over. . . . [I] clasped my heels about the horse with all my strength. . . . He rose into daylight, and struck out splendidly to the opposite shore, describing a great curve before he reached the landing. He bounded to the high land, and at once shook his skin."[18]

Even an experienced Pecos cowboy sometimes resorted to desperate measures in swimming his horse.

"They'd get to splashing and flopping around sometimes," remembered cowhand Jim Witt, who frequently crossed at Emigrant Crossing on horseback in the 1920s. "It was something new to them, and they'd want to turn back. If you got in trouble swimming your horse, you'd just slide off of him, go off over him backwards, and grab his tail. And he'd go on and pull you out."[19]

Not only did the Pecos present problems in crossing, but merely in *watering* cattle or saddle stock. "In the course of 240 miles, its [Texas] length," noted the October 4, 1884, *San Angelo Standard*, "there are but few places where an animal can approach . . . [the waters] in safety."[20] Even if travelers went to the trouble of cutting away the banks, they succeeded only in opening a quagmire for unwary hooves. It was a dilemma which sometimes forced U.S. Army contingents, such as that of Lieutenant Francis T. Bryan in 1849, to water their mules and horses by means of buckets and camp kettles.[21]

Such an undertaking would have been impossible with a cattle herd, so drovers had to heed the advice of James Campbell, who first drove the California Trail in 1853. "Look out," he wrote of the Pecos, "for best places to water."[22]

Drovers seeking watering places—not only on the California Trail's river frontage, but on later routes upstream—learned to pay careful attention to the bends. "The Pecos was mean to water at . . . ," noted W. H. Boyd, who trailed a herd up the Pecos to Fort Sumner, New Mexico, in 1867. "But on the lower side of the bends of the river, the banks were often sloping and we could get down to the water."[23]

Still, there was a technique to watering a herd, as nine-year-old Jim Lane Cook learned when he accompanied his father on a drive up the Pecos to New Mexico in 1867.

"Our cowboys . . . turned the steers' heads up the river," he related, "as, in all cases when you throw a herd of cattle on the water, if it is a running creek or river, cattle cannot drink good going downstream."[24]

Sometimes, however, thirsty cattle were unmanageable, especially as they neared a Pecos crossing after negotiating days of arid hell. Even if they didn't plunge over the sheer bank upriver or downriver of a ford, the lead animals might forge into the waters and be forced on across by those behind before they could drink. Turning, they might swim back to midstream, each animal again pushed by the one at its hindquarter, only to meet more splashing into the Pecos.[25] Milling in the treacherous waters, even the strongest steers might drown.

Along the California Trail's Pecos frontage—a distance requiring three to four days to negotiate[26]—drovers could pinpoint only three water holes. Ten miles upriver of Lancaster Crossing, recorded Campbell in 1853, "you will find a watering place at the mouth of a hollow, gravelly beach."[27] Another five or six miles upstream, "at a bend of the River," noted Michael Erskine of Seguin, Texas, in 1854, lay a second water hole.[28] Serving as a landmark to the site, observed Campbell, was a "bluff of a mountain" one-half mile upstream.[29]

Cowboys also could water their droves at the point the trail left the river,[30] a site which James G. Bell described in 1854 as "about 20 yards [wide], depth from 10 to 20 feet, current very rapid." Bell also included another observation: "The water is very muddy and filthy for drinking and cooking."[31]

The quality of the Pecos water was always unpredictable. Although Rip Ford judged it to have an "agreeable taste" in 1849,[32] cowhands generally cursed it even while forcing it down. "It'd get awful bad in the summertime," remembered Bill Eddins of his days on the Pecos in the 1910s and 1920s. "In the wintertime, you *could* drink it if you wanted to, kind of a salty sweet taste."[33]

Reaching the Pecos after a long dry stretch in 1876, Nathaniel A. Taylor assessed its taste similarly: "The first sensation in the mouth is a slimy saltiness, as if salt had been melted in soapy water; next a faint sweetness, followed by a distinct bitter, finally winding up with a distinct taste of lye."

Taylor's companion, Jones Johns, cut more to the heart of the matter: "All them buffaloes and wild horses is camped on this river," he said, "and their dreenage [*sic*] has pisened [poisoned] it!"[34]

Finally, in 1932, the Bureau of Economic Geology concluded what old-time cowhands had known all along. Ten times saltier than the sea and highly impregnated with minerals, said Dr. C. L. Baker, the Pecos had the "world's worst" water.[35]

Nevertheless, a thirsty cowhand usually had no choice but to dip his hat brim in its currents and cup up a mouthful, or many mouthfuls. And when he did, it often had a powerful effect on his gastrointestinal system.

"The Pecos water," noted Army Second Lieutenant John Bigelow Jr. in 1878, "is very apt to loosen one's bonds and cause pain in the belly."[36]

Cowhand Jim Witt put it in terms a cowboy could understand: "We didn't carry canteens in those days, and hell, we'd go ride 10 or 12 hours in a day and you'd get pretty thirsty in July. I couldn't stand it any longer—I'd go over there and get a drink of that river water and it'd give me the runs every time."[37]

Travelers could do little about the purgative powers of the Pecos, but they were always on the lookout for ways to improve its taste. "It has a tendency to make both men and animals sick," noted Second Lieutenant Thomas C. Davenport, who marched along the old ruts of the California Trail in 1874. "A few drops of the

Jim Witt in 1996. COURTESY OF THE AUTHOR

extract of ginger gives a very pleasant flavor to the water and promotes health."[38]

Even if palatable, it still contained an enormous amount of suspended sediment. "When we was working, we had to use river water . . . ," noted J. Arthur Johnson, who took charge of the TX outfit on the Pecos in 1887. "All you had to do was clarify it . . . with fires. It [the mud] would settle in five minutes."[39]

As early as the 1849 expedition of Major Robert S. Neighbors and Rip Ford, travelers sometimes used prickly pear leaves in clarifying the water.[40] "The cook . . . would slice off the peeling along with the thorns," explained cowhand M. H. Loy, "then slice the leaves into the water and stir it up. The slimy juice seemed to collect the mud and settled to the bottom, leaving the water clear."[41]

Cattle and horses, however, had no alternative but to drink the water as it was. For animals unaccustomed to its alkali content—especially animals weakened by long, dry drives—the consequences sometimes were fatal.[42] Nevertheless, some cowhands believed the water to have medicinal properties. It was said to cure not only athlete's foot and rashes, but serious diseases.

"It's good medicine—it sure is that," offered Billy Rankin, a cowhand of the 1920s. "I've known two different people that had venereal disease that couldn't get doctors back in the '20s, and they'd just drink a little of that water and go a-swimming in it, and it cured them up."

Pecos livestock, as well, may have benefitted medicinally. "Take cattle, or sheep—you know, they have stomach worm bad," said Rankin. "But sheep that watered in that river never was bothered with stomach worm . . . back in the '20s."[43]

James Campbell of San Antonio, pointing his herd west down the California Trail from Eagle Pass on June 12, 1853,[44] didn't worry about the "putrid Pecos potion" (as one old-time Pecos hand termed it);[45] he just wanted to see his herd through to the river and on to the West Coast. Reaching Warner's Ranch, fifty-five miles from San Diego, in exactly four months, he returned to tell of his success and pass along a written description of the route and its water holes.[46]

Encouraged in part by his drive, Texas cattlemen pushed numerous herds down the California Trail in 1854. In late April, Michael Erskine set out with 1,054 head, including work oxen.[47] One month later, a drove of 700 head passed through Victoria, Texas, to follow in their wake.[48] The fate of that herd is lost to history, but by June 2, storms and stampedes had cut the Erskine drove to 934 head.[49] Another two animals fell by the wayside before the herd reached the Pecos on June 14. Forging upstream for four days, Erskine made daily entries in his diary, and twice he included observations that revealed his concern: "*No Indians.*"

In later years, few Pecos drovers, especially those New Mexico-bound, would be able to make such a statement.

Twelve days behind Erskine (who eventually reached California with 814 head)[50] was the drove of John James, whose party included twenty-two-year-old James G. Bell and other emigrants anxious to reach the West Coast. Fording Lancaster Crossing June 26 and holding the animals overnight at a grassy spot three miles upstream, they learned why experienced drovers watered their herds only at natural water holes. "Lost some cattle at watering," Bell noted in his diary the next morning.

Preparing to leave the Pecos after a three-day push upstream, Bell expressed a sentiment shared by virtually every Pecos drover: "We leave about one o'clock and am sure no one of the party will regret it in the least."[51]

In mid-July, James Campbell headed out from San Antonio with his second California-bound herd in thirteen months, prompting a Matagorda, Texas, newspaper to note, "The speculation of driving beef cattle from our State to California still continues, and doubtless a regular trade will be made of it for some years to come."[52]

To protect the California Trail and Lower Road, the U.S. Army set up a series of posts along the Texas stretch in the 1850s—Fort Clark, 127 miles west of San Antonio; Fort Lancaster, 4 miles east of Lancaster Crossing; Fort Stockton, 46 miles west of the Pecos; and Fort Davis, 74 miles west of Stockton.[53] Oversupply of cattle, however, began to drop beef prices in California as early as 1855, a year in which West Coast buyers paid only six to seven dollars a head for Texas steers.[54]

Ironically, military concerns both encouraged drovers to continue pushing west, and finally led them to abandon the venture entirely. In the summer of 1857, for example, soldiers from Forts Clark, Lancaster, and Davis escorted beeves to New Mexico and hungry Regiment One troops.[55] But soon after Texas seceded from the Union and aligned with the Confederacy in 1861, the nation plunged into a civil war that dealt a death blow to beef trade with California.

And upon war's end, Texas cowhands would again point their herds to the Pecos and blaze one of the truly legendary trails of the Old West.

NOTES

Unless otherwise indicated, all towns, counties, and map quadrangles throughout notes are in Texas.

1. By the latter 1850s, the Upper Road pushed upstream on the east side and crossed near the New Mexico line at newly opened Pope's Crossing, rather than at Horsehead. For a study of Horsehead Crossing, see Dearen, *Crossing Rio Pecos*, 43–60; and Patrick Dearen, *Castle Gap and the Pecos Frontier* (Fort Worth: Texas Christian University Press, 1988), 35–61.
2. For a study of Emigrant Crossing, see Dearen, *Crossing Rio Pecos*, 31–42.
3. For a study of Lancaster Crossing, see Dearen, *Crossing Rio Pecos*, 87–107.
4. Census figures for 1850 as reported in *Texas Almanac 1970–71*, 379. Of that total, 1,161,018 were stock cattle.
5. Haley, *Goodnight*, 256.
6. Haley, "Log of the Texas-California Cattle Trail," 209.
7. See Whiting's journal in Bieber, *Exploring Southwestern Trails*, 243–350.
8. This study of the Lower Road-California Trail route is based on: report of Captain S. G. French, *Reports of the Secretary of War with Reconnaissance of Routes from San Antonio to El Paso*, 31st Cong., 1st sess., Senate Executive Document No. 64 (Washington: 1850), 52; report of Lieutenant Colonel J. E. Johnston, including "List of encamping places on the southern route from San Antonio to El Paso, with distances," *Reports of the Secretary of War*, 27, 29; journal of Captain Edward S. Meyer in Escal F. Duke, ed., "A Description of the Route from San Antonio to El Paso by Captain Edward S. Meyer," *West Texas Historical Association Year Book* (hereinafter, *WTHA Year Book*) 49 (1973), 128–141; log of James G. Bell in Haley, "A Log of the Texas-California Cattle Trail," 211–237; log of Michael Erskine in Haley, ed., *The Diary of Michael Erskine* (Midland: The Nita Stewart Haley Memorial Library, 1979); and Brevet Lieutenant Colonel Thomas B. Hunt, "Journal showing the Route taken by the Government Train accompanying the 15th Regiment U.S. Infantry from Austin, Texas to Fort Craig, New Mexico and returning to San Antonio, July–December 1869," U.S. Department of War, Civil Works Map File, Q-154, Record Group 77, National Archives, Washington, D.C.
9. Log of James G. Bell, 219.
10. Billy Rankin, videotaped interview with author, Rankin, 29 April 1991.
11. Rankin, composite of statements, interviews, 9 August 1989 and 29 April 1991.
12. L. B. Eddins, interview.
13. Rankin, interview, 29 April 1991.
14. Young Bell, *Seventy Years in the Cow Business in Texas, New Mexico, Old Mexico, and Arizona* (Pecos: Elliott Printing Company, 4th edition, 1987), 36–37.
15. Hudson "Bud" Mayes, videotaped interview with author, 30 April 1991, Ozona.
16. Patterson, interview, 29 April 1991. Patterson cowboyed in the Pecos country in the 1920s and 1930s.

17. Otis D. Coggins, taped interview with author, Alpine, 3 March 1990. Coggins crossed the Rio Grande with herds in 1933 and 1934.

18. Taylor, *Coming Empire*, 297.

19. Jim Witt, taped telephone interview with author, Loving, New Mexico, 22 July 1995.

20. "Tom Green County," *San Angelo Standard*, 4 October 1884.

21. Report of Lieutenant Francis T. Bryan, *Reports of the Secretary of War*, 20.

22. Haley, ed., *Diary of Michael Erskine*, 160 ("Memo of Mr. Campbell's Route to California").

23. W. H. Boyd, interview with Haley, Sweetwater, 24 January 1932, Haley Collection, Haley Library, Midland.

24. Jim Lane Cook, as told to T. M. Pearce, *Lane of the Llano* (Boston: Little, Brown & Company, 1936), 8.

25. Such an incident occurred on Charles Goodnight's first drive to the Pecos in 1866. See Charles Goodnight, "Recollections II," 70, typescript, Haley Library.

26. See log of Michael Erskine, and log of James G. Bell.

27. Haley, ed., *Diary of Michael Erskine*, 160 ("Memo of Mr. Campbell's Route to California"). Erskine's log gives the distance as 12 miles. Campbell also noted the availability of water at Pecos Spring, just west of the river at a point "6 or 7 miles" upstream of Lancaster Crossing.

28. Log of Michael Erskine, 49.

29. The ambiguity of Erskine's diary regarding distances leaves open the possibility that the "bend of the River" water hole mentioned by Erskine, and that marked by a bluff as noted by Campbell, were separate sites. However, the fact that both men describe a "bluff" as marking the watering place suggests that the locations were one and the same.

30. Log of Michael Erskine, 49.

31. Log of James G. Bell, 221.

32. John S. Ford, "Letters and Documents, Opening Routes to El Paso, 1849," *SHQ* 48, No. 2 (October 1944), 265.

33. L. B. Eddins, interview.

34. Taylor, *Coming Empire*, 301.

35. "'World's Worst' is Pecos Water," *Pecos Enterprise*, 15 April 1932, microfilm, Permian Basin Petroleum Museum, Library, and Hall of Fame, Midland. For a new assessment of water quality in the Pecos River, see Patrick Dearen, *Bitter Waters: The Struggles of the Pecos River* (Norman: University of Oklahoma Press, 2016).

36. "Scout made by a detachment from Company B, 10th Cavalry, under command of 2nd Lt. John Bigelow Jr. under an order dated April 25, 1878," journal of marches, scouts, and expeditions, Fort Stockton. The "April 25" date is questionable, due to variant interpretations of Bigelow's script.

37. Witt, interview, 22 July 1995.

38. "Journal of march of detachment, Company M, 9th Cavalry, commanded by 2nd Lt. Thomas C. Davenport, 9th U.S. Cavalry, from Fort Stockton, Texas to Independence Creek viz. old Fort Lancaster . . . pursuant to special order number 14 . . . February 4, 1874," journal of marches, scouts, and expeditions, Fort Stockton.

39. J. Arthur Johnson, interview with Haley, Midland, 27 March 1946, Haley Collection, Haley Library, Midland.

40. Ford, "Opening Routes to El Paso," 265.

41. M. H. Loy, manuscript dated 7 January 1930, Haley Collection, Haley Library, Midland.

42. Barney Hubbs, who emigrated to a Pecos ranch in 1908, attributed the river's reputation as a "graveyard" to its "bitter water," among other factors. (Barney Hubbs, videotaped interview with Mike Cox, Pecos, 21 October 1991, copy in author's possession.)

43. Rankin, interview, 29 April 1991.

44. *The Colorado Tribune* (Matagorda), 21 July 1854, transcript, Haley Collection, Haley Library, Midland.

45. Paul Patterson (foreword), in Dearen, *Crossing Rio Pecos*, x.

46. *Colorado Tribune*, 21 July 1854; and "Memo of Mr. Campbell's Route to California" in Haley, ed., *Diary of Michael Erskine*.

47. Introduction by Haley in Haley, ed., *Diary of Michael Erskine*, 31.

48. *The Galveston Journal*, 26 May 1854, transcript, Haley Collection, Haley Library, Midland.

49. "Cattle on Hand" in Haley, ed., *Diary of Michael Erskine*, 69.

50. Haley, ed., *Diary of Michael Erskine*, 34, 49, 69.

51. Log of James G. Bell, 219–221. Bell's age is from Haley's introduction to the log, 210.

52. *The Colorado Tribune*, 21 July 1854.

53. These distances, in wagon road miles, are from the journal of Thomas B. Hunt.

54. *Texas State Gazette*, 21 April and 18 August 1855, as cited by Haley, ed., "A Log of the Texas-California Cattle Trail," 210.

55. Post returns, July 1857, Fort Lancaster, National Archives, Washington, D.C.

CHAPTER THREE

The Goodnight-Loving Trail

THEIR LIVELIHOOD TAKEN AWAY BY WAR, THE TEXAS COWHANDS WHO rode the California Trail returned home or were mustered into service to face military action. Almost none of it took place along the Pecos, which—with the abandonment of Forts Lancaster, Stockton, and Davis—reverted to the domain of the Comanche.[1] By 1867, when the Pecos again had a meaningful military presence,[2] the western frontier in Texas had retreated as much as one hundred miles toward the state's interior.[3]

Moreover, the South's foredoomed defeat in 1865 left Texas with little cash but a lot of potential money-on-the-hoof. For Texas was a superb breeding ground for cattle—three million wild and ornery longhorns by 1866[4]—and territories to the north had lush grasslands for maturing, the promise of railroads to come, and, most importantly, money. The result was inevitable:

"There were no cattle in the western world and Texas cattle stocked the country from southern Utah to the Arctic Circle," Charles Goodnight recalled in the 1920s.[5]

Indeed, in the twenty years following the end of the Civil War, trails bearing north from Texas would carry 5,713,976 cattle,[6] 250,000 of them up the Pecos to New Mexico Territory and perhaps beyond.[7] Although the Pecos trail someday would bear Goodnight's name, other men of courage would be the ones to blaze it through unchallenged Indian country.

While the Civil War still raged, two important events set the stage for the Goodnight-Loving Trail. In 1864 merchants of Chihuahua, Mexico, commissioned the delivery of 1,000 cattle from stockmen in the Texas Hill Country. Trail boss William A. Peril, who was only nineteen, pushed the animals to Presidio del Norte, Chihuahua (adjacent to modern Presidio, Texas) by way of the Middle Concho River, the dreaded "Staked Plains," Castle Gap, and Horsehead Crossing.[8] And in June of that year, thirty-one-year-old James Patterson of New Mexico ventured into Texas to enlist stockman William C. Franks in a plan to supply beef to two New Mexico forts: Sumner on the Pecos River and Stanton near present Ruidoso.[9] Beef was in demand not just by troops, but by 9,000 Navajos and Mescalero Apaches who faced starvation at Bosque Redondo Reservation at Sumner.[10]

It is unclear exactly when the first Patterson-Franks herd pushed up the Pecos, but by late summer of 1865, Patterson already had delivered two droves and was readying to return to Texas for a third.[11] Franks, meanwhile, was driving the trail also, either in concert with Patterson or with separate herds. Three decades later, he recalled that in 1865 he was "living in Texas and New Mexico, on the trail on the Staked Plains, coming here [to New Mexico] . . . all the time with stock . . . and going back . . . to Texas to get some more."[12]

Nevertheless, the two men's efforts only whetted New Mexico's demand for cattle. On September 2, 1865, Brigadier General James H. Carleton, commander of the Department of New Mexico, wrote, "It is desirable to encourage the introduction of cattle from Texas to New Mexico, now partly reduced in stock from Indian depredations, and this enterprise of getting cattle across the plains from that state [Texas] . . . is the beginning only, it is hoped, of a great and profitable trade."[13]

Six weeks later on October 17, three men from the North Texas settlement of Fort Davis (not to be confused with the Trans-Pecos military post) set out for Mexico on one of the most ambitious and daring drives in history. While herds generally required a minimum of seven to ten hands, especially in Indian country, George Reynolds, W. R. St. John, and Si Huff had only each other on whom to rely. Bearing southwest from Stephens County and the Brazos River country, they reached the Concho

River with a small herd of big steers, only to hear rumors that Mexico had little demand for beef. Veering for New Mexico Territory along a route that would take them up the Pecos, they met up with soldiers on the plains.

"The soldiers asked them where they were going," seventeen-year-old Susan E. Newcomb, a fellow townsman, related in her diary. "When they told them, they asked if them three were all that was going. They said yes.

"'Well,' said the men, 'I glory in your spunk, but I don't go anything on your judgment.'"

Spending impossibly long hours in the saddle, they pushed up the Pecos through a land ruled by Comanches and Apaches. "They must have had a hard time of it," wrote diarist Samuel P. Newcomb, Susan's husband, "guarding their cattle every night, one at a time, one-third of the night each."

Nevertheless, Reynolds, St. John, and Huff saw the herd through, all the way up the Pecos to within seventy-five miles of Santa Fe. Selling the cattle, the men still faced a treacherous ride home. On January 7, 1866, the horse on which St. John had started to Mexico showed up riderless at its home range in North Texas, alarming residents of Fort Davis.

"The horse . . . is back at Greer's Ranch in very good order, and it is reported that the boys are killed," Susan Newcomb lamented in her diary that day. "But we hear so many flying reports that we don't know whether to believe it or not, although it is very likely they are."

One week later, however, Reynolds and Huff came riding back in to Fort Davis to tell townspeople that "they did not meet with any Indians nor much bad luck," wrote Susan. Furthermore, they explained that St. John had parted with them in New Mexico, with the intention of proceeding to Denver and Missouri. Finally, on March 12, St. John reached home looking "exactly like he always did," recorded Susan.[14]

On November 11, 1865, almost a month into their drive, twenty-nine-year-old Charles Goodnight had visited civilian Fort Davis,[15] which lay only twenty or so miles south of his cattle range on Elm Creek, a tributary of the Brazos.[16] Having planned a drive of his own to New Mexico and Colorado since the previous spring,[17] he undoubtedly was aware of the Reynolds-Huff-St. John venture and likely learned details of their route upon their return.

At any rate, in Young County in the spring of 1866, Goodnight pooled herds with fifty-four-year-old Oliver Loving,[18] an experienced cowman who had trailed cattle to Louisiana, Illinois, and Colorado before the Civil War.[19]

With 2,000 steers and breeding cows (all under separate ownership),[20] the two men and eighteen hands set out June 6 from a point twenty-five miles southwest of Fort Belknap for "the mountains" of Colorado. By direct route, it would have been a long, hard drive to Denver, much of it through dangerous Comanche and Kiowa territory. But Goodnight had a daring plan. Although it would virtually double the distance, he would avoid occupied Indian country by hooking south and west to the Pecos and bearing upstream[21]—essentially the same route trailed by Reynolds, Huff, and St. John seven months before.

For much of its course, wagon ruts already pointed the way. Emigrant and military parties had traveled stretches of the trail as early as the Gold Rush days, and for several months in 1858 and 1859, Butterfield Overland Mail stages had traced it from Fort Belknap, near present Newcastle, all the way to Pope's Crossing and the New Mexico line.[22]

Nevertheless, forging as it did into an unforgiving wilderness to share its ruts none-too-briefly with the Comanche War Trail,[23] it remained little traveled in the early post-war era. Even the U.S. Army shunned it, and would do so for another year before reoccupying Fort Stockton.

As a cattle trail, the route came to be known to historians as the Goodnight or Goodnight-Loving, although it is unlikely that drovers of the day knew it by that name or any other. Terms for landmarks along it, however, were recognizable far and wide. From Fort Belknap on the Brazos, the trail bore southwest, striking the abandoned military posts of Camp Cooper and Fort Phantom Hill, cutting through forested Buffalo Gap, and pressing on past empty Fort Chadbourne. It crossed the North Concho River near modern Carlsbad, Texas, and pushed across a divide to the Middle Concho. Turning west, it traced the flowing stream through an increasingly arid and forbidding country to the river's so-called headwaters, immediately east of the present Irion-Reagan county line.

Charles Goodnight. COURTESY OF J. EVETTS HALEY COLLECTION, N. S. HALEY MEMORIAL LIBRARY, MIDLAND, TEXAS

Looming ahead was a seventy-nine-mile stretch of hell known as the Staked Plains—waterless, treeless, and treacherous for animals accustomed to watering daily.[24] At the normal pace of a drive, ten to fifteen miles a day, it would mean a dry drive of almost a week—a death sentence to even the strongest steer.

Goodnight and Loving, reaching the headwaters that June day in 1866, realized the desert would test their mettle and demand careful herd management. Holding the drove at the last pools for long hours, they let the beeves water and graze and water some more. Finally, under the blazing afternoon sun, they forged on into a "shoreless ocean of desolation," as one traveler described it.[25]

They kept the herd moving on into dark, and by dawn the alkali dust again rose from the flinty hooves. It crawled down the men's collars and choked their throats, but the cowhands kept the herd pointed west on into another sunset. They held the herd again that night, only to see the thirsty animals mill instead of rest. At dawn on the third day out, Goodnight and Loving realized they would have to drive the cattle unceasingly if any were to survive. So the sun climbed and fell, and still they kept the animals pointed west, marking the trail all the way with carcasses, 300 to 500 in all by the time they crossed the Staked Plains.[26]

In pitch black, two hours past midnight, they reached Castle Gap, a narrow pass yawning open to the hidden Pecos, twelve miles to the south-southwest.[27] As rimrocked mesas, 431 feet high, squeezed in on either side, the crazed cattle smelled dampness and stampeded. Giving chase through the dark, Goodnight rode down the leaders and saved the herd.

They held the animals in the gap the rest of the night, and at daybreak Goodnight loped his horse across the sandy flats to scout the Pecos. Near where the trail began its curve upriver, he found a deadly alkali pond, and not far beyond, equally dangerous Horsehead Crossing.[28] Returning to the herd, he enlisted the aid of four of his best hands and brought the stronger cattle—about two-thirds of the herd—on to the river. Wild for water, the beeves bypassed the pond and stampeded into Horsehead and on across without drinking. Goodnight, swimming his horse at the head of the frenzied mass, reached the far bank in time to wheel his animal and turn the herd back into the river.

"They readily went in again, this time drinking as they swam across," related Goodnight. "The cattle crossed in such volume and force that the water was halfway up the bank in a perfect flood."

Returning to Castle Gap, Goodnight helped Loving point the 500 drags toward the Pecos and Horsehead's narrow cut. But the wind shifted, and the maddened animals smelled water and pressed on without respect for the desperate cowhands who tried to turn them from the sheer bank ahead.

"When they reached the river," related Goodnight, "they poured right over the bank, never halted. . . . We all followed the cattle into the water and tried to float and drive them down to where they could get out. We kept this up for two days and finally concluded that our men could not endure this any longer."

When they finally pointed the herd upriver on the east side, they left more than a hundred mired animals to die below the impossibly steep banks.[29]

The trail upstream, while following the river's general bearing, made no attempt to snake bend-for-bend along the sinuous Pecos. Sometimes, when the channel wheeled sharply westward (as viewed from downstream),[30] the trace held to a direct course across the desert and intercepted the Pecos at a return bend, whose lower side might harbor a natural watering. In the approximately 123 trail miles between Horsehead and Pope's Crossing,[31] there were only six well-known sites where an animal might drink safely; and as herd after herd trailed upriver, cowhands came to know them by name.[32]

The first water hole, thirty-six miles above Horsehead and five miles west of present Grandfalls, was at a sharp crook called Dagger Bend. In the latter part of 1858, Butterfield had established a small relay camp here, taking advantage of what 1870s drover W. R. "Jake" Owen termed "a big watering."[33]

Five air miles upstream, at the point at which the present Reeves-Pecos county line intersects the river, herds could water at Pecos Falls, later known as Great Falls. One of the few crossing points in Texas, Pecos Falls (which no longer exists) offered a brief moment of grandeur in an otherwise bleak and despairing river. "Saw a grand sight at the falls of the river," emigrant Maria Shrode wrote in her diary in 1870. "The water falls about 10 feet in six rods [33 yards]." Twenty-one years earlier, Brevet First Lieutenant Francis T. Bryan had described the cataract in slightly more detail, noting that "the water tumbles over several steps of rocks."[34]

Emigrant Crossing, twelve miles southeast of present Barstow, would have been the next available watering,[35] but the Goodnight-Loving Trail bypassed its miry east bank[36] and bore straight for a wicked twist in the Pecos eighteen wagon miles upstream of Pecos Falls. "We called the place Adobe Walls ... ," recalled drover A. T. Windham. "The river and the hills come right in together." Indeed, with a sharp, fifty-foot bluff squeezing in on the northeast side and the sheer bank of the Pecos suddenly falling away on the other, this quarter-mile stretch known as the Narrows barely permitted passage for herds.

Situated thirteen miles east of the present city of Pecos, Adobe Walls, like Dagger Bend, had been the site of a Butterfield stage stand. When westbound passenger Waterman L. Ormsby reached the station in the dark of September 26, 1858, he found "a very fine 'adobe' corral" already completed and an adobe house under construction.[37]

A mile upstream, the river channel veered sharply into sunset, and the trail pushed ahead into the low Quito Hills and didn't intercept the river again for approximately sixteen miles—a hard day's drive.[38] Even then, the sheer bank repelled any notions of watering for another nine miles until, south-southwest of present Mentone, the river leaned westward and cut a large, sweeping curve. At its southernmost point, "Texas Bend" arched almost languidly, but a mere mile or two upstream or downstream, the Pecos again slithered like a rattler. In those twists, remembered W. R. Owen, lay "a good big watering, with a sand bank."[39] The first drover to identify Texas Bend and turn a herd into its coil was Robert K. Wylie,[40] who took 3,200 steers to Fort Sumner in the fall of 1865.[41]

Upriver from Texas Bend, another tough day's drive, lay the fifth watering, Narbo's Crossing, presumably ten and one-half miles southeast of present Orla.[42] There, the Pecos intercepts a northeast-trending draw known today as Narrow Bow[43]—likely a corruption of *Narbo*. "It was a good watering ... ," recalled J. K. Millwee, who drove the trail in 1868. "It had been a wagon crossing and was a dandy."[44] In fact, some herds crossed at Narbo's before pushing on upstream, although most droves held to the sunrise side.[45]

Their bellies once more bloated, beeves forged another twelve miles upriver to water at Sand Bend, where low, broken hills mark yet another sharp crook into the sunset.[46] Leaving the Pecos to its own meanderings, the animals cut a trace ten miles northwest to yet another landmark on the river—Pope's Camp,[47] headquarters for an ambitious drilling project initiated in 1855. In a three-year, disaster-plagued operation, U.S. Army Captain John Pope sank three wells along the Texas-New Mexico line in a futile search for artesian water.[48] In 1858 and 1859 the stone and adobe buildings served as a Butterfield station,[49] but by the mid-1860s only rattlesnakes and scorpions frequented the walls.

From the ruins, which lay on a rounded limestone rise,[50] the trail descended toward a point on the river three miles northwest. Here between red-tinted bluffs, one air mile south of New Mexico, a fist of rock marked not only a sharp bend, but Pope's Crossing immediately downstream.[51] With the upstream bluffs soon to give way to choppy sand hills, the trail now crossed to the west side where the footing was better.[52]

Cowhands welcomed also the firm, rock bottom underlying Pope's Crossing. "We drive cattle across this crossing, because it is one of the best spots to get them across the Pecos," a cowhand wrote home in April 1867.[53]

From the ford, herds traced one last bend four or five miles and gained the New Mexico line,[54] a location marked by 1869 with "a long

A trail herd watering at Pope's Crossing about 1910. COURTESY OF J. EVETTS HALEY COLLECTION, N. S. HALEY MEMORIAL LIBRARY, MIDLAND, TEXAS

flat rock placed upright on a mound of earth perhaps three feet high," observed drover Henry Pelham Kellogg. "On one side is cut deep in the stone the letter *T.* On the other, *N.M.*"[55]

Once in New Mexico, drovers could look to additional landmarks as guides. Two and one-third air miles into the territory, the trail crossed Delaware River 100 to 200 yards from its confluence with the Pecos.[56] At a westering bulge in the Pecos, three and one-half trail miles farther north, herds could water at Red Bluff, where a 100-foot prominence sentinels the approach of east-trending Red Bluff Draw.[57]

Another three miles upstream, the trail left the coiling river in favor of a more direct route, but returned in time to cross Black River about 300 yards from where it empties into the Pecos, 1.6 miles northeast of present Malaga.[58]

The trail then forged straight for Loving's Bend (later known as Wildcat Bluff) where Dark Canyon Draw spills into the river from the west. Now in Carlsbad, New Mexico, the site offered a watering so friendly that herds could have crossed,[59] though most drovers preferred pushing on up the west side one more day to Patterson's Crossing. Here, approximately two miles shy of the Pecos–Seven Rivers confluence, a draw entering from the east created a natural ford for drovers eager to avoid Apache raiders from the west-lying Guadalupe and Sacramento mountains. With their herds again on the sunrise side, drovers could turn to the moat-like channel as a buffer against attack.[60]

On upstream, near the U.S. Highway 70 bridge seventeen miles northeast of present Roswell, New Mexico, the trail skirted the site of later Lloyd's Crossing,[61] but kept to the east side another fourteen crow-flight miles to a cottonwood grove known as Bosque Grande—"Big Timbers."[62] Forty-seven air miles farther upriver,[63] at a point 700 trail miles from the Brazos country of Texas,[64] herds finally gained Fort Sumner and a reservation filled in the 1860s with starving Navajos and Mescaleros.[65]

Whether Goodnight and Loving, in planning their first drive, were aware of Sumner's demand for beef is unclear.[66] But when they reached the isolated outpost in July they found government contractors Thomas S. Roberts and James Patterson eager to buy their steers.

Red Bluff watering place in 1996. COURTESY OF THE AUTHOR

"Dressed beef was bringing sixteen cents per pound, they could not get enough to properly feed the Indians," Goodnight related. "They paid Mr. Loving and me eight cents per pound on foot."[67]

In an era in which cattle could be purchased in Texas for $3 to $5 a head,[68] it was an astounding price, totaling $12,000 for the steers alone. Within a year, however, as drovers followed Goodnight and Loving to Sumner, it would plummet to 2.5 cents per pound on foot—a price still good enough to attract Texas cowmen.[69]

As Goodnight rode back for Texas to trail another herd up the river, Loving proceeded north with the 700 to 800 unsold cows and calves. He drove through the New Mexico settlement of Las Vegas, entered Colorado at Raton Pass, and hugged the eastern fringe of the Rockies en route to the Denver area and a buyer.[70] Goodnight, in later pushing the Goodnight-Loving Trail into Wyoming, modified the route north from Fort Sumner.

"My trail . . . left the Pecos 30 miles above Sumner and turned pretty much near to north," he detailed in 1925. "It passed the Capulin Mountain [now a national monument near Capulin, New Mexico], passed west of Deadman Crossing, the east end of the Raton Mountains through the Trinchera Pass . . . and crossed the Arkansas River [in Colorado] about 40 miles [east-southeast of] Pueblo. From there it led on to the South Platte near Crow Creek and on to Cheyenne [Wyoming]."[71]

By hoof and courage, the Goodnight-Loving Trail had been cut, and now it waited to carry in its trace a herd of Pecos cowhands who would live out a golden moment in western history.

NOTES

Unless otherwise indicated, all towns, counties, and map quadrangles throughout notes are in Texas.

1. No evidence has surfaced to corroborate a lower Pecos River skirmish between Texas State Troops and 300 to 500 lawless Californians and deserters, as reported in R. H. Williams, *With the Border Ruffians: Memories of the Far West, 1852–1868* (London: John Murray, 1908), 343–348, 363–373. For a discussion see Patrick Dearen, *Devils River: Treacherous Twin to the Pecos, 1535–1900* (Fort Worth: TCU Press, 2011), 184–185.
2. The U.S. Army reoccupied Fort Stockton July 7, 1867. See post returns, July 1867, Fort Stockton, National Archives, Washington, D.C.

3. Mary G. Crawford, "A History of West Texas," *1990–1991 Texas Almanac* (Dallas: *The Dallas Morning News*, 1989), 44. Four of every five frontier ranches had been abandoned by 1866. See *Waco Register*, 21 April 1866.

4. *The Texas Almanac for 1867* (Galveston: The Galveston News, 1857).

5. Charles Goodnight, "The Cattle Trail and Its Effect on Finance and Civilization," manuscript statement taken by Haley, Haley Collection, Haley Library, Midland.

6. "The Cattle Movement," *Texas Live Stock Journal*, 5 December 1885, 2.

7. Goodnight, "The Cattle Trail."

8. T. U. Taylor, "Olive and W. A. Peril," *Frontier Times* (July 1979, reprint of 1939 article), 24.

9. Charles Kenner, "The Origins of the 'Goodnight' Trail Reconsidered" (including a letter from Brigadier General James H. Carleton, headquarters, Department of New Mexico, to Captain William R. Shoemaker, Fort Union, New Mexico, 2 September 1865), *SHQ* Vol. 77, No. 3 (January 1974), 392–394.

10. John P. Wilson, *Fort Sumner, New Mexico* (Santa Fe: Museum of New Mexico, 1974), 4.

11. Carleton to Shoemaker, in Kenner, "Origins of the 'Goodnight' Trail," 393–394.

12. Kenner, "Origins of the 'Goodnight' Trail," 392, quoting deposition of William C. Franks, February 18, 1898, Indian Depredation Claim Number 5622, William C. Franks and James Patterson vs. the U.S. and Mescalero Apache Indians, Records of the United States Court of Claims, Record Group 123, National Archives, Washington, D.C.

13. Carleton to Shoemaker, in Kenner, "Origins of the 'Goodnight' Trail," 393–394.

14. Diary of Susan E. Newcomb (entries for 17 October 1865, and 7 January, 14 January, and 12 March 1866), and diary of Samuel P. Newcomb (entry for 14 January 1866), in "Diary of Samuel P. Newcomb," bound typescript, Haley Library, Midland.

15. Diary of Susan E. Newcomb (entry for 11 November 1865), in "Diary of Samuel P. Newcomb." Goodnight was born 5 March 1836. See Haley, *Charles Goodnight*, 4.

16. Goodnight, "Recollections II," 68.

17. Haley, *Charles Goodnight*, 119.

18. Goodnight, "Recollections II," 68. Loving's age is from Haley, *Charles Goodnight*, 127.

19. Haley, *Charles Goodnight*, 20-21.

20. Ibid., 147. The number of cattle is from Goodnight, "Recollections II," 68.

21. Goodnight, "Recollections II," 68; Haley, *Charles Goodnight*, 126–127; and Oliver Loving to R. M. Garden, Weatherford, 22 May 1866, original letter, Haley Library, Midland. Garden's last name is in question due to variant interpretations of Loving's script.

22. See Waterman L. Ormsby, *The Butterfield Overland Mail* (San Marino: Huntington Library, 1955). Ormsby, a through passenger on the first westbound stage, gives a detailed log of sites and incidents along the route. In 1859, Butterfield officials revised the route to cross the Pecos at Horsehead rather than proceed upstream. See Roscoe P. Conkling and Margaret B. Conkling, *The Butterfield Overland Mail, 1857–1869 Vol. 1* (Glendale: Arthur H. Clark Company, 1947), 375.

23. See O. W. Williams, *Pioneer Surveyor-Frontier Lawyer*, 278.

24. This study of the opening stretch of the trail is based on: Goodnight, "Recollections II," 68; Ormsby, *Butterfield Overland*, 46–64; Conkling and Conkling, *Butterfield Vol. 1*, 319–360; and Haley, *Charles Goodnight*, 127–129. The distance across the Staked Plains is from the journal of Thomas B. Hunt, 9–10. Hunt determined it to be 78.97 wagon road miles.

25. Albert D. Richardson, *Beyond the Mississippi* (Hartford: American Publishing Company, 1867), 232. Richardson rode a westbound Butterfield stage in 1859.

26. Goodnight assesses the loss at 300 head in "Goodnight Recollections" (no volume number), Charles Goodnight file, Haley Collection, Haley Library, Midland; and at 500 head in Charles Goodnight, interview with Haley, Clarendon, 5 June 1925, Haley Collection, Haley Library, Midland.

27. For a study of Castle Gap, see Dearen, *Castle Gap and the Pecos Frontier*, 3–34; and Dearen, *Crossing Rio Pecos*, 16, 43, 45, 47, 49, 51–55, 79–81.

28. For a study of Horsehead Crossing, see Dearen, *Castle Gap and the Pecos Frontier*, 35–61; and Dearen, *Crossing Rio Pecos*, 43–60.

29. This account of the drive across the Staked Plains to Horsehead is drawn primarily from Goodnight, "Recollections II," 68–71, although I also consulted Haley, *Charles Goodnight*, 130–134.

30. The following discussion is from the viewpoint of an upstream-bound traveler, who would consider the course of the river channel in regard to his own course. For example, although I indicate the channel "wheeled sharply westward," the current's flow actually would have been *out* of the west.

31. Distance is from Conkling and Conkling, *Butterfield Vol. 1*, 376, 386. For the upper stretch of this course (from Pecos Falls to Pope's Crossing), I also consulted Second Lieutenant John Bigelow to adjutant general (hereinafter, AG), 9 December 1879, journal of marches, scouts, and expeditions, Fort Stockton. Bigelow gives specific distances between watering places on the river.

32. W. R. Owen, interview with Haley, Carlsbad, New Mexico, 2 March 1933, Haley Collection, Haley Library, Midland. Owen drove the trail in 1875 and later cowboyed up and down the river. See W. R. Owen, interview with Haley, Carlsbad, New Mexico, 12 August 1926, Haley Collection, Haley Library, Midland.

33. W. R. Owen, interview, 2 March 1933; W. R. Owen, interview with Haley, Carlsbad, New Mexico, 12 January 1927, Haley Collection, Haley Library, Midland; Conkling and Conkling, *Butterfield Vol. 1*, 377; "Map of Scout to Pecos Falls by 2nd Lieutenant T. C. Davenport, 9th U.S. Cavalry" (supplementing the journal of Thomas Davenport, pursuant to special order dated 16 March 1874), journal of marches, scouts, and expeditions, Fort Stockton; and U.S. Geological Survey (hereinafter, U.S.G.S.), Grandfalls Southwest Quadrangle, 7.5-minute series, 1969 (topographic map).

34. W. R. Owen, interview, 2 March 1933; U.S.G.S. Rio Pecos Ranch Quadrangle, 7.5-minute series, 1963, rev. 1981 (topographic map); U.S.G.S. Grandfalls Southwest Quadrangle; Bigelow to AG, 9 December 1879, journal of marches, scouts, and expeditions, Fort Stockton; Maria Shrode diary in Sandra L. Myres, ed., *Ho for California! Women's Overland Diaries from the Huntington Library* (San Marino: Huntington Library, 1980), 270; report of Francis T. Bryan, *Reports of the Secretary of War*, 20; and

Clayton Williams, *Texas' Last Frontier: Fort Stockton and the Trans-Pecos, 1861–1895* (College Station: Texas A&M University Press, 1982), 208.

35. For a study of Emigrant Crossing, see Dearen, *Crossing Rio Pecos*, 31–42.

36. As described by Brevet Captain John Pope in "Diary of the Expedition of John Pope," *Reports of Explorations and Surveys to Ascertain the Most Practicable and Economical Route for a Railroad from the Mississippi River to the Pacific Ocean, Vol. II*, 33rd Cong., 2nd sess., House of Representatives Executive Document No. 91 (Washington: 1855), 70.

37. This study of Adobe Walls on the Pecos is based on: W. R. Owen, interviews, 12 January 1927 and 2 March 1933; A. T. Windham, interview with Haley, Pecos, 10 January 1927, Haley Collection, Haley Library, Midland; Bigelow to AG, 9 December 1879, journal of marches, scouts, and expeditions, Fort Stockton; Ormsby, *Butterfield Overland*, 70; Conkling and Conkling, *Butterfield Vol. I*, 377–378; and U.S.G.S. Quito Draw Quadrangle, 7.5-minute series, 1963, rev. 1981. A second Adobe Walls lay well downstream near present Girvin. See Dearen, *Crossing Rio Pecos*, 112. Neither was associated with well-known Adobe Walls in the Texas Panhandle.

38. U.S.G.S. Pecos Quadrangle, 1:250,000, 1954, limited revision 1963 (topographic map); U.S.G.S. Mentone Quadrangle, 7.5-minute series, 1961, revised 1981 (topographic map); and Conkling and Conkling, *Butterfield Vol. 1*, 378.

39. This study of Texas Bend is based on: Bigelow to AG, 9 December 1879, journal of marches, scouts, and expeditions, Fort Stockton; Conkling and Conkling, *Butterfield Vol. 1*, 378; U.S.G.S. Pecos Quadrangle, 1:250,000, 1954, limited revision 1963 (topographic map); U.S.G.S. Mentone Quadrangle, 7.5-minute series, 1961, revised 1981 (topographic map); and W. R. Owen, interview, 2 March 1933.

40. James Cox, *Historical and Biographical Record of the Cattle Industry and the Cattlemen of Texas and Adjacent Territory* (St. Louis: Woodward and Tiernan Printing Company, 1895), 330.

41. Irbin H. Bell, interview with Haley, El Paso, 18 March 1927, in "Notes Upon the Cross Timber Country," bound typescript, Haley Library, Midland.

42. W. R. Owen, interview, 2 March 1933. John Bigelow's log indicates a distance of 15 miles between Texas Bend and Narbo's. See Bigelow to AG, 9 December 1879, journal of marches, scouts, and expeditions, Fort Stockton.

43. U.S.G.S. Orla Southeast Quadrangle, 7.5-minute series, 1961 (topographic map).

44. J. K. Millwee, interview with Haley, Lubbock, 13 September 1932, transcript, Haley Collection, Haley Library, Midland.

45. For a discussion on Narbo's Crossing, see Dearen, *Crossing Rio Pecos*, 118–119.

46. W. R. Owen, interview, 2 March 1933; W. R. "Jake" Owen, interview with Haley, Carlsbad, New Mexico, 24 June 1937, transcript, Haley Collection, Haley Library, Midland; Bigelow to AG, 9 December 1879, journal of marches, scouts, and expeditions, Fort Stockton; Conkling and Conkling, *Butterfield vol. I*, 378–379; and U.S.G.S. Orla Northeast Quadrangle, 7.5-minute series, 1968 (topographic map). Almost due east of Orla, a northeast-trending arroyo known as Sand Bend Draw strikes the Pecos a few miles downstream of the site I have pinpointed for Sand Bend watering. Owen, in the 24 June 1937 interview, indicated that Sand Bend watering was located "where the

[southbound] trail first hit the river after leaving Pope's [Camp]." For the Butterfield road—which the Goodnight-Loving Trail traced—that point lay at a "sharp bend . . . west" ten miles below Pope's Camp, according to Conkling and Conkling, 378–379.
47. Bigelow notes a distance of eight miles between Sand Bend and Pope's Crossing, while Conkling and Conkling indicate a distance of ten miles from Sand Bend to Pope's Camp, and another three miles between Pope's Camp and Pope's Crossing. Ormsby corroborates the latter distance. See Bigelow to AG, 9 December 1879, journal of marches, scouts, and expeditions, Fort Stockton; Conkling and Conkling, *Butterfield vol. I*, 379, 386; and Ormsby, *Butterfield Overland*, 72.
48. Lee Myers, "Pope's Wells," *New Mexico Historical Review* 38, No. 4 (October 1963), 282, 283, 284–295.
49. Ormsby, *Butterfield Overland*, 72.
50. Conkling and Conkling, *Butterfield vol. I*, 379.
51. For a study of Pope's Crossing, see Dearen, *Crossing Rio Pecos*, 9–29. The completion of Red Bluff Dam on the Pecos in 1936 inundated both Pope's Camp and Pope's Crossing.
52. Goodnight, "Recollections II," 71–72.
53. Jake to Dear Ones, in Carpenter, "Letter from 1867," *The Pecos Independent and Enterprise*, 17 May 1962.
54. U.S.G.S. Orla Quadrangle, 1:62,500, 1931, reprint 1949 (topographic map).
55. Henry Pelham Kellogg, "Pocket Journal Belonging to Henry Pelham Kellogg, Wheelock, Texas," 8, typescript, Haley Collection, Haley Library, Midland.
56. U.S.G.S. Red Bluff Quadrangle, Eddy County, New Mexico, 7.5-minute series, 1985 (topographic map); and W. R. Owen, interview, 2 March 1933.
57. Bluff Quadrangle, Eddy County, New Mexico (topographic map); and W. R. Owen, interview, 2 March 1933. Guided by landowner Evelyn Cooksey, I personally inspected Red Bluff watering hole on 15 July 1996.
58. U.S.G.S. Malaga Quadrangle, New Mexico, 7.5-minute series, 1985 (topographic map); and W. R. Owen, interview, 2 March 1933.
59. W. R. Owen, interview, 2 March 1933; U.S.G.S. Loving Quadrangle, New Mexico, 7.5-minute series, 1985 (topographic map); and U.S.G.S. Carlsbad East, New Mexico, 7.5-minute series, 1985 (topographic map).
60. W. R. Owen, interviews, 2 March 1933 and 12 January 1927; Goodnight, "Recollections II," 72; U.S.G.S. Lake McMillan South Quadrangle, New Mexico, 7.5-minute series, 1955 (topographic map); U.S.G.S. Seven Rivers Quadrangle, New Mexico, 7.5-minute series, 1954 (topographic map); and U.S.G.S. Carlsbad West Quadrangle, New Mexico, 7.5-minute series, 1985 (topographic map). Possibly named for early drover James Patterson, the crossing may have been known also as Ninety-Mile Crossing in consideration of its distance in trail miles from Bosque Grande. See Millwee, interview, 13 September 1932. Owen, in the 12 January 1927 interview, noted that a trail continued up the river's west side as well.
61. For information on Lloyd's Crossing, see: U.S.G.S. Acme Quadrangle, New Mexico, 7.5-minute series, 1962, rev. 1982 (topographic map); U.S.G.S. Melena Quadrangle, New Mexico, 7.5-minute series, 1962, rev. 1982 (topographic map); J. D. Hart and Bob

Beverly, interview with Haley, ranch near Lovington, New Mexico and Monument, New Mexico, 24 June 1937, Haley Collection, Haley Library; Midland; Lucius Dills, interview with Haley, Roswell, New Mexico, 5 August 1937, Haley Collection, Haley Library, Midland; Edgar Harral file, 23, Haley Collection, Haley Library, Midland; J. D. Hart file, 1, Haley Collection, Haley Library, Midland; Frank Lloyd, interview with Haley and Hervey Chesley, Tularosa, New Mexico, 12 June 1939, Haley Collection, Haley Library, Midland; W. Wier and Bob Beverly, interview with Haley, Monument, New Mexico, 22 June 1937, Haley Collection, Haley Library, Midland; Cox, *Historical and Biographical Record*, 301; Court of Claims, Indian Depredations Claim Number 5388, James Chisum, administrator of estate of John S. Chisum, versus the United States and Comanche and Mescalero Apache Indians, 238, National Archives, Washington, D.C.; J. Evetts Haley, *George W. Littlefield, Texan* (Norman: University of Oklahoma Press, 1943), 147–149; and Lily Klasner, *My Girlhood Among Outlaws* (Tucson: University of Arizona Press, 1972), 58–61.

62. U.S.G.S. Eightmile Draw Quadrangle, New Mexico, 7.5-minute series, 1982 (topographic map); and U.S.G.S. Cottonwood Draw Quadrangle, New Mexico, 7.5-minute series, 1982 (topographic map).

63. U.S.G.S. Fort Sumner East Quadrangle, New Mexico, 7.5-minute series, 1982 (topographic map); U.S.G.S. Bonner Lake Quadrangle, New Mexico, 7.5-minute series, 1968 (topographic); U.S.G.S. Eighteenmile Hill Quadrangle, New Mexico, 7.5-minute series, 1982 (topographic map); U.S.G.S. Conejo Creek East Quadrangle, 7.5-minute series, 1967 (topographic map); U.S.G.S. La Espia Peak Quadrangle, New Mexico, 7.5-minute series, 1982 (topographic map); and U.S.G.S. Deering Place Quadrangle, New Mexico, 7.5-minute series, 1967 (topographic map).

64. Haley, *Charles Goodnight*, 139.

65. Goodnight, "Recollections II," 72; and Wilson, *Fort Sumner*, 4.

66. There is no direct evidence that they were aware of the demand.

67. Goodnight, "The Cattle Trail." The names of the contractors are from Carleton to Shoemaker, 2 September 1865, in Kenner, "Origins of the 'Goodnight' Trail," 393.

68. *Texas Almanac for 1867*, 197.

69. Haley, *Charles Goodnight*, 140, 148.

70. Goodnight, "Recollections II," 72; and Haley, *Charles Goodnight*, 198.

71. Goodnight, interview, 5 June 1925.

CHAPTER FOUR

The Pecos Trail Hand

"We had driven to the Pecos, the weather being fine;
We had camped on the south side in a bend."
—"LITTLE JOE THE WRANGLER,"
A SONG OF THE GOODNIGHT-LOVING TRAIL

THROUGH CAREFUL STUDY OF THE COW BRUTE AND OF THE GOOD-night-Loving Trail's special demands—as well as through trial and error—cowmen such as Charles Goodnight refined cattle driving into a near-science in the early post-war era.

Herd management, first and foremost, demanded a keen understanding of Texas longhorns.

"They were a breed to themselves," observed Barney Hubbs, who emigrated to a Pecos River ranch in present Reeves County, Texas, in 1908. "They were pretty wild animals . . . [and] they were big, had long horns, sometimes a span of four feet."[1]

The longhorn's endurance, self-sufficiency, and fiercely independent nature sometimes manifested itself in remarkable ways. Goodnight, driving up the Goodnight-Loving Trail, once lost a cow at Horsehead Crossing. When he returned to Palo Pinto County, Texas, he found the bovine back on its old Brazos River range; alone, it had crossed the waterless plains and trod hundreds of miles.[2] Two John Chisum steers displayed an even more remarkable homing instinct, trailing for weeks back down the Pecos from New Mexico to Coleman County, Texas.[3]

With independence, though, came a fighting spirit that tested a cowboy's skill and mettle.

"Those old longhorn cattle were 10 times as hard to work as these cattle we have now [in the 1950s]," said Julius D. Henderson, who cowboyed on the Pecos at the turn of the twentieth century. "They could run like a deer, and an old cow would run around the roundup, stop, try to dodge behind your horse, and it sure did take a good horse to cut them out."[4]

Managing an entire herd demanded not only insight into longhorn psychology, but anticipation, planning, and a readiness to act quickly. A trail boss, upon throwing together a typical herd of 2,000 or 3,000 head, positioned his cowboys at strategic points. On either side of the lead or "point" rode two of his best hands, who kept the herd on course. In a haze of dust at rear, three steady hands rode "drag," bringing up the slower animals and ensuring that the stronger cattle ahead did not impede their progress. Between point and drag were the "swing" men, who rode along on either side of the beeves. Under normal conditions, a herd lengthened

Bringing up the drags on a cattle drive from south of Midland to the L-Ranch near the Pecos in Loving County about 1923. COURTESY OF J. EVETTS HALEY COLLECTION, N. S. HALEY MEMORIAL LIBRARY, MIDLAND, TEXAS

out to half a mile while narrowing to only fifty or sixty feet. From a high hill in broken country, the mass would have appeared to trail along like a slithering rattler.

Goodnight, aware that "the nearer the point the lighter the work" for men and horses, devised a system to divide the labor for all positions except point and drag. "Three hundred miles of the Pecos was bad with alkali dust," recalled Goodnight, "and the men not only shifted their positions daily, but reversed their sides of the herd."

In a dry or new country, or if it were storming, the trail boss scouted ahead, returning to direct any course changes with signals easily understood from afar. The mule-drawn chuck wagon, driven by the cook, started out behind the herd every morning, but soon rumbled ahead of point, where the chuck and bedrolls wouldn't soak up quite so much alkali. Off to the side, the wrangler rode along with the remuda, which averaged 30 horses for every 1,000 cattle.[5]

For the first couple of weeks southwest from the Brazos country, a Goodnight-Loving Trail hand sat a horse no differently than a drover

Pecos country chuck wagon and cowboys moving out about 1895. COURTESY OF SOUTHEASTERN NEW MEXICO HISTORICAL SOCIETY, CARLSBAD, NEW MEXICO

on any other trail. But once he reached the head of the Middle Concho to face the seventy-nine-mile desert that stretched to equally forbidding Horsehead Crossing, he had to call upon all his wits and stamina.

The Staked Plains would never be obliging to either man or animal, but a good trail boss learned from his own experiences and those of others. Only weeks after Goodnight had watched 300 to 500 beeves die on the plains in his first drive in 1866, he was back at the Middle Concho's last pool, ready to point another herd into hell. But this time he had a carefully devised plan.

"We left the Concho about noon, having first allowed the cattle to drink all they would," he related. "We then put them to the trail and kept them moving until just before sundown, then gave them all the grass they could eat while we had our supper. Cattle will not drive well if hungry. We then drove them all night. The next morning we again grazed them until they were full, then trailed. After that they do not want to eat much as they commence to get dry. We moved them all that day and the following night.

"Just before day we were in the Castle Mountain Canyon [Castle Gap]. We held them in the canyon until daylight so we would have daylight for watering. We never lost a head after learning this system of crossing the plains."[6]

Goodnight also employed a practice known as "squeezing down" in making the dry drive. The pace of a drove was dictated by the swing men—the closer they flanked the column of beeves, the narrower it became and the faster it marched. "Therefore," he noted, "when we had a long drive to make between watering places, the men rode in closer to the line. . . . Narrowing the string was called 'squeezing them down.' Ten feet was the lowest limit, for then gaps came, and the cattle would begin trotting to fill up the spaces. . . . They were never allowed to trot."[7]

Although many discerning trail bosses employed these procedures in pushing west from the Middle Concho, the desert still proved so deadly that, in 1876, a traveler would curse it as "Skeleton Plain."[8]

Even if a cowboy saw a herd through to the Pecos at the expense of three straight days in the saddle ("You got to where you could sleep on a horse without any trouble," said Goodnight),[9] he was far from home free. There remained the problem of coping with the beeves' inevitable plunge over the sharp bank—"like turtles off a log," said one drover.[10] While Horsehead's quicksands and the imprisoning walls never would be denied their share of carcasses, smart trail bosses learned to minimize their losses.

When eighteen-year-old Joe D. Jackson got within six miles of the Pecos one night in 1879, his herd smelled water and rushed forward in a frenzy. Pushing his horse hard, he stayed ahead of the beeves and led them to Horsehead's narrow cut. Gaining a sandbar in midstream, he remained half the night, discouraging the watering beeves from drifting downstream to the steep banks and quicksand.[11]

A cowboy could get his fill mighty quickly riding daybreak to dark with a dusty herd. Unfortunately, even when he threw his bedroll on the ground, his work wasn't finished—he still had to ride night guard for a couple of hours.

"Two men stood guard on the cattle at a time, which was all that was needed around 3,000 head," noted John Rumans, who drove the Goodnight-Loving Trail. "They would go in opposite directions and just keep a-riding. There were about three reliefs. Sometimes we had watches, but sometimes we stood by 'heart,' but some of the hands didn't have any heart."[12]

While necessary to the success of the drive, riding night guard was not relished by any cowboy of the Pecos.

"This guarding business is pretty hard on us," one drover noted in his journal after only three days on the Goodnight-Loving Trail. "To drive all day and stand guard half the night is wearing on the constitution slightly and I am getting tired of it already."[13]

The Pecos, cursed by cowboys for its treachery, offered one decided advantage to weary drovers starved for sleep. "In many places the river would bend back until it almost touched itself," recalled Jim Lane Cook, who at age nine in 1867 went along on a drive up the Pecos. "I have seen these bends curve around more than two thousand acres of land with not more than one-fourth of a mile across from the river above to the river below. The cowboys would put from two to three thousand cattle into one of these river bends, turn them loose, and guard the narrow gap through the night."[14]

Sometimes the gap was so narrow that it required but a single rider.

"In some places . . . you could stand between two bends and pop your cow whip from one bend over into the other . . . ,"recalled W. H. Boyd, who drove up the river in 1867. "We herded our cattle in these at times as they were easy to hold in such a place."[15]

W. R. Owen recalled one such site in particular—Texas Bend. "The river described a big bend and came very close together," he said, "probably only thirty steps across the mouth. . . . You could put a big herd in it."[16]

Not only did the bends allow cowhands to gain precious sleep, they were God-sends when the cattle were spooky or cattle thieves were on the prowl. Most stampedes came early in a drive, before the beeves were "trail-broke." However, on stormy nights or in Indian country, they might jump and run at any moment, even if the trail boss called out every hand.

In the late 1890s or early 1900s, Julius D. Henderson and his fellow guards could have used a Pecos "horseshoe," as a bend was called,[17] but they had bedded their herd near present Penwell, Texas, twenty-eight miles north-northeast of the river. Related Henderson:

> *It began to cloud up in the evening; by night there was one of the blackest clouds I ever saw. It rained a little, and about dark it began to thunder and the lightning just rolled on the ground. We were all out there and expected those steers to run every minute. There were balls of lightning as big as my fist just rolling around everywhere. One would roll against a bush and just go* bang! *like a bomb. . . . I expected to be killed at every clap of thunder.*
>
> *There was a blue blaze on the point of my horse's ears, and I put my hand on his neck and it blazed up like a gas flame. It was on the points of those old steers' horns too, and when a ball of lightning would roll close to one, he would jump and snort.*

It was so dark between lightning flashes, said Henderson, that when another horse brushed his own, he couldn't even see its rider.

"About that time," Henderson continued, "there was an awful clap of thunder right over us and the lightning lit up everything around there,

Julius D. Henderson as a young man. COURTESY OF PERMIAN HISTORICAL ARCHIVES, UNIVERSITY OF TEXAS OF THE PERMIAN BASIN, ODESSA, TEXAS

and we could see we were right in the middle of the herd. It was the boss. He said, 'I'll quit and let them go.'"

Amid spooked longhorns ready to trample anything in their path, they quickly gathered the other hands for the return to camp, only to realize the cook had failed to place a lighted lantern atop the chuck box.

> *I said, "I don't know where the wagon is, but I'll bet you old Hornet (my mount) knows." So we took off and someone kept saying, "Let's stop and let it rain—that horse don't know where that wagon is." But . . . pretty soon he [Hornet] stopped, and I got down to feel to see what he had stopped for. His head was at the chuck box.* [18]

Sometimes a herd would stampede at even the drop of a hat. On the Pecos one night in 1888, drover Tex Crosse was riding guard around a herd already spooked by an approaching cloud. A stiff wind suddenly blew his hat off and across the backs of a couple of steers. In an instant, the entire herd was up and thundering away. [19]

In such an event, a good cow horse would go wild, jumping and running with its rider at the first blur of cattle. Suddenly, cowboy and horse were one, racing alongside the stampeding mass in the pitch black of night. "You could feel your horse's heart a-beatin' against your leg," remembered one cowhand. [20] Riding blindly after the leaders to turn them and save the herd, a cowhand never knew when a sudden hole would land him in a shallow grave. "How I dread," lamented one Pecos drover, "the idea of a death . . . away from home and friends." [21]

It took a special breed to endure a cowboying life so demanding and treacherous.

"A certain type of men could handle it; weaklings could not," observed Barney Hubbs, who drove a chuck wagon on a drive to the Pecos in 1908. [22]

A journal kept by Henry Pelham Kellogg on a drive up the Good-night-Loving Trail in 1869 gives rare insight into this class of men. Like most drovers—white, black, or Mexican—he was young: twenty-three. Like some, he was troubled. Returning to Wheelock, Texas, after serving in the Civil War, he killed a Negro who allegedly had insulted his mother.

Fleeing Reconstruction law, he reached the Stephenville, Texas, area, and on May 26, 1869, he sought out cowmen making up a drive to New Mexico. "I am afraid if I go away for so long and without any communication with home," he wrote that day, "the suspense will kill Mother. . . . The very idea of going off to be gone so long unnerves me."

Nevertheless, three days later he signed on with a "pretty rough set" of drovers for $30 a month. "Imagine it will be pretty hard work," he noted, "but I can stand it."

Cow-hunting and dodging Indians for six weeks, Kellogg and his fellow hands finally pointed the herd down the trail July 15. Only a day later, he observed that "there is nothing much interesting in the life of a beef driver." On July 20, however, between Hord's Creek and the Colorado River, excitement struck with the fury of a storm. "There came up a violent rain and . . . it required all hands to hold the cattle . . . ," he wrote. "That night . . . it rained again and we had a hell of a time generally— cattle stampeded and frightened away the loose horses. . . . A miserable night."

Frustrated by a rise on the Colorado that delayed them for a day, Kellogg complained on July 22 that "this is rather slow traveling and I don't like it much, but as it is the best I can do I shall continue on the weary monotony of my way."

Pushing on to Fort Concho, which by 1869 had been established at present San Angelo, Kellogg let his "naturally hot blood" get him in trouble again. At camp, he exchanged words with a Negro soldier and would have shot him had the man remained in revolver range. Kellogg fled a pursuing cavalry contingent and soon found himself "in a h__l of a fix" in Indian country unknown to him. "I have often wished for some wild adventure of this kind," he wrote, "and I am likely now to be gratified." Eating only wild grapes and prickly pear for more than forty-eight hours, he finally rejoined the herd as it moved west.

Trailing up the Middle Concho, Kellogg endured "the hottest day" he had ever known on July 30 and reached the headwaters July 31. Laying over "to rest the cattle, horses, and men, and to prepare for the plains," they forged onward August 2 through unusual summer rains. On the morning of August 5, Kellogg found Castle Gap "a wild mountain pass," and at three o'clock that afternoon, they turned the herd into Horsehead Crossing. "Here," he wrote, "I saw several fresh moccasin tracks and we were careful about guards that night for the first time."

Nevertheless, as they pushed upstream for the Rio Hondo (which strikes the Pecos near present Roswell, New Mexico), Kellogg found little worth writing about. "It seems nothing of any interest will ever occur," he wrote on August 16. "Just the same old thing all the time."

On August 18 they forded the Pecos, presumably at Pope's Crossing.[23] Although Kellogg did not discuss the matter in his journal, a drover's duties included crossing not only the herd and remuda, but the chuck wagon, which came into prominence only after the Civil War.[24] To do so, he had to secure the wagon bed to the frame to prevent it from floating away. He accomplished this, front and back, by stretching a rope across the bed and securing it to the wheels, according to 1880s Pecos hand F. S. Millard.[25] Bill Eddins, who crossed a chuck wagon at likely Narbo's Crossing in 1921, detailed the procedure thereafter.

"There was two horses, two men, tied on to the end of the tongue," he explained, "and [the cook] put me and another boy on the up[stream] side of the river—tied on to the wagon bed—and he had two on the lower [downstream] side tied on it. We was tied on to it when he drove down in there. We was out 30 feet ahead of it. We was about near out of the swimming water [by the] time the chuck wagon got *in* to swimming water. That wagon just floated. Our beds was wet and everything else was wet in there."[26]

On Kellogg's drive of 1869, the chuck wagon apparently crossed without mishap. Shortly after the herd entered New Mexico on August 19, however, threat loomed—Kellogg sighted an Indian on a hill one-half mile away. Still, the drive upriver turned out to be so monotonous and tiresome that he neglected his journal except for a final entry: "On the Hondo. We arrived here all right on the evening of the 29th [of August]."[27]

Like Kellogg, most cowboys found the Goodnight-Loving Trail an odd blend of boredom and excitement, monotony and danger. Many also found their own shallow graves along the way, dug all too often by the treachery of the very men who rode with them. Wrote J. Frank Dobie:

"If in the old days a man said of another, 'He is a cowboy of the Pecos,' that might mean . . . that he ran the risk of being 'pecosed' either for his integrity or the lack of it; on the other hand, it might mean that he had helped to 'pecos' some other rider of the range."

Such callous disregard for life led to a mournful old song of the river:

"On the rocky banks of the Pecos,
they will lay him down to rest,
with his saddle for a pillow,
and his gun across his breast."[28]

In his nine years of riding the Goodnight-Loving Trail,[29] Charles Goodnight grew familiar with the graves of violence. "In passing over the desert between the Concho and the Pecos," he said, "I used to see two graves, and at Horsehead Crossing there were 13 others, all the result of pistol shots but one. I shall never forget the impression made upon me by those lonely graves, where rested cowboys killed in battle with one another after having fallen out while crossing the long stretch without water."[30]

W. H. Boyd, in his 1867 drive up the Goodnight-Loving Trail, saw the graves too, some with dirt still fresh. "Near Phantom Hill we saw a fresh grave and a new cowboy saddle that didn't look like it had ever been rained on, sitting a-straddle of the grave," he related in 1932. "We saw one on the Concho and one on the plains and one or two between Castle Mountains and the [Pecos] river. The grave on the plains had a board at the head. The man's name was written on it with a note that he was killed by the Indians."

Despite the marker, Boyd later learned that Indians had not been involved. The victim, in fact, had been "straw boss" of a "bunch of outlaws" dispatched by John Hitson to repossess cattle which Indians had stolen in Texas and then traded in New Mexico. One evening as their herd approached a water hole, the straw boss rode ahead to drink and water his horse before the cattle muddied the site. At the same time, a mere kid-of-a-hand reached the watering place and began filling canteens dispatched by other drovers.

"The straw boss," reported Boyd, "threatened to cowhide him [whip him with his leggings] and started toward him. The boy shot him off his horse."[31]

Not all killings were justifiable, of course, but in a time and place in which "the first thing a man did when he got up was to buckle on his six-shooter," as one drover said, shootings were inevitable.[32]

Charles Goodnight, for one, believed a trail boss bore a responsibility to protect his hands not only from the dangers of the trail, but from each other. "I never had any trouble with the cowboys on the trail," he related. "They signed a contract before they started out. If a man used a gun, he was to be hung. He was to be tried by the outfit and hanged on the spot, if found guilty. I never had a man shot on the trail. The contract was sometimes verbal and sometimes written. When we started on the trail, each man was given a list [of rules] so that he could not forget them."[33]

Among the rules Goodnight enforced to discourage violence was a ban against certain vices. "I never allowed my men to gamble on the trail . . . ," he said. "That made me very unpopular with the saloon men, for I would not let them drink either."[34]

As J. Arthur Johnson of the old TX Ranch on the Pecos put it, "Cards and whiskey don't go where there is work to be done."[35]

To characterize the Pecos trail hand as prone to violence would be an injustice. Most were honest, loyal to their bosses, and could be counted on to trail a herd all the way to hell and back.

"I cannot resist mentioning the high ideals and good character of the men I contacted . . . on the plains of New Mexico and Texas," noted B. A. Oden, a Pecos cowhand in the 1880s. "The world will never know another generation in kind, noted for its sterling honesty, high ideals, and business sagacity."[36]

In the sunset of his life, Goodnight eulogized the cowhands who had risked their lives in driving the Pecos trail:

It is lamentable that the class of men who followed the trail are so rapidly passing away, never to return, as the conditions have gone that made such men. It required good cool judgment and some degree of courage to start out into an unknown wilderness, defying the elements, swollen streams, and the savages of the unknown territory. In carrying out this work, more credit is due the cowboy than is generally given him by those who do not understand him. Their loyalty and courage is beyond comprehension.[37]

In face of the threat which Indians would bring to the Pecos in the late 1860s, cowhands would need every ounce of that courage, and more.

NOTES

Unless otherwise indicated, all towns, counties, and map quadrangles throughout notes are in Texas.

1. Hubbs, interview with Cox, 21 October 1991.
2. Charles Goodnight, interview with Haley, Clarendon, 8 April 1927, Haley Collection, Haley Library, Midland.
3. John Nichols, interview with Haley, Lampasas, 15 May 1927, Haley Collection, Haley Library, Midland.
4. Henderson, "Life of an Oldtimer," prologue, 14.
5. This study of herd management is drawn primarily from Charles Goodnight, as quoted in Haley, *Charles Goodnight*, 245–248, 254–255. Information about the remuda is from Goodnight, "The Cattle Trail."
6. Goodnight, "Recollections II," 77.
7. Goodnight, as quoted by Haley, *Charles Goodnight*, 248.
8. Taylor, *Coming Empire*, 290.
9. Haley, *Charles Goodnight*, 180.
10. D. N. Arnett, interview with Haley, Colorado City, 18 October 1926, in "South Plains Interviews," bound typescript, Haley Library, Midland.
11. J. Marvin Hunter, ed. and compiler, *The Trail Drivers of Texas* (Austin: University of Texas Press, reprint, 1985), 466.
12. John Rumans, interview with Haley, Amarillo, 13 December 1928, Haley Collection, Haley Library, Midland.
13. Kellogg, "Pocket Journal," 4.
14. Cook, *Lane of the Llano*, 10.
15. Boyd, interview.
16. W. R. Owen, interview, 2 March 1933.
17. Report of Francis T. Bryan, *Reports of the Secretary of War*, 20.
18. Henderson, "Life of an Oldtimer," book two, 10–11.
19. J. Frank Dobie, *The Longhorns* (Boston: Little, Brown & Company, 1941, 16th printing), 117.
20. Tom Blasingame, taped interview with author, JA Ranch, Armstrong County, 26 July 1989. Blasingame began cowboying in the Texas Panhandle in 1916.

21. Kellogg, "Pocket Journal," 7.

22. Hubbs, interview with Cox, 21 October 1991.

23. Kellogg, "Pocket Journal," preface, 1–8.

24. Charles Goodnight, interview with Haley, site not recorded, 14 December 1928, Haley Collection, Haley Library, Midland. Prior to his first drive in 1866, Goodnight constructed the first wagon chuck box he had ever seen. See Haley, *Charles Goodnight*, 122.

25. Millard, *Cowpuncher*, 21.

26. L. B. Eddins, interview.

27. Kellogg, "Pocket Journal," 8.

28. Dobie, *Vaquero*, 275.

29. Haley, *Charles Goodnight*, 217.

30. Ibid., 258–159.

31. Boyd, interview.

32. G. W. Roberson, interview with Haley, Vega, 30 June 1926, Haley Collection, Haley Library, Midland.

33. Composite of statements, Goodnight, interview, 8 April 1927, and Haley, *Charles Goodnight*, 258–259.

34. Goodnight, interview, 8 April 1927.

35. Paul Patterson, "A Forgotten Empire of the Pecos," *The Cattleman* (May 1943), 24.

36. B. A. Oden, "Early Cowboy Days in New Mexico and Texas," typescript, Haley Library, Midland.

37. Goodnight, "The Cattle Trail."

CHAPTER FIVE

Hoof and Arrow

FOR THE LONG, DANGEROUS DRIVE THROUGH INDIAN COUNTRY ON THE Pecos, Charles Goodnight looked for one particular trait in a cowhand. "I want the fellow that is always looking for Indians," he said, "for he will fight when he runs onto them."[1]

Trail bosses had plenty of chances to test a cowhand's fighting spirit in 1867, for Comanches had discovered the hoof-cut trace of the Goodnight-Loving route and knew the longhorn as a favored item for barter with *comancheros*—native New Mexican traders.[2] In eagerly accepting beeves, *comancheros* handed out ammunition, arrow points, knives, calico, tobacco, coffee, whiskey, and trinkets. Already, Comanches had driven so many stolen beeves from the Texas interior to New Mexico that A. B. Norton, superintendent of Indian affairs, considered the Territory "filled with Texas cattle."[3] Now, the outlook for illegal trade was even brighter. By blazing a cattle trail to New Mexico, cowmen had rendered the Comanches' arduous trek to and from the Texas frontier unnecessary. The warriors needed only to turn to the Pecos, especially at Horsehead Crossing, and capture beeves already well on their way to *comanchero* country. Then the war parties could escape with the droves by heading northwest across the sands to east-central New Mexico's Portales Valley (present Roosevelt and Curry counties) before pressing on for settlements and traders.

Incredibly, Comanches even seized Fort Sumner–bound steers and carried them to the post themselves.

The vicinity of Horsehead Crossing in 1995. COURTESY OF THE AUTHOR

"I was there ... one day [in 1867]," recalled Charles Goodnight, "and looked up and saw six ... steers that I had lost [at Horsehead] coming across the parade ground. The Indians had driven them straight across the country to the Portales and then had driven them across to trade at Sumner."[4]

Even if a drove safely negotiated Comancheria, more danger lurked in southeastern New Mexico, where the west-lying Guadalupe and Sacramento (or White) mountains signaled Apache country. But to a cowhand anxious to see home again, it at least was a lesser peril, for Apaches did not enjoy the same trade relations with *comancheros* as did Comanches.[5]

Whether the threat was from Comanche arrow or Apache, it was a ride through hell for cowboys on the Pecos trail in 1867. Assessing the situation August 5, Edward Hatch of the U.S. Army lamented, "During the last year I am informed that every drove of cattle intended for the posts of New Mexico were captured when passing ... [Horsehead Crossing]."[6]

Hatch's information was exaggerated; some trail bosses did pass unscathed, through luck or through the skill of a Goodnight, who took special precautions in Indian country. When driving, he would tighten up the herd, making it less vulnerable, and when holding, he would protect the remuda by positioning it between the herd and camp.[7]

The bosses of four herds procured by Andy M. Adams of Fort Union, New Mexico, could have used luck, skill, and more in driving the Pecos trail in the spring of 1867. Seeking to fulfill Adams's contract for delivery of beef to Fort Sumner at 2½ cents per pound on foot,[8] George W. Hepburn and nine hands (including Thomas Turner and Richard Fowler) pointed 656 beeves west from the Middle Concho headwaters on April 17. About 10 p.m. six days later, the exhausted cowhands finally reached Horsehead, only to see 365 head spirited away into the night by fifty to seventy-five Comanches. When day broke, Hepburn and a few hands pursued and recovered thirty-eight beeves, but Indians raided again on the night of April 26 and seized fifteen horses.[9]

On May 4, Adams's bookkeeper and confidant, Edwin B. Hepburn, struck out from Spring Creek in present Tom Green County with 471 beeves.[10] A day or so ahead of him were more than 1,000 cattle in the charge of Ben F. Gooch, and another 700 head owned by James Whitehead. On May 6 near the Middle Concho headwaters, 150 to 300 Indians seized the Gooch and Whitehead herds and captured drover Billy Dumas, literally skinning the poor man and leaving him to die an agonizing death. Gooch and other drovers escaped by hiding in a thicket, but Whitehead, his family, and a man named James Watson (who suffered a severe neck wound) had no choice but to fight back from behind a breastwork of wagons, oxen, and a horse. Holding off the hostiles until the next morning, the Whitehead party finally escaped.[11]

Just one day later, the Edwin Hepburn drove reached the head of the Middle Concho. "That night while holding the cattle under close herd," he recounted in an affidavit two months later, "the Indians charged us, capturing the herd. Don't know what tribe they belong to, but suppose them to be Kickapoos. The next day we gathered 103 head that the Indians dropped or lost."[12]

Adams's third herd, in the charge of Joel D. Hoy of Camp San Saba, trailed out 1,014-head strong from Spring Creek May 15 with eleven drovers, including James S. Bourland, 41, of Llano, and brothers Nathan A. Cavin, 22, and Byron H. Cavin, 19, both of Burnett County. Rumbling alongside was a wagon carrying Hoy's wife and their four children, whom the trail boss believed would be safer with an armed party than at home.

About May 24, the drovers reached Horsehead Crossing, where they laid over for water, rest, and forage. At approximately 1 p.m. the next day, as Byron Cavin was riding guard around the herd, Hoy's six-year-old daughter Kate saw "a cloud of dust" and realized it was a "band of Indians who were trying to steal our horses." Byron, in face of 150 hostiles, put spurs to his horse and rode hard for camp.

"The Indians," recalled Nathan Cavin in 1892, "fired a few shots, passed on to the herd, and divided it into several parts and drove it off. The warriors then came back."

Kate would never forget what happened next.

"Before the Indians reached us," she related decades later, "my father put the children and myself in the wagon and told us to drive down in a gully while they prepared to fight. Mother loaded the guns for the twelve men, while the Indians made an attack on us. The Indians used both bows and arrows and guns. They would send about three Indians by at a time just as fast as they could possibly ride. One of our men killed an Indian."

The warriors wounded three drovers, including Nathan Cavin and Bourland, who narrowly escaped death when a metal arrow point ripped through his coonskin cap and bent against his skull. Another arrow imbedded in Mrs. Hoy's hip or thigh, but the heroic woman "continued to load the guns," said Kate, "until she became so weak from the loss of blood that she had to have immediate attention." With a pocketknife, Bourland cut the arrowhead free.

As the Indians withdrew, the able-bodied drovers pushed and pulled a wagon bearing the wounded to a set of adobe walls—the ruins of a Butterfield stage stand around a bend upstream from Horsehead. There they huddled, day and night, placing all their hopes on a cowhand who presumably slipped over the walls for help. Yards away, he gained the river only to drown.

"No food nor water . . . passed the lips of these people during the three days siege," noted John Warren Hunter, an eyewitness to the breaking of the siege. "During the day they were consumed by the burning sun, and the night brought no rest as every man had to stand to arms and maintain the utmost vigilance. For three days and nights, they held their own against fearful odds."

Finally, on the morning of the fourth day, little Kate looked toward Castle Gap's cleft and saw "another cloud of dust"—a 100-man prospecting party led by Jacob Schnively and Colonel William Dalrymple.

"[We] heard shots and yells that indicated that a fight was in progress . . . ," related Hunter, one of the prospectors. "We rallied and were on the eve of making a charge, when the Indians discovered us bearing down on them, [and] picked up and left double quick. . . . When we came to their relief . . . [Mrs. Hoy] was in a state of delirium from the effects of pain, thirst, and high fever."

Outfitted by the prospectors, the drovers recovered 60 stray steers and tallied their losses: 954 beeves, 23 horses and mules, a loaded wagon, and 4 yoke of oxen.[13]

On May 15 near Llano, the snake-bit Adams operation dispatched its fourth herd for the Pecos, in the charge of twenty-seven-year-old Orville A. Oatman of Llano. Driving the beeves were ten cowhands, including Jim Moss, Charley Moss, Allen Roberts, and Mort Holton. One hundred thirty-five steers bolted away in a stampede, reducing the herd to 800 by the time they reached Horsehead Crossing. There on May 28, 100 to 150 Comanches and Kiowas—with whom Comanches were allied—overpowered the drovers and seized the herd, as well as fifteen horses or mules later valued at $2,250. They also torched two commissary wagons worth $2,650. The drovers, including two wounded, took refuge in a sinkhole and survived a days-long siege.[14]

Charles Goodnight and Oliver Loving, returning down the Pecos that spring with about nine drovers after wintering in New Mexico and forming a partnership, met a hail of Comanche bullets as they neared Horsehead Crossing. One slug split the crown of cowhand Frank Willburn's hat and creased his forehead, but the cowboys escaped and slipped through dangerous Castle Gap by night. Meeting a westbound herd on the Staked Plains the next day, Goodnight sought out the trail boss and warned him of Indians ahead.

"Let them come," snapped the man. "I'd like to sample those damned Comanches."

In disgust, Goodnight pushed on to the east to gather another herd, leaving the trail boss to ride straight into Castle Gap and an ambush that cost him his cattle and wagons.[15]

These were desperate times, and with Forts Sumner and Stanton in New Mexico suffering the consequences in lost beef, the U.S. Army decided to respond. A thirty-one-man escort, from a Middle Concho outpost near present Arden, Texas, reached Horsehead Crossing June 18 with three herds, and by early July, a twenty-one-man guard had seen a fourth herd through to the Pecos.[16] Finally, the Goodnight-Loving route had a military presence.

July 7 would bring more good news for cowhands: the U.S. Army reoccupied Fort Stockton, thirty-four miles southwest of Horsehead.[17] Post officials soon moved to protect the beleaguered trail, spurred in part by a warning issued July 27 by District of Texas headquarters in Galveston: "It having been reported that *Indians are assembling at points on the Pecos River* with view to raid on the settlements, you will keep your command . . . alert."[18]

Two days later, Captain George Gamble and forty men tracked a large raiding party to Horsehead and staved off a sure attack on a pair of cattle herds. On August 5, post commander Edward Hatch informed his superiors of the importance of guarding Horsehead "when cattle intended for government use in New Mexico are passing. . . . When notified of the probable time when cattle are to reach this crossing . . . , I can readily protect them."[19]

But in this vast wilderness where communiques traveled at the pace of a horse or wagon, the Army's plan to protect the trail came too late to help Goodnight and Loving, already driving hard for Sumner with 2,500 beeves road-branded with a circle.

From the start, it seemed a foredoomed drive. Barely out of the frontier settlements, Indians swooped down and stampeded their herd. Recovering the runaways, Goodnight rejoined the drove and sought much-needed sleep, only to awaken to a second attack. This time it cost Goodnight and Loving not only 262 steers, but a cowhand—Joe Loving (no relation to Oliver Loving), who caught a nonfatal arrow in the neck. Pushing on through a night rain to avoid more trouble, the cowboys soon found themselves chasing the lead steers through a fierce storm. Night after night, the beeves continued to run, even thundering right through camp one daybreak near Buffalo Gap. But it remained for the Pecos to summon up real tragedy.

The very first hours on the river portended things to come. Bedding the animals 200 yards from Horsehead Crossing, the weary cowboys tried to hold the herd through a driving rain. Breaking free, the beeves lured the cowhands on a dangerous chase through a hard dark that hid the river's sharp, winding bank.

At daybreak, they counted the herd 162 short and took up the runaways' trail. More than twenty-five miles distant, "One-Armed Bill" Wilson and other cowhands found the beeves in the hands of Indians and were content to escape with their scalps.

Goodnight and Loving pushed on up the Pecos into late July, when, still a few days' drive below the New Mexico line, Loving and Wilson rode ahead for Santa Fe to secure beef contracts. Wary of Comanches, they traveled only by night as far as the Black River-Pecos confluence, and then proceeded by day. Somewhere near present Otis, New Mexico, where the trail crossed an open plain well to the west of the meandering Pecos, they suddenly saw a large raiding party bearing down from the southwest. The two men reined their horses off-trail and rode hard for the nearest approach of the river, where they hoped for a natural bulwark from which to fight back.

Presumably two and one-half miles east-northeast of present Otis, at a point at which the plain suddenly falls away thirty-five feet to form a mile-long bluff fronting the Pecos from as little as 200 feet away, they made their stand in a shallow gully at river's edge. In late evening a bullet shattered Loving's wrist and cut a skin-deep gash across his side. Believing the torso wound fatal, he begged Wilson to flee by night and carry word of his demise to his family. As the moon fell and plunged them into darkness, Wilson slipped into the Pecos and escaped.

Oliver Loving. COURTESY OF J. EVETTS HALEY COLLECTION, N. S. HALEY MEMORIAL LIBRARY, MIDLAND, TEXAS

Three days later, barefoot and half-dead, Wilson met up with the herd near Adobe Walls watering in Texas and told Goodnight of the siege. Riding desperately through an evening and a night, Goodnight and five men reached the site between two and four o'clock the following afternoon to find evidence of the struggle but no hint of Loving's fate. Presuming him dead, they returned to the herd and forged on for Sumner.

But Loving, incredibly, was still alive. Through a second and third day, he fought off Comanches before slipping into the river and making his way upstream, evidently to the next trail watering at Loving's Bend (Wildcat Bluff) in present Carlsbad, New Mexico. There, he survived another three days before wagoners happened upon him. Despite reaching Fort Sumner and gaining medical attention, Loving died of his wounds September 25.[20]

Twenty-four days later, W. E. Cureton and his father embarked from Coleman County with a herd of mature steers. At Horsehead Crossing, Indians stormed into the drove and seized eleven saddle horses. Trying to regroup, the Cureton outfit saw the dust rising against Castle Gap and found not only another herd approaching, but an escort of one sergeant and eighteen men. Gaining the crossing, the escort turned back for Fort Chadbourne in present Coke County, leaving the Cureton party to face the dangerous trek upriver with tired mounts and a depleted remuda.

"We went up the river together," recalled W. H. Boyd, who was with the second herd, "camping about half a mile apart, with our wagons camped between the two herds to keep them from mixing."

At present Roswell, New Mexico, the Curetons turned up the Hondo River, while the Boyd outfit continued to Sumner and delivered 1,160 beeves November 7.[21]

At the end of November, W. E. Cureton and five hands—mounted on Spanish mules and trailing two pack animals—headed back for Texas. As they reached the headwaters of the Middle Concho, they found a gruesome sight.

"There in a depression a little way from the road," recalled Cureton in 1922, "lay Jim and John Ketchum of San Saba and . . . other cowboys, dead. The Indians had killed them two days before as they were returning from New Mexico."

On December 21, Lieutenant George A. Thurston and twenty-two enlisted men from a U.S. Army camp at present San Angelo removed four bodies from the gully and a fifth from the nearby chaparral. Identifying four of the victims—the Ketchum brothers, William Truman, and Thomas Darnell—Thurston oversaw their burial in a common grave.[22] The fifth casualty may have been a man named Compare from the San Saba area.[23]

The massacre of the drovers marked a violent end to the drive of 1867. By all routes, 35,000 beeves had started out from Texas,[24] uncounted thousands of them down the Goodnight-Loving Trail. Never again would drovers find the Pecos trace quite so bloody, but neither would Comanches readily give up *comanchero* barter as long as beeves still stirred its alkali dust.

NOTES

Unless otherwise indicated, all towns, counties, and map quadrangles throughout notes are in Texas.

1. Charles Goodnight, "Indians at Castle Canyon," typescript statement, Charles Goodnight file, Haley Collection, Haley Library, Midland.
2. For a study of the *comancheros*, see Haley, *Charles Goodnight*, 185–197.
3. Wallace and Hoebel, *The Comanches*, 267–268, citing A. B. Norton (superintendent of Indian affairs, New Mexico) to commissioner of Indian affairs, 24 August 1867, *Annual Report*, 1867, 194–195.
4. Goodnight, "Indians at Castle Canyon."
5. Ibid.
6. Edward Hatch to acting assistant adjutant (hereinafter, AAA) general, District of Texas, 5 August 1867, letters sent, Fort Stockton.
7. Haley, *Charles Goodnight*, 249, 158.
8. Ibid., 148. Information regarding Adams's home is from Orville A. Oatman's 2 November 1867 deposition in an Indian depredations case, as quoted in Frank Rigler, "The Andy M. Adams Story, Part 2," *The Highlander*, 18 January 1973, section B, 1–2.
9. George W. Hepburn, statement before Charles A. Brown (notary public, County of San Miguel, Territory of New Mexico), Fort Sumner, New Mexico, 5 July 1867, as filed in an Indian depredations case and quoted in Rigler, "Andy M. Adams Story," 1. Information regarding Turner and Fowler is as paraphrased by Rigler from their own corroborative statements.

10. Rigler, "Andy M. Adams Story," 1; and Edwin B. Hepburn, statement before Charles A. Brown (notary public, County of San Miguel, Territory of New Mexico), Fort Sumner, 5 July 1867, as filed in an Indian depredations case and quoted in Rigler, "Andy M. Adams Story," 1.

11. Judge John Beasley, McCulloch, McCulloch County, to General D. R. Gurley, 10 July 1867, Throckmorton Papers, Texas State Library, Austin; and James E. Rauk, San Antonio, to Governor E. M. Pease, 17 August 1867, Pease Papers, Texas State Library, Austin.

12. Edwin B. Hepburn, statement, 5 July 1867, in Rigler, "Andy M. Adams Story," 1. Beasley to Gurley, 10 July 1867, indicates the attack on the Edwin Hepburn outfit occurred May 7, not May 8. Rauk to Pease, 17 August 1867, indicates that several drovers were wounded, though none mortally, and that Indians also took the remuda and camp equipage.

13. This account of the siege of the Hoy party is based on: Joel D. Hoy, statement before Charles A. Brown (notary public, County of San Miguel, Territory of New Mexico), Fort Sumner, 5 July 1867, and statements of Nathan A. Cavin and Byron H. Cavin before John C. Oatman (attorney for claimant) and Thomas Ball (attorney for the U.S.), Llano, 18 June 1892, all as filed in Indian depredations case[s] and quoted by Rigler, "Andy M. Adams Story," 1; Beasley to Gurley, 10 July 1867; Rauk to Pease, 17 August 1867; Boyd, interview; Kate Longfield [Hoy's daughter], "Pioneer Woman Tells of Perilous Trip," *Frontier Times* Vol. 14, No. 2 (November 1936), 56–57 (originally published as "Three Days in 'Dobe Walls," *The Lampasas Record*, 3 September 1931); John Warren Hunter, "The Ill-fated Schnively Expedition," *Frontier Times* Vol. 2, No. 1 (October 1924), 18–19 (originally published in *Hunter's Magazine*, 1911); A. Whitehurst, "Reminiscences of the Schnively Expedition of 1867," *SHQ* Vol. 8, No. 3 (January 1905), 270–271; Cora Melton Cross, "Tells of Indians and Cattle Thieves," *Frontier Times* Vol. 3, No. 2 (November 1925), 5 (originally published in *Dallas Semi-Weekly News*, 21 May 1925); Goodnight, "Recollections II," 83–91; and Haley, *Charles Goodnight*, 159–160. Beasley to Gurley indicates the attack occurred on May 27. Beasley to Gurley also states that four party members were wounded, but Rauk to Pease indicates that five persons were wounded. The latter letter may include the drowned drover among the wounded. Hunter and Whitehurst both record the name of the wounded woman as Hoyett rather than Hoy.

14. Orville A. Oatman, deposition, 2 November 1867, as filed in an Indian depredations case and quoted in Rigler, "Andy M. Adams Story," 1; and John Oatman (Orville A. Oatman's father and owner of part of the cattle), deposition, 6 March 1897, Indian Depredations Claim Number 1187, quoted in Rigler, "Andy M. Adams Story," 2.

15. Goodnight, "Recollections II," 83, 87–89; Goodnight, "Indians at Castle Canyon;" and Haley, *Charles Goodnight*, 155–158. Information on the Goodnight-Loving partnership is from Haley, *Charles Goodnight*, 147.

16. Lieutenant P. M. Boehm to Charles A. Vernon, 19 July 1867, Records of the War Department, Fort Concho, National Archives, Washington, D.C., as quoted in Haley, *Fort Concho and the Texas Frontier* (San Angelo: San Angelo Standard-Times, 1952), 124–125.

17. Post returns, July 1867, Fort Stockton, National Archives microfilm, Southwest Collection, Texas Tech University, Lubbock. Distance is from journal of Thomas B. Hunt, who determined it to be 33.75 trail miles.

18. Brevet Major General Griffin to commanding officer, 27 July 1867, letters and telegrams received, Fort Stockton.

19. Edward Hatch to AAA general, District of Texas, 5 August 1867, letters sent, Fort Stockton; and post returns, Fort Stockton, July 1867.

20. This account of the 1867 Goodnight and Loving drive, the Loving-Wilson Indian fight, and Loving's demise is drawn from: Goodnight, "Recollections II," 91–114; Goodnight, interviews, 5 June 1925 and 8 April 1927; Goodnight, "Indians at Castle Canyon;" Hunter, *Trail Drivers*, 908–913 (W. J. "One-Armed Bill" Wilson's narrative) and 903–908 (Charles Goodnight's narrative); Charles Goodnight, "Recollections I," 37–48, and 52–59 (W. J. Wilson's narrative titled "Wilson's Getaway from the Indians"), Haley Library, Midland; Charles Goodnight's narrative in Grace Miller White, "Oliver Loving, the First Trail Driver," *Frontier Times* Vol. 19, No. 7 (April 1942), 273–275; Cox, *Historical and Biographical Record*, 307–308 (entry for Oliver Loving) and 478 (entry for Charles Goodnight); and Haley, *Charles Goodnight*, 162–183. Goodnight, in the 8 April 1927 interview, indicated the Loving-Wilson Indian fight occurred "on the west side of the river about four or five miles below the site of Carlsbad [New Mexico]." In his *Trail Drivers* account of his search and rescue mission, Goodnight further details that it occurred at a location where the plain "drops abruptly some one hundred feet" at a distance of 150 feet from the river bank. Haley, *Charles Goodnight*, 170, gives the latter distance as "about one hundred yards." Goodnight, in White, "Oliver Loving," 273, again says the plains "break off abruptly" at the location. In my study of topographic maps of the vicinity, the lone site which suggests the location described by Goodnight is situated near Otis, New Mexico, as I have detailed. In my personal inspection of the site 15 July 1996, I found it consistent with Goodnight's accounts, although this bluff drops only thirty-six feet, from an elevation of 3,081 feet to 3,045 feet. The flat between the base of the bluff and the river is now in cultivation. The upstream end of this bluff is situated 5.2 miles from Wildcat Bluff in present Carlsbad. See U.S.G.S. Otis Quadrangle, New Mexico, 7.5-minute series, 1985 (topographic map); and U.S.G.S. Carlsbad East Quadrangle, New Mexico (topographic map).

21. William E. Cureton, "Westward I Go Free: The Memoirs of William E. Cureton," recorded 8 February 1922, *SHQ* Vol. 81, No. 2 (October 1977), 174–175; Hunter, *Trail Drivers*, 54 (narrative of W. E. Cureton); and Boyd, interview.

22. Cureton, "Westward I Go," 175; and Haley, *Fort Concho*, 155–156, citing George A. Thurston to Captain G. C. Huntt, December 27, 1867, Fort Concho files.

23. Fayette Tankersley, "Route Traversed by Southern Trail," *Mertzon Weekly Star*, undated clipping, Haley Collection, Haley Library, Midland. Tankersley, who was born in 1859, inspected the graves on numerous occasions.

24. "The Cattle Movement," *Texas Live Stock Journal*, 5 December 1885, 2.

CHAPTER SIX

Thundering Herds

DESPITE THE INDIAN THREAT, THE GOODNIGHT-LOVING TRAIL QUICKLY became a major route to the unstocked ranges of the West. Not only could Texas cowmen drive north to Colorado and Wyoming by way of the Pecos, and from Wyoming to the Pacific Coast, but also to California again. By trailing up the Pecos to the Hondo River confluence at modern Roswell, New Mexico, they could veer into the sunset and catch the old California Trail near the Rio Grande.[1]

To guard increased trade and extend the frontier, the U.S. Army established Fort Concho 134 miles east of Horsehead Crossing late in 1867.[2] From its location at the juncture of the Concho rivers, the cavalry could scout the Goodnight-Loving Trail west up the Middle Concho and discourage hostiles.

Soon, the Army inched nearer the Pecos with garrisons. In the spring of 1868, officials set up an outpost, Camp Charlotte, at the mouth of Kiowa Creek, eight miles from the Middle Concho head.[3] By late July, down-trail in the dreaded Staked Plains, the Army occupied Middle (Centralia or Central) Mail Station thirty-four miles shy of Castle Gap.[4] On the Pecos itself, a Fort Stockton company of infantry had dug in by April where the threat was greatest: Horsehead Crossing. The picket's presence, which continued on into summer,[5] did deter Indian depredations at the ford, but cowmen such as John Simpson Chisum learned that the vast, lonely Pecos offered other points just as vulnerable.

Successful in a fall 1867 drive to New Mexico, where he wintered his 600 to 900 beeves about eight miles below Bosque Grande,[6] forty-three-

John Simpson Chisum about 1866. COURTESY OF SOUTHEASTERN NEW MEXICO
HISTORICAL SOCIETY, CARLSBAD, NEW MEXICO

year-old Chisum secured a beef contract with Fort Sumner contractor James Patterson in the spring of 1868. For every Texas steer Chisum delivered to Bosque Grande, Patterson would pay him $35. Chisum immediately set about purchasing 1,165 head of cattle in northern Texas from veteran Pecos drover Robert K. Wylie and others. Four to eight years old, each beef averaged 700 pounds and cost $20.

When the herd reached Horsehead Crossing, Chisum's brother Pittser asked the picket for an escort up the river. Denied protection, the Chisum outfit nevertheless pushed safely through Texas, only to meet disaster in New Mexico at the Black River-Pecos confluence. There on June 12, 150 Indians swept in and seized the drove and a saddle mule. The cowboys recovered 65 steers and trailed the main herd twenty miles up the Black River, where they found 200 cattle carcasses bearing the Chisum brand. Although John Chisum initially believed that Comanches were responsible, he later blamed Mescalero Apaches, toward whose Guadalupe Mountains haunts the tracks had led.[7]

Even as the drive was under way, the Army negotiated a new treaty at Sumner with the Navajos, almost 3,000 of whom had died in their four years of captivity on the Pecos. On June 18, 1868, six days after the incident at Black River, the U.S. government finally closed Bosque Redondo Reservation and allowed the Navajos to return to their homeland in northwestern New Mexico.[8]

The action abruptly ended the demand for beef at Sumner, a circumstance which led the man who would become cattle king of the Pecos— John Simpson Chisum—to form a partnership with the dominant figure of the Pecos trail—Charles Goodnight. Only months before, the two men had wintered herds on the river within eight miles of one another. Now, for a fifty-fifty split plus a dollar a head, Chisum would drive Texas cattle up to Bosque Grande and deliver them to Goodnight, who in turn would trail them to buyers throughout the western Great Plains.[9]

As drives continued, cowboys learned to be wary of not only Comanches and Apaches, but badmen who saw in the lawless Pecos a place to ply their treachery. In mid-August 1868, for example, twelve armed Mexicans rode through Fort Stockton en route to the Pecos. Although they claimed to be hunting Indians, they nevertheless streaked their faces with war paint and prowled Horsehead Crossing for two weeks, waiting for a chance to steal stock. Drovers bound for El Paso with a cattle herd suffered the consequences, losing four horses to the gang. Captain George Gamble of Fort Stockton took up the chase and captured nine of the *bandidos*, but the others fled toward Mexico with the horses.[10]

Regardless of the dangers, cowboys kept the Pecos trail well-beaten that fall. In one twenty-four-hour stretch, five droves—each with 1,000 to 3,000 beeves—forged up the Middle Concho past Camp Charlotte, whose poorly rationed garrison usually levied a tax of one beef per herd,[11] a small price to pay for a temporary measure of security.

One of those herds may have been bossed by J. H. Wheeler, for whom seventeen-year-old Jim K. Millwee helped drive 1,200 beeves to Bosque Grande that season. Gaining the Pecos, the ten-man outfit used a variation of the Goodnight-Loving Trail.

"From Horsehead Crossing . . . we kept up the east side to Narbo's Crossing, where we crossed to the west side . . . ," Millwee recalled in 1932. "From there we drove up to the Delaware, then to Black River and to the next watering place at Loving's Bend. We kept on the west side and crossed back to the east at Sixty-Mile Crossing [presumably sixty miles from Bosque Grande]."[12]

The Black River–Pecos confluence and its environs, far from any military outpost, continued to bedevil drovers. On the evening of March 1, 1869, emigrant Robert Adam Casey Sr. and his wife, Ellen Eveline, along with their children and Mexican hands, bedded 1,500 beeves and a flock of sheep on the flats three miles north of the watering place. Alongside was a herd of 2,500 animals owned by James E. Rauk and guarded by an eighteen-man outfit bossed by brothers Lace and Joe Bridges. The next morning, in the dense fog of pre-dawn, Apaches suddenly stampeded the larger herd and attacked the Bridges camp, which lay fifty yards from the Casey covered wagon.

"Us children were poking our heads out from under the sheet [wagon tarp]," recalled Casey's son Robert Adam, who was eight at the time. "And they thought we was men, and that kept them away from us."

As the assault wore on, the Bridges brothers seemed resigned to die. At the elder Casey's urging, however, Joe Bridges and his hands rolled

Robert Adam Casey Sr. and Ellen Eveline Casey. COURTESY OF SOUTHEASTERN NEW MEXICO HISTORICAL SOCIETY, CARLSBAD, NEW MEXICO

their chuck wagon to the emigrants' camp and formed a breastwork. From the Casey wagon, young Robert Adam watched the Apache leader Jose de la Paz, who sported a red blanket on his shoulders, ride in to stampede the sheep.

"Father says to Mother, 'They've got your sheep!'" related the younger Casey in 1937. "Well, she was loading the shotgun, and she dropped it and grabbed a pan and put some corn in it and rattled it and called the sheep back. That surprised [de la Paz]. . . . He just stopped. . . . Father got a bead on him, and as he turned to go, Father shot him in the back. . . . Brother said, 'I saw the dust fly from his blanket!'"

After the Apaches lifted the almost-two-hour siege, the trail outfits regrouped and pushed on, minus the entire Bridges herd and 1,000 Casey beeves.[13]

A cowhand's return trip continued to be as dangerous as the drive. Reaching California that June with R. F. Tankersley and his herd of 2,500 beeves, cowhands Tom Compton, Jim Cummings, and Sam

Burleson turned back down the trail for Texas. Burleson, one of many black cowboys who drove the Pecos trail, was leading a pack horse as they entered Castle Gap and suddenly came under Indian attack. As feathered arrows rained down from the bluffs, Compton fell dead beside him and Cummings took a fatal arrowhead to the skull. Cutting the pack animal free, Burleson put spurs to his horse and escaped.[14]

Camped at Dagger Bend on the Pecos September 23, 1870, after driving a John Chisum herd to New Mexico, three cowhands—identified by a contemporary San Antonio newspaper as "Rhodes, Sloan, and Chisum [obviously a brother to John Chisum]"—awakened to a daybreak assault by fifty Indians. Luckily, the Texans escaped injury, but they lost fifty-six of their fifty-eight horses and mules.[15]

The cattle they had delivered represented a part of John Chisum's ever-growing herd, which he began moving drove-by-drove from Texas to his budding ranch at Bosque Grande after fulfilling his contract with Goodnight in 1870.[16] Even as Chisum's indebtedness grew (he had acquired many cattle on credit and would suffer stock losses of $150,000 to Indians), he was building a vast empire on the Pecos in New Mexico.[17]

Goodnight, meanwhile, had driven the Pecos trail for the last time, though he continued trailing herds along other stretches of the Goodnight-Loving route through 1874.[18] Decades later he would recall his years on the trail as the "happiest" he ever spent. "There were many hardships and dangers, of course, that called on all a man had of endurance and bravery," he reflected, "but when all went well there was no other life so pleasant."[19]

In the desperate moments of a spring day at Horsehead Crossing in 1871, twenty-two-year-old G. F. Banowsky, thirteen fellow drovers, and two emigrants were not concerned with living pleasantly; they just wanted to stay alive any way they could. Throwing their 3,000 longhorns and 40 horses away from the river to graze, they pitched camp near the old adobe walls of the stage stand for a much needed rest after the waterless ordeal from the Middle Concho.

"Shortly after the noon meal, when we were taking our ease, half of us asleep, we were startled by the Apache warwhoop," related Banowsky in 1930. "We ran for the wall, firing as we went, and found ourselves opposed by about 100 Indians."

While the warriors besieged the party, another 100 Indians drove away the remuda and cattle, including 100 beeves owned by a Colorado-bound man and his wife.

"Early in the battle," recalled Banowsky, "the woman received a bullet in the fleshy part of her hip. The incident completely unnerved the man, who threw down his gun and was of no further service in the fight. But it only enraged the woman, who fired faster than ever, and abused the Indians for everything she could lay her tongue to, and there is no doubt that she got several of them."

For more than an hour after seizing the stock, the Indians fought the drovers and emigrants for a yoke of oxen between the ruins and nearby river. Finally, the hostiles retreated with their casualties, leaving the oxen, two wagons, and a store of provisions.

"We dressed the woman's wound as best we could," related Banowsky, "and placing her and our supplies in one of the wagons, we left the other wagon and set out afoot for Fort Concho."[20]

Attacks on Pecos drovers intensified in 1872. Trailing back to Texas from Chisum's Bosque Grande Ranch in June, Charlie Rankin, John Barnes, and four other cowhands nooned at Horsehead Crossing's west bank as their 120 horses and 30 mules grazed a flat 200 to 300 yards away. Only two mules, hitched to the chuck wagon, remained in camp. Suddenly forty or fifty Comanches or Mescalero Apaches swept between the wagon and remuda. The cowhands put up a fierce fight, but Rankin fell to a wound in the hip and the Indians made off with all the grazing animals. For days, the able-bodied men walked the desert, all the way back to Trickham, Texas, as the cook brought up the wagon bearing the wounded man and their saddles.[21]

The depredations were not limited to the Pecos stretch of the trail. Sometime that spring, a Dr. Bartlett (or Bartley) lost a herd to Indians on the Middle Concho at Johnson's Mail Station, twenty-six and one-half miles west of Fort Concho. Persistent, Bartlett proceeded to join a trail outfit bossed by Madison Tucker of Erath County, and 10 a.m. on July 6 found the drove four miles below Pecos Falls. Riding 300 yards ahead of the lead steers, Bartlett suddenly met thirty Indians streaked with war paint. Wheeling his horse, he fled for the chuck wagon, but the warriors quickly rode him down and killed him.

Through the rising dust came more hostiles, as many as 300 in all, adorned in feathers and wearing deer and buffalo horns on their heads. The band divided, one-third capturing the herd and the others pursuing the fleeing drovers. At the wagon, the seven cowboys made their stand against bow and arrow. Fighting to keep their last four horses, they felled two Indians, including one they presumed to be a chief because of his numerous feathers. After two hours, the Indians withdrew far enough to induce the cowboys to back away from a few broken-down animals. The warriors then seized the animals and rode off, leaving Bartlett's body mutilated and burned.

After burying Bartlett, the drovers turned back for the frontier settlements July 7. Downriver, they found a drove of almost 2,000 head rounded up in a bend as a precaution against attack; the night before, owners Spiller and Miller had detected Indians prowling about their camp. Spiller and Miller also feared for a Brown County cattleman named Hoffman and his six hands, who had been at Horsehead Crossing with 650 beeves July 5 and had been expected to join them upstream the next day.

Learning that the missing outfit was armed only with one rifle and one shotgun, a cowhand named Roberts—who had survived the siege near Pecos Falls—rode on to Horsehead with Spiller. Reaching the crossing after nightfall, they found dead cattle but no sign of the drovers, spurring Roberts and two other men to seek help at Fort Stockton. Losing their way in the dark, they did not reach the post until July 10, the same day that stage passengers arrived to report meeting an eastbound herd five miles west of the Middle Concho headwaters. Possibly Hoffman's, the outfit had no wagon and only 200 cattle.

Seeking the herd taken near Pecos Falls, Captain F. S. Dodge and a cavalry troop—equipped with 100 rounds of ammunition per man and rations for twenty-six days—reached the site of the siege on July 11. Finding the Indians' trail too old to warrant a chase, Dodge followed orders and escorted the Spiller-Miller outfit and other droves upstream to Seven Rivers, New Mexico,[22] an adobe trading post established near Patterson's Crossing in late 1867.[23]

In this year of 1872, Captain Joseph Rendlebrock and a contingent of cavalry from Fort Concho also rode guard up the Pecos for several herds, including the trail's largest of record—12,000 head.[24] Some of these droves may have belonged to John Chisum, who moved more than 10,000 Texas beeves to his Bosque Grande ranch that season.[25]

Meanwhile, thirty-six-year-old Robert K. Wylie had ranching aspirations of his own in New Mexico, and turned loose 9,000 Texas cattle in 1872 at Eighteen-Mile Bend on the Pecos, thirty-two miles above Chisum's Bosque Grande headquarters. The next year, however, Wylie sold out to Chisum and returned to Texas.[26]

In extreme southern New Mexico, meanwhile, other cattlemen brought herds to the river's open range and stayed. By 1873 Milo L. Pierce of Buffalo, New York, and Lewis Paxton had set up a cow camp at the mouth of Pierce Canyon, five miles southeast of present Malaga and thirteen miles north of the Texas line. At first, they had brands of their own, but soon they went into partnership.[27] Like most early ranchers on the Pecos, they chose the east side for their grazing operation. Not only did the river serve as a buffer against Apaches from the west-lying mountains, it also marked a vegetative boundary.

"It was better country and better grass on the east side—it always was," noted W. R. "Jake" Owen, who came to the Pecos country in 1875.[28]

From the start, the Paxton-Pierce herd may have ranged south into Texas, for in 1873 George Owens and the 24th Infantry—marching with Colonel Ranald Mackenzie—found cattle grazing at Pope's Crossing. Far downstream, infantryman Owens also found three men living in dugouts and tending cattle along the river. The Roberts brothers, near Pontoon Crossing, and a McLaughlin, near Juan Cordona Salt Lake ten miles north of Horsehead, were among the first cowmen to dig in along the Pecos in Texas.[29] However, cowboys may have ridden herd over free-ranging cattle at Pope's Crossing much earlier, if an intriguing letter ostensibly penned by a man in April 1867 is to be believed.

Published (evidently in its entirety) in a 1962 Pecos, Texas, newspaper, the letter bears the signature "Jake" and is directed to the man's family members. "Am making quite a cowhand now," he wrote, "not as inexperienced as I was when I first came to the Pecos River. Am working for an outfit now near Pope's Crossing."[30]

At any rate, soon after Paxton and Pierce turned their cattle loose near Malaga, Joe H. Nash of Mississippi (and later Crosbyton, Texas) brought a herd to southern New Mexico. At first, he evidently partnered with Nathan Underwood near Seven Rivers, but by 1875 he had gone into business with H. J. "Jim" Ramer of Indiana and set up camp with Paxton and Pierce at Pierce Canyon.

Before the year was over, both outfits had moved downstream to uppermost Texas, where Nash and Ramer established a ranch at Pope's Crossing and soon built a rock headquarters. With the Roberts and McLaughlin ventures having failed, Nash-Ramer and Pierce-Paxton had the Texas coils to themselves. Still, for mutual support, perhaps, they chose to share the same Pecos range land straddling the Texas–New Mexico line.[31]

"The cattle was all running together in them days—[everybody] just rode lines," noted W. R. Owen.[32]

Meanwhile, a Robert K. Wylie outfit—in the charge of a man named Yopp—returned to the Pecos about 1873, working out of a west-side camp four to five miles above the Black River confluence. By 1875 the seldom-present Wylie had 2,500 beeves and controlled thirty miles of east river front, from the salt lake east of present Loving, New Mexico, up to Seven Rivers.[33] His domain, however, paled in comparison to the kingdom which cattle baron John Simpson Chisum was carving out for himself.

From his Twelve-Mile Bend cow camp above Bosque Grande, Chisum dispatched an outfit down the Pecos in April 1873 to bring back the last of his Texas cattle. With a chuck wagon and a remuda of seventy horses and thirty-five mules, trail boss George King and his hands reached Horsehead and crossed to the east side without incident. Pushing on, they reached the west edge of Castle Gap and pulled rein.

"We camped about sundown and the horses were out feeding," related cowhand John Barnes, who had survived an attack at Horsehead the year before. "We hadn't pulled our saddles off. The Indians run in and cut them off. A few shots were fired on both sides, and we lost our horses and never did get them back. They'd taken all the horses we had except six or eight saddle horses, and all the mules."

Chisum foreman George Teague, waiting at Trickham with the cattle herd, had to purchase more horses and mules from the Coggin brothers before undertaking the drive to New Mexico.[34]

Such depredations led Captain F. S. Dodge, on May 13, 1873, to declare the Goodnight-Loving route unsafe from Johnson's Station on the Middle Concho to Seven Rivers in New Mexico. Dodge added his conviction that drovers too often looked to the Army for protection rather than arm themselves properly "Last year," he reported, "I saw a party of fifteen or twenty men in charge of about 1,000 cattle who had, in addition to their pistols, only two or three worn-out muskets in their party."[35]

Forging unescorted up the Pecos in July with the last Chisum herd, Teague had neither the firepower nor the men to fend off disaster. As the 1,600 beeves reached Adobe Walls watering, Indians attacked and captured the remuda of seventy-two horses and twenty-five mules, leaving the cowhands with only the horses they were riding and the mule team hitched to the chuck wagon. As a rider named Motto rode hard for the distant Chisum ranch to secure more animals, the drovers and their exhausted mounts pushed the herd on upstream. Gaining Black River, they met Motto and other Chisum hands hurrying down the Pecos with thirty to forty fresh horses.[36]

Pope's Crossing proved just as dangerous as Adobe Walls. In an attack near the ford about August 1, Indians severely wounded a drover. The incident prompted agent Bushnell, of the Mescalero Indian Agency near present Ruidoso, New Mexico, to investigate depredations along the river.

"From the finding of stolen stock and property in their [the Mescaleros'] possession near the agency," he wrote, "and from the apparent fact that the number of horses and mules was very great, and constantly increasing, the conclusion was fair that these Indians . . . shared in the profits of the thefts, if not entirely responsible for all."[37]

The events of September 28, 1874, opened the way for greater depredations by Mescalero Apaches. On that day, Colonel Ranald S. Mackenzie and his command attacked five Comanche and Kiowa villages in
Palo Duro Canyon in the Texas Panhandle. By destroying their supplies
and capturing more than 1,000 horses and mules,[38] Mackenzie forced the
Indians to their reservation in present Oklahoma and effectively ended
their forays along the Pecos in Texas. With Comanches finally yielding
the territory after 125 years of bloody rule, Mescalero Apaches were free
to raid the river from their Guadalupe Mountains stronghold and New
Mexico reservation.

G. F. Banowsky, who had survived an Indian attack at Horsehead
Crossing in 1871, was among the unlucky drovers who could testify to
the increased Apache threat. Returning down the Pecos in 1875 after
driving a herd to New Mexico, he and eleven other men were caught
unawares by 50 to 200 Apaches two miles above Grand Falls, a onetime
cataract near present Grandfalls, Texas.

"I was lying under the wagon, reading an old magazine," he related
in 1930. "One of the boys near me suddenly leaped to his feet, and said:
'Better get ready; the Indians are coming!'"

Knowing the man was prone to joke, Banowsky disregarded the
warning. The next moment, however, guns began to crack.

"The Indians fired first, and then raised the warwhoop, and began
to circle us," said Banowsky. "They outnumbered us and had better guns
than we had, but as they rode at full speed, they shot wild. I saw several
of them tumble off their horses, and saw several horses go down. But they
gave us a good whipping, and ran off all our horses but one."

The next day, the drovers fortunately met up with a cow outfit and
bought an additional horse. Hitching the animals to a wagon, they turned
the reins over to the teamster, who had but one leg. For Banowsky, it must
have seemed like *déjà vu*—for the second time in four years, he set out
afoot with fellow drovers for Fort Concho (this time more than 170 miles
away) to tell of losing an Indian fight on the Pecos.[39]

John Chisum, despite setbacks of his own, saw his Pecos herd grow
to an incredible 60,000 head in the mid-1870s.[40] In 1875 the *Las Vegas
Gazette* described his domain at its height:

John Simpson Chisum.

The Chisum ranch . . . extends south along the river near Fort Sumner to Seven Rivers, a distance of 150 miles. . . . East and west it reaches as far as a man can travel on a good horse during a summer [ride]. . . . The home ranch is at Bosque Grande. . . . At this point a general store is kept, buildings and large corrals constructed. At convenient points up and down the river from the home ranch are . . . cow camps. . . . Not less than 100 employees take care of the cattle.[41]

That same year, however, Chisum not only moved his headquarters to South Springs River near present Roswell, New Mexico, but transferred ownership of his cattle to the St. Louis firm of Hunter and Evans, which assumed his debts of more than $200,000. In the next five years, the beef commission house would trail 50,000 onetime Chisum beeves from the banks of the Pecos to Kansas.[42]

Although his brothers, Pittser and James, would continue ranching the Pecos in southern New Mexico,[43] John Chisum no longer had a role in the story of the river.[44] Soon, though, would come other outfits, flooding the Texas coils with cattle and furthering the legend of the Pecos cowboy.

NOTE

Unless otherwise indicated, all towns, counties, and map quadrangles throughout notes are in Texas.

1. Haley, "Log of the Texas-California Cattle Trail," 210.
2. Haley, *Fort Concho*, 128. Distance is from journal of Thomas B. Hunt, 8–10.
3. Haley, *Fort Concho*, 156. Distance is from journal of Thomas B. Hunt, 9.
4. Haley, *Fort Concho*, 157. Distance is from journal of Thomas B. Hunt, 10.
5. San Antonio *Herald*, 18 April 1868, as cited by Clayton Williams, *Last Frontier*, 91; and Ruth Shackleford diary as contained in Holmes, *Covered Wagon Women* Vol. 9, 191–192.
6. Hunter, *Trail Drivers*, 951; Haley, *Charles Goodnight*, 203; and Cox, *Historical and Biographical Record*, 300. Some accounts, including *The New Handbook of Texas*, Vol. 2 (Austin: The Texas State Historical Association, 1996, six volumes), 91, say Chisum's first drive up the Pecos occurred in 1866.
7. Cox, *Historical and Biographical Record*, 301; and Indian Depredations Claim Number 5388, 241 (petition of John Chisum, 31 January 1870), 242 (statement of James Patterson, 26 September 1873), 243 (petition of John Chisum, 27 July 1874), 243 (statement of Robert K. Wylie, n.d.), and 243 (petition of John Chisum, May 1884). Pittser Chisum's name is sometimes spelled Pitzer. In questioning on 19 January 1883

(page 244 of claim number 5388), the claimant stated that "the Mescaleros inhabited the Guadalupe Mountains west of the Pecos River and close by, and drove the stock in that direction, which is evident to me that they were Mescalero Apaches." Aware of the *comanchero* trade enjoyed by Comanches, the claimant further noted that "Comanches would not have killed so great a number of cattle all at one time and place." However, George E. Tabbs, in testimony on 24 July 1871 (page 242 of claim number 5388), indicated that a herd of 450 cattle, seized from Comanche traders in New Mexico and held at that time at Fort Bascomb, contained "quite a number" of beeves bearing Chisum's brand. These cattle, however, may have dated from a later raid.

8. Gregory Scott Smith (manager, Fort Sumner State Monument), telephone interview with author, Fort Sumner, New Mexico, 17 February 1996; and Wilson, *Fort Sumner*, 4.

9. Haley, *Charles Goodnight*, 204.

10. Captain George Gamble to Lieutenant C. E. Morse, AAA general, 31 August 1868, letters and telegrams sent, Fort Stockton.

11. So reported San Antonio *Herald* correspondent H. C. Logan after his stage trip to El Paso during the latter part of 1868. See Clayton Williams, *Last Frontier*, 103–104. Logan's series of articles appeared in the *Herald* 20 and 26 of October, and 3, 10, 12, 17, 24, 26, and 27 November 1868.

12. Jim K. Millwee, interview with Haley, Lubbock, 3 July 1932, Haley Collection, Haley Library, Midland.

13. Robert Adam Casey, interview with Haley, Picacho, New Mexico, 25 June 1937, Haley Collection, Haley Library, Midland; and Klasner, *My Girlhood*, 32–35. Date of the attack is from Indian Depredations Claim Number 2429, as cited in a 1 March 1996 letter to the author from Michael E. Pilgrim with the Archives I Reference Branch, Textual Reference Division, National Archives, Washington, D.C.

14. Hunter, *Trail Drivers*, 765; and Tankersley, "Route Traversed."

15. Clayton Williams, *Last Frontier*, 139, quoting *Daily New Mexican* (Santa Fe, New Mexico), 3 November 1870, reprinted in *Pioneer News-Observer* (Kerrville), December 1972. W. C. Cochran may have referred to the same incident in "A Trip to Montana in 1869" (Haley Collection, Haley Library, Midland). Cochran, who drove up the Pecos in 1869, tells of a daybreak attack by forty Indians on a "Captain John Slone of San Saba" and other hands on their return trip with the remuda in 1870. He places the attack at Adobe Walls watering place, however, rather than at Dagger Bend. "There were two mules left," said Cochran, who was not present, "and the man that owned them kept them chained to his wagon every night. Everything in his outfit was burned except what two mules could pull. The men all walked to Fort Concho."

16. Cox, *Historical and Biographical Record*, 301, 478.

17. *New Handbook of Texas*, 91; and Haley, *Charles Goodnight*, 233.

18. Haley, *Charles Goodnight*, 217.

19. Haley, *Charles Goodnight*, 259.

20. G. F. Banowsky as quoted in W. S. Adair, "Texas Pioneer Tells of Fights with Indians," *Dallas Morning News*, 8 June 1930. This incident bears a striking resemblance to the siege of the Hoy party at the adobe ruins at Horsehead in 1867, but they seem to have been separate incidents.

21. Indian Depredations Claim Number 5388, claimant's brief and request for finding of facts, 25 (testimony of Charles Nebo), 25–26 (testimony of J. B. Miller), 26 (testimony of John Barnes), and 26 (testimony of B. F. Chisum). Nebo and Miller, along with Barnes, were eyewitnesses to the attack.

22. Zenas Bliss to AAA general, Department of Texas, San Antonio, 11 July 1872, letters sent, Fort Stockton; and Captain F. S. Dodge to post adjutant, Fort Stockton, 3 August 1872, letters received, Fort Stockton. The distance from Fort Concho to Johnson's Mail Station is from journal of Thomas B. Hunt, 8.

23. W. R. Owen, interview, 24 June 1937; and Clayton Williams, *Last Frontier*, 86.

24. Clayton Williams, *Last Frontier*, 164, citing Bliss to AA general, 19 November 1872, Army Commands, RG 98, National Archives, Washington, D.C.

25. Indian Depredations Claim Number 5388, claimant's brief and request for finding of facts, 23 (deposition of John Chisum, 19 January 1883).

26. Cox, *Historical and Biographical Record*, 299, 301. Location of Eighteen-Mile Bend (later spelled Eighteenmile Bend) is from Indian Depredations Claim Number 5388, 211.

27. "Pecos County 28 Years Ago," *The Fort Stockton Pioneer*, 17 September 1908 (reprint of an article in the San Antonio *Texas Sun*, November-December 1880); Klasner, *My Girlhood*, 65–66; and W. R. Owen, interviews, 12 August 1926, 2 March 1933, and 24 June 1937. Pierce, who was born in 1839 in Illinois, came to New Mexico in the fall of 1872. He already may have been ranching on the river by the end of the year. See Frederick Nolan, *The Lincoln County War: A Documentary History* (Norman: University of Oklahoma Press, 1992), 479.

28. W. R. Owen, interview, 24 June 1937.

29. George Owens, interview with Haley, Pecos, 10 January 1927, Haley Collection, Haley Library, Midland.

30. Marj Carpenter, "Letter from 1867 Reveals Early Pecos River Deeds," *The Pecos Independent and Enterprise*, 17 May 1962. The letter confounds the general notion that cowmen undertook ranching operations on the Pecos in Texas no sooner than the 1870s. Although I could not locate the original, I found no reason to question the letter's authenticity. Even if "1867" were taken to be a typographical error (either on the part of the cowhand or newspaper), the text of the letter includes a reference which still pinpoints its date of composition as the 1860s: "It has now been almost four years since brother died in the war." Nor is there any textual evidence to indicate that the cowhand was merely delivering herds to Pope's (or receiving them) for trailing on up to Fort Sumner or elsewhere. Indeed, several references suggest otherwise. In a 10 May 1996 letter to the author, Marj Carpenter could not recall any details regarding the original letter.

31. W. R. Owen, interviews, 2 March 1933 and 24 June 1937; James P. Jones, interview with Haley, Rocky Arroyo, New Mexico, 13–14 January 1927, in "Notes on the History of Southeastern New Mexico," bound volume, Haley Library, Midland; Walter Cochran, interview with Haley, Midland, date not known, in "Panhandle Notes, Volume I," bound volume, Haley Library, Midland; Klasner, *My Girlhood*, 66; journal of George A. Armes in George A. Armes, *Ups and Downs of an Army Officer* (Washington:

publisher not known, 1900), 464; *Fort Stockton Pioneer*, 17 September 1908; and Nolan, *Lincoln County War*, 62–63 (map), 121, 143. According to Nolan, 496, Nash was born in Alabama in 1855. The Roberts and McLaughlin operations evidently had left the Pecos by sometime in 1875, for W. R. Owen, in driving cattle upstream from Lancaster Crossing to New Mexico that year, found "not a person living" from "the state line on south to the Rio Grande." See W. R. Owen, interview, 12 August 1926.

32. W. R. Owen, interview, 24 June 1937.

33. Jones, interview; W. R. Owen, interviews, 12 August 1926, 2 March 1933, and 24 June 1937; and Klasner, *My Girlhood*, 66. Owen, a Wylie cowhand under a foreman named Yopp, worked out of a rock house line camp in the latter 1870s. At that time, the outfit's lower camp was about twelve miles below Loving's Bend at east-lying Old Wylie's Bluff. Owen once witnessed the ransacking of their lower camp by Indians who rolled their wagon over the drop-off to the river below. See W. R. Owen, interview, 24 June 1937.

34. Indian Depredations Claim Number 5388, claimant's brief and request for finding of facts, 23 (deposition of John Chisum), 29–30 (testimony of J. B. Miller), 30 (testimonies of John Barnes, George King, and P. M. Chisum), 30–31 (testimony of B. F. Chisum), 31 (statement of John Chisum), and 36 (statement of George E. Teague). Miller and King, in addition to Barnes, were eyewitnesses to the attack. Miller stated that they managed to retain eight or ten horses and four mules.

35. Captain F. S. Dodge to AA general, 13 May 1873, letters and telegrams sent, Fort Stockton.

36. Indian Depredations Claim Number 5388, claimant's brief and request for finding of facts, 33 (testimonies of P. M. Chisum, B. F. Chisum, and Alijo Herrera), 33–34 (testimony of Charles Nebo), 34 (testimonies of T. P. Weathered and J. B. Miller), 34–35 (testimony of John Barnes), 35 (testimonies of George King, E. B. Peter, and James M. Reynolds); and 37. Nebo, Weathered, Miller, Barnes, and perhaps King were eyewitnesses to the attack.

37. Indian Depredations Claim Number 5388, claimant's brief and request for finding of facts, 22–23, quoting Bushnell's annual report for 1873. W. D. Crothers, later the agent of the Mescalero Indian Agency, reported on 20 June 1876 that Mescaleros would trade the stolen animals to Comanches. See brief, 22.

38. Mary G. Crawford, "A History of West Texas," 1990–91 *Texas Almanac*, 47; and *New Handbook of Texas* Vol. 5, 28, Vol. 4, 416.

39. Adair, "Texas Pioneer," *Dallas Morning News*, 8 June 1930.

40. Cox, *Historical and Biographical Record*, 299, 302.

41. Mary Whatley Clarke, *John Simpson Chisum: Jinglebob King of the Pecos* (Austin: Eakin Press, 1984), 31, quoting a contemporary edition of *Las Vegas Gazette*.

42. Cox, *Historical and Biographical Record*, 302; Clarke, *John Simpson Chisum*, 32; and *New Handbook of Texas*, 91.

43. Harwood Hinton, interview with author, Midland, 9 July 1996. William Robert managed the James and Pittser Chisum outfit.

44. John Chisum died 22 December 1884. See Cox, *Historical and Biographical Record*, 299.

CHAPTER SEVEN

Cattle Kings Come to the Pecos of Texas

FROM THE EARLIEST TRAIL DRIVES, COWMEN HAD LOOKED UPON THE Texas stretch of the Pecos as a graveyard through which to hurry, not tarry. Now, in the late 1870s, things were changing, even as the Pecos country remained wild and dangerous. After all, Apaches and outlaws were still on the prowl, and with the military deterrent limited, the chances of a cowboy hanging on to his horse or his scalp were sometimes only as good as his aim. Too, even with enormous Pecos County organizing in 1875[1] and claiming the river for its eastern boundary from New Mexico to the Rio Grande, it remained a lonely land. The only settlement for hundreds of miles was adjacent to Fort Stockton, which itself was a hard day's ride from Horsehead Crossing and many days' ride from Pope's Crossing.

Nevertheless, cattlemen now took herds to the Pecos in Texas and stayed, carving dreams out of courage and sweat. Like Paxton-Pierce and Nash-Ramer, several of the earliest cowmen already had tried the New Mexico coils and simply drifted south, where the arid range land—which would remain unfenced for decades—demanded close ties with the river.

The RB outfit, owned by Henry M. Beckwith and his sons Robert and John, originated near Seven Rivers and Lakewood, New Mexico, and dropped down below the big salt lake near present Loving, New Mexico, in 1876 or 1877. From there, RB cattle grazed south along the Pecos to a point thirty miles inside Texas. Robert Beckwith met with a violent death in the Lincoln County War in New Mexico in 1878, but by August 18, 1879, his twenty-four-year-old brother John had set up camp at Sand Bend and incurred tax for 800 beeves, which evidently

85

Robert Beckwith. COURTESY OF ROBERT N. MULLIN COLLECTION, N. S. HALEY MEMORIAL LIBRARY, MIDLAND, TEXAS

ranged on the west-lying Pecos County side. Officials valued his herd at $5,600, or $7 an animal. John, however, never lived to pay the tax, for at the Nash camp at Pierce Canyon on August 26, he too died violently, the victim of a bullet fired by a cowhand in a dispute over cattle owner-ship. Nevertheless, by the fall of 1880, 1,600 head of "Beckwith Ward"

John Beckwith. COURTESY OF ROBERT N. MULLIN COLLECTION, N. S. HALEY MEMORIAL LIBRARY, MIDLAND, TEXAS

cattle (apparently a joint operation involving his father) ranged along the river.[2]

Another outfit, the AHB of Wallace Olinger and Charlie Krieling, also originated near Seven Rivers in the mid-1870s. On August 17, 1878, in yet another episode of bloodshed involving a Beckwith, Olinger severely wounded Henry M. Beckwith near Seven Rivers after Beckwith had killed a man and threatened Olinger's life. Venturing down the Pecos, Olinger and Krieling grazed cattle above Pope's Crossing before establishing a camp at Sand Bend by 1878 or 1879. In August of the latter year, Pecos County officials taxed "Krieling & Co." for 750 beeves valued at $4,500. By 1880 the AHB herd had grown to 1,000 head.[3]

About 1877, veteran New Mexico cowman Robert K. Wylie trailed his herd down the Pecos and turned it loose at the most infamous and threatening landmark on the river—Horsehead Crossing. His brand, a T-like cross on the shoulder and an X on the hip, soon became known as the TX, and cowhands dubbed the operation the Horsehead Outfit. In the late 1870s Wylie sold the TX herd to A. B. "Sug" Robertson, who set up a lower camp at Horsehead Crossing to keep the cattle from drifting downstream.

While the twenty-five-year-old Robertson grazed only 1,800 beeves in 1880, the TX soon controlled twenty-five to forty miles of riverfront on both sides and was on its way to becoming a giant. After Robertson relinquished his interest in the TX brand in 1882 to John Dawson (and Henry Byler and Tom Word, evidently), the operation grew until it ran 20,000 cattle on the east side and 10,000 on the west. A TX hand "riding line" out of headquarters—a two-story bunkhouse and cistern one and a half miles upstream of Horsehead—might find a TX cow as far north as Pecos Falls or as far south as Pontoon Crossing, ten miles northwest of present Iraan.[4]

In the late 1870s another huge outfit—the JM—turned loose a herd near the mouth of Live Oak Creek adjacent to present Sheffield. Owned by brothers Mayer and Solomon Halff, the JM soon claimed more than forty miles of east riverfront from Pontoon Crossing on the north to Independence Creek on the south.[5]

Upstream, meanwhile, at a point forty miles north-northwest of Fort Stockton, John Gibson's Hookity-Hook Ranch was in operation by 1878.

"He branded the '66'—they called it the Hookity-Hook," recalled R. H. Crosby, who trailed a herd past the Gibson spread in 1878. "There was a big pen . . . on the east side of the river. That was the only one from there on up to Bosque Grande."

TX Ranch cowboys with remuda in background. COURTESY OF SCHARBAUER
COLLECTION, N. S. HALEY MEMORIAL LIBRARY, MIDLAND, TEXAS

Within two years, Gibson and his partner, Narbo (possibly Pete Narbo), would see their herd grow to 4,000 head.[6]

In 1879 drovers with two outfits struck out from present Abilene, Texas, with three herds bound for the Pecos. The Jim and Lish Carter operation, with 2,500 beeves, was sizable, but the Hash Knife company, owned by John Simpson of Dallas and successive partners J. R. Couts and William E. Hughes, would become an empire. On the banks of the Pecos, its cowboys would burn the Hash Knife into what would become the largest herd under one brand in the United States.

Ironically, it was the Carter outfit, not the Hash Knife, that got its pick of the Pecos range land.

"I came with the first [Hash Knife] herd . . . ," recalled A. T. Windham, who was nineteen in 1879. "The three came together for protection and [Jim] Carter and Simpson agreed that the man who got in the lead when they got to the river country could turn loose where he wanted to and the other man would go on. Carter had more steers and less calves in his herd and could out-drive us, so he turned loose . . . [at Adobe Walls]."

Near the point of a bluff, the Carters established their headquarters and lower line camp. Nine to ten miles upstream of the present city of Pecos, where the river flows out of the sunset, they established their "west ranch" camp. With the addition of a second herd in 1880, the Carters saw their beeves range on the east side of the river between Adobe Walls and the New Mexico line.[7]

That same year, Jim Carter moved his wife out to headquarters.

"We had five *chozas*, sort of dugouts that were built back in the hill, walled with rock and covered with dirt and mesquite bushes," Mrs. Carter recalled in 1927. "We had fireplaces in these, a place for a door, but no doors. Each *choza* was about 14 feet square. No two of them connected. We had bedrooms [and] kitchens. . . . When we went out, I did make them carry my cookstove, as I did not know how to cook on a fireplace."[8]

The Hash Knife outfit, meanwhile, became the first large-scale operation to see promise in the river's west side in upper Texas, and turned loose its 5,370 beeves across from present Mentone. Establishing headquarters near later Arno, the outfit looked to the Pecos-Delaware confluence in New Mexico for its upper camp and to the Grand Falls of the Pecos (near the present city of Grandfalls) for its lower camp. By the end of 1881, another four Hash Knife herds had trailed to the Pecos and the outfit had assumed legendary proportions. Approximately 105 miles long from northwest to southeast, the ranch soon employed twenty-five cowboys at $35 to $75 a month (a dollar a day was typical cowhand wages), and grazed 525 saddle horses and an incredible 100,000 cattle. In 1882 cowhands burned the Hash Knife into 11,000 calves,[9] a figure which would rise to a phenomenal 38,000 in 1884.[10]

Even so, the Hash Knife—like many other early outfits—never had a legal claim to any of its grazing range.

"[The Hash Knife] owned no land and never leased any, that I know of . . . ," recalled Windham. "The company never made any improvements or put up any fences. . . . The wagon was your home."[11]

During the same period, however, the Western Union Beef Company—a cattle syndicate from up north—burned its "7D" mark of ownership into east-side riverfront in then-unorganized Crockett County.

A wagon camp on the W spread on the Pecos. COURTESY OF J. EVETTS HALEY
COLLECTION, N. S. HALEY MEMORIAL LIBRARY, MIDLAND, TEXAS

Under the nurturing of owners John T. Lytle and T. M. McDaniel, the
7D quickly grew into yet another giant outfit, with its cattle ranging on
both sides of the river from near present Toyah to the Rio Grande.[12]

Across the river from Crockett County and the deeded Western
Union Beef land, 4,000 cattle bearing the Mule Shoe brand of Hart
Mussey and Jesse H. Presnall were grazing around Pecos Spring and
present Sheffield by 1880.[13] Mussey alone incurred Pecos County taxes
that year for 2,100 head valued at $14,700, as well as for 20 horses or
mules valued at $400.[14] Soon, the Mule Shoe outfit would claim 18,000
beeves,[15] which reportedly ranged as far north as Grand Falls.[16]

Even as all these outfits took root on the Pecos, however, Mescalero
Apaches continued their raids and the U.S. Army launched counter-
measures. "As the Indians are committing depredations throughout the
country," wrote Colonel George A. Armes of Fort Stockton on March
31, 1879, "I have been ordered to hold my command in readiness to take
the field."[17]

Marching toward the Pecos on April 7, Armes entered into a long
and frustrating campaign against hostiles who always stayed a step
ahead.[18] Nevertheless, cowhands welcomed the military presence. "The
cowboys," noted Armes upon crossing Horsehead April 23, "are very glad
to see us looking out for their protection and [are] much encouraged."

Nevertheless, the raids endured, even as Armes was in the field. Setting out from the Emigrant Crossing vicinity on May 9, he and his men marched seventy-five miles in an unsuccessful attempt to overtake what Armes described as "the band of Indian marauders who have been stealing cattle through this section." Forty days later, Armes learned late in the evening that Indians had been at Horsehead Crossing. With his command and fifteen cowboys, he trailed the hostiles to Castle Gap by night. Again, it proved fruitless. "The Indians," Armes wrote, "have scattered into the [Castle] mountains, and it is impossible to find them."[19]

Not only did Mescaleros persist in stealing horses, they sometimes forced cowmen to bargain for their return. In late August or early September, Milo L. Pierce and a cowman named Van Wyke paid $2 a head to reservation Apaches in New Mexico for eighteen horses the Indians had stolen from their outfits. Although a Fort Stockton detachment oversaw the transaction and knew the circumstances, the soldiers did not challenge the extortion. Indeed, Second Lieutenant John Bigelow even called the payment "nominal."[20]

Although neither Armes nor Bigelow engaged hostiles in eight months of searching, an Indian-Army skirmish stemming from a raid along the Pecos was yet to come. On the night of March 30, 1880, Indians swooped down on a cow camp near Pecos Falls and made off with several head of stock. Marching past the site the next day, Colonel B. H. Grierson learned of the raid and dispatched Lieutenant Calvin Esterly and a Tenth Cavalry contingent in pursuit. Overtaking the marauders three days' ride to the northwest, the detachment from troops F and L killed one Indian and recovered eight stolen animals before giving up the chase.[21]

W. R. "Jake" Owen, a twenty-three-year-old cowhand working out of the Nash-Ramer rock headquarters at Pope's Crossing the same year, lived through a raid that could have cost him his life.

"We had two bunches of horses," he related fifty-seven years later. "We kept one of six or seven hundred head on one side of the river and six or seven hundred on the other side, so they [the Indians] wouldn't get them all."

An Army beef contractor named Briggs and four or five hands, waiting to receive a small cattle herd for trailing to Fort Davis (ninety-five air miles south of Pope's), had set up camp on the river's west side across from Owen and the Nash-Ramer house. Briggs, who ranched at Blue Spring five miles east of present Whites City, New Mexico, rode on up to check on his spread, only to lose his horse to Indians and walk all the way back.

"He got in there about three o'clock in the afternoon . . . ," related Owen. "I says, 'By George, what did you come down here for? Don't you know they followed you all the way down? They'll get the balance of our horses tonight.'"

While Briggs and his hands set about staking, hobbling, and guarding their remuda, Owen corralled the east herd and waited. As night fell, he turned the horses out and ran them five or six miles up a canyon emptying out of the east. Returning, he threw his bedding on the ground between the house and river and staked his horse at his head.

"I had two of the best dogs that a man ever saw in the world, and I . . . [stayed] there with my horse and them dogs slept with me . . . ," recalled Owen. "I had my gun laying right by the side of me. . . . I had a pot of coffee at the house, and every once in a while I'd go up and get a little coffee and go back and lay down. . . . I didn't aim to go to sleep, but I dropped off. . . . At the very break of day—it was just gray in the east—I heard the darnedest shooting across the river. It wasn't more than a couple of hundred yards [away]."

Owen discovered something else upon awakening—not only had his dogs wandered off, but the horse he had guarded so jealously was gone.

"While I was asleep there," he related, "one of my 'friends' [an Indian] come up there and cut the rope right at my head. . . . The knife that cut the rope could have cut my throat."

Before the gunfire ended across-river, the Apache band had spirited away another fifteen to twenty horses.[22]

By early the next year, the Mescalero threat along the Pecos had ended, finally relieving a sleepy cowhand of at least one worry in a precarious life

W. R. "Jake" Owen in 1932. COURTESY OF SOUTHEASTERN NEW MEXICO HISTORICAL
SOCIETY, CARLSBAD, NEW MEXICO

in which he still might bed down in the path of a rattler or an outlaw's bullet.

In the fall of 1880, the *Texas Sun* of San Antonio took stock of the Pecos River's budding cattle industry. Although syndicates such as Continental Cattle Company (which assumed a one-third interest in the Hash Knife herd that year) escaped notice,[23] the publication listed eighteen river outfits with 1,500 horses and 23,320 beeves. Lewis Paxton of the Paxton-Pierce operation drew particular attention: "Ranch located 130 miles north of Stockton with a range on the Pecos of 20 miles long by 8 miles in width—good rock houses—1,400 head of improved stock with best-blooded Durham bulls."

Other outfits listed by the *Texas Sun* included Payner and Powell, 500 head of cattle; Vaumick (or Vanmick or Van Wyke), 1,000 head; C. Slaughter, 1,000 head; Reuben Richards and Francis Rooney, 1,300 head; H. C. Tarty [or Tarde], 1,800 head; and Cesario Torres and brother, 400 head.[24]

The number of cattle grazing along the Pecos soon would increase dramatically, for across the flats, the twin rails of the Texas and Pacific Railroad already were crawling out of the rising sun. In 1881 the track bridged the Pecos near present Barstow, and by the end of the year, laborers had driven the last spike and created a transcontinental line.[25] On January 12, 1883, another railroad gang did the same for the Southern Pacific at a location three miles west of the Pecos–Rio Grande confluence.[26] Not only did the two lines open up the Pecos to the nation, they also lured more cattle outfits to its banks.

By 1882 Nub Pulliam held range on the west side from a point seven or eight miles below the ruins of Fort Lancaster (which the U.S. Army had garrisoned sporadically in the 1870s) up to Horsehead Crossing. His outfit, managed by his brother-in-law, W. H. Holmsley, burned three S's across every calf and was known as the S Ranch. The ranch, in turn, lent its name to S Crossing eight miles northwest of present Iraan.[27]

On to the south, around Independence Spring and the confluence of the Pecos with east-trending Independence Creek, the T5 turned loose a herd that grew to 12,000 in the 1880s.[28] Up at Pope's Crossing, meanwhile, shootist Clay Allison took up the old Milo L. Pierce range after acquiring Pierce's P brand. Until Allison's death in a wagon accident on the Pecos in 1887, the reformed gunman operated out of the old Nash-Ramer rock headquarters and grazed 700 to 2,000 cattle.[29]

By 1883 the Quien Sabe—known to cowboys as the "Kin Savvy"—relocated from the Rio Grande to the east side of the Pecos above Horsehead Crossing and the TX range. Sam Cress managed the Quien Sabe for its initial owner, a Major Hewett of New York.[30]

The year 1884 saw the Seven Rivers Cattle Company trail 10,000 cattle down the Pecos from the Seven Rivers region of New Mexico and set up headquarters a few miles upstream from present Mentone. Organized in 1883, the English syndicate was associated with Union Trading Company, which had offices in Colorado City, Texas.

"We ran nearly all Texas cattle [longhorns] but began breeding them up . . . ," recalled A. T. Windham, foreman of the outfit for nine years beginning February 16, 1884. "We branded Lazy Y on the side and hip. . . . We branded 5,500 calves in 1884, 6,500 in 1885."[31]

Even while ranches were taking root along the Pecos, cattle continued to cut the Goodnight-Loving Trail ever deeper. The trace itself constituted the only registry of drives, but the *San Antonio Express* of the day reported that 12,000 beeves forged up the river in the first six months of 1876.[32] By the 1880s, many of the drives originated on the Pecos, as outfits trailed their beeves to markets or ranges in locations such as Kansas, Oklahoma, Colorado, Montana, and the Dakotas.

"We sold nothing but steers," recalled Windham of his days working with the Hash Knife brand as Continental manager. "There were 13,000 sold in 1882. These ranged from yearlings up to 25 years old. We drove them to the northern ranches—the Hash Knives had northern ranches of their own in Montana and Dakota and drove lots of cattle every year." Later, as boss of the Seven Rivers outfit, Windham annually cut out 2,200 steers for trailing to the Seven Rivers' ranches in South Dakota and Colorado.[33]

The big trail drives would endure only a few more years, but ranching was on the Pecos to stay, creating a need for the open range cowboy and nurturing his legend as no other place could.

NOTES

Unless otherwise indicated, all towns, counties, and map quadrangles throughout notes are in Texas.

1. *New Handbook of Texas*, Vol. 5, 121.

2. W. R. Owen, interviews, 12 January 1927 and 2 March 1933; Klasner, *My Girlhood*, 67; Armes, *Ups and Downs*, 464 (journal entry); Bigelow to adjutant general, 9 December 1879; Pecos County tax roll, 1879 (dated 18 August 1879); *The Fort Stockton Pioneer*, 17 September 1908 (reprint of *Texas Sun*, November–December 1880); and Nolan, *Lincoln County War*, 121, 330, 394, 445, 496, 513, 518.

3. Wier and Beverly, interview; Windham, interview; Pecos County tax roll, 1879; *The Fort Stockton Pioneer*, 17 September 1908 (reprint of *Texas Sun*, November–December 1880); Klasner, *My Girlhood*, 67; Nolan, *Lincoln County War*, 344, 445; and W. R. Owen, interviews, 2 March 1933 and 24 June 1937. Owen worked for Charlie Krieling in 1878 or 1879. See W. R. Owen, interview, 24 June 1937. Krieling's name is also spelled Kreeling, Kruling, or Creeling.

4. This study of the TX is based on Patterson, "Forgotten Empire," 24–25; Henderson, "Memories of an Old Cowboy," 21–22; Henderson, "Life of an Oldtimer," book four, 8; Millard, *Cowpuncher*, 31; Windham, interview; Newland, interview; W. R. Owen, interviews, 2 March 1933 and 24 June 1937; W. C. Cochran, "Walter C. Cochran's Memoirs of Early Day Cattlemen," Betty Orbeck, ed., *The Texas Permian Historical Annual* Vol. 1, No. 1 (August 1961), 41; O. H. Nelson, "Judge O. H. Nelson, Pioneer: Breeder of High Grade Herefords," 38, typescript, Haley Collection, Haley Library, Midland; Fount Armstrong, interview with Haley, Odessa, 2 February 1965, Haley Collection, Haley Library, Midland; J. A. Johnson, interview; *New Handbook of Texas*, Vol. 5, 615; and Tad Moses, "Some Texas Cattlemen and Their Operations," pamphlet reprinted from *The Cattleman*, November and December 1947, and January and February 1948, 10. Word's name is spelled "Ward" or "Werd" in some accounts.

5. Cochran, "Walter C. Cochran's Memoirs," 41; Ivan Murchison and K. F. Neighbours, "Ranching on the Pecos at the Turn of the Twentieth Century," *WTHA Year Book* Vol. 53, 1977, 127; Moses, "Some Texas Cattlemen," 8, 9, 10; Newland, interview; W. H. Holmsley, interview with Haley, Midland, 17 October 1926, Haley Collection, Haley Library, Midland; and Graham, E. V., interview with Haley, place and date not known, Haley Collection, Haley Library, Midland. For a thorough discussion of the JM's origins, see Patrick Dearen, *Halff of Texas* (Austin: Eakin Press, 2000) 35–42.

6. R. H. Crosby, interview with Haley, Kenna, New Mexico, 4 August 1937, Haley Collection, Haley Library, Midland; and *The Fort Stockton Pioneer*, 17 September 1908 (reprint of *Texas Sun*, November–December 1880). Pete Narbo is mentioned in Millwee, interview, 13 September 1932.

7. Windham, interview; *New Handbook of Texas* Vol. 3, 498–499, and Vol. 5, 1055–1056; *The Fort Stockton Pioneer*, 17 September 1908 (reprint of *Texas Sun*, November–December 1880); Bigelow to adjutant general, 9 December 1879; and Mrs. J. W. Carter, interview with Haley, Dimmit, 31 October 1927.

8. Mrs. Carter, interview.

9. Windham, interview.

10. Henderson, "Life of an Oldtimer," book four, 8.

11. Windham, interview.

12. Moses, "Some Cattlemen, 8." The *New Handbook of Texas* Vol. 5, 979, says the 7D brand originated with Cesario Torres and family in 1869 on Comanche Creek near Fort Stockton, and that the operation was sold first to Jesse H. Presnall and Hart Mussey 18 March 1886, and then to Western Union Beef Company 19 July 1890, and finally to John T. McElroy in 1899.

13. *The Fort Stockton Pioneer*, 17 September 1908 (reprint of *Texas Sun*, November–December 1880).

14. Pecos County tax roll, 1880 (dated 6 August 1880).

15. Millard, *Cowpuncher*, 31.

16. Clayton Williams, *Last Frontier*, 300.

17. Armes, *Ups and Downs*, 462 (journal entry).

18. Colonel George A. Armes to AA general, 8 September 1879, journal of marches, scouts, and expeditions, Fort Stockton.

19. Armes, *Ups and Downs*, 463, 466, 474 (journal entries).

20. Bigelow to adjutant general, 9 December 1879. Van Wyke is probably the "Vaumick" whom the November–December 1880 *Texas Sun* listed as grazing 1,000 head of cattle on the Pecos. See reprint of the *Texas Sun* article in *The Fort Stockton Pioneer*, 17 September 1908.

21. "Record of Engagement with Hostile Indians in Texas, 1868–1882," WTHA Year Book Vol. 9 (October 1933), 115–116; and Clayton Williams, *Last Frontier*, 235.

22. W. R. Owen, interviews, 2 March 1933 and 24 June 1937.

23. Windham, interview. Hash Knife owners John N. Simpson and William E. Hughes, along with John W. Buster, formed Continental Cattle Company and shared ownership with several smaller stockholders. Windham, in the interview, stated that he became manager for Continental in 1880. However, *New Handbook of Texas* Vol. 2, 295, says that Continental was not formed until 1881, a date which, if correct, could explain Continental's absence from the *Texas Sun* list.

24. *The Fort Stockton Pioneer*, 17 September 1908 (reprint of *Texas Sun*, November–December 1880).

25. *New Handbook of Texas*, Vol. 6, 385.

26. "The Last Spike Driven and the Southern Pacific Route is Complete," *San Antonio Daily Express*, 13 January 1883.

27. Holmsley, interview; and Clayton Williams, *Last Frontier*, 300. For a study of Fort Lancaster, see Dearen, *Crossing Rio Pecos*, 87–107. For a study of S Crossing, see Dearen, *Crossing Rio Pecos*, 114–118.

28. Millard, *Cowpuncher*, 36–37; and Clayton Williams, *Last Frontier*, 300.

29. Windham, interview; Oden, "Early Cowboy Days;" W. R. Owen, interviews, 2 March 1933 and 24 June 1937; Huling Ussery, taped interview with Richard Mason, Carlsbad, New Mexico, 22 February 1982, Southwest Collection, Texas Tech University, Lubbock; Haley, *Rough Times-Tough Fiber* (Canyon: Palo Duro Press, 1976), 148–149;

and Barney Hubbs, "The Day Clay Allison Died," in Chuck Parsons, *Clay Allison, Portrait of a Shootist* (Seagraves: Pioneer Book Publishers, 1983), 84–85.

30. J. A. Johnson, interview; Cochran, interview; and Cochran, "Walter C. Cochran's Memoirs," 41.

31. Windham, interview.

32. *San Antonio Express*, 19 July 1876, transcript, Clayton Wheat Williams Collection, Haley Library, Midland.

33. Windham, interview. The quote is a composite of statements.

CHAPTER EIGHT

The Open Range Cowboy of the Pecos

COWBOYING ON THE OPEN RANGE OF THE PECOS DEMANDED NOT ONLY insight into the nature of the cow brute, but a keen understanding of the region and how the bovine interacted with it.

Although as early as 1880 Pecos cowmen experimented with "blooded stock" by introducing Durham bulls,[1] the longhorn continued to be the breed of choice for decades. This hardy animal was ideal for the Pecos country, which cowmen regarded as strictly a breeding range. "As such, [the Pecos] has no equal on Earth, not even excepting Australia and South America," reported the *Dallas News* in 1886. "The average increase [in herd size through calving] is 90 per cent [a year]."[2]

Such a breeding rate was typical for longhorn cows, which could produce calves even at age twenty-five.[3] With outfits generally holding back the heifers and trailing the steers northward to maturing ranges or to market,[4] the cow soon became the critter which demanded most of a cowboy's day-to-day attention.

Although travelers in pre-ranching days sometimes praised the grasses of the Pecos country as "abundant and excellent,"[5] overgrazing took its toll. Catching only nine to twelve inches of rain a year, this region was arid at best, and a desert at worst.[6] Either way, the range could not replenish itself quickly. As early as May 1879, when Colonel George A. Armes scouted the Pecos region from present Grandfalls to Seven Rivers, forage already was scarce everywhere except along Black River. Armes laid the blame directly on cow outfits, noting "the great number of cattle herded throughout the country."[7]

The situation not only induced the longhorn to turn to salt-laden grass on the Pecos flood plain—or worse, to goldenrod poisoned with alkali[8]—it also forced the animal to range increasingly farther from the river.

"There was no water back from the river, and they [the cattle] took the grass as far as they could reach it, some twenty miles back from water," recalled A. T. Windham of the Hash Knife, Continental, and Seven Rivers outfits. "These high-blooded cattle won't range like that."[9]

Even though ranching generally was limited to a forty-mile-wide band split by the Pecos, the absence of fences left cattle prone to drift. Fortunately, cowmen trying to "hold range" along a single bank could look to two natural boundaries as deterrents against straying—the river, which cattle would not cross on their own, and the waterless country beyond the twenty- or twenty-five-mile mark, into which cattle seldom roamed. However, the animals instinctively drifted along the river, particularly downstream during wintery conditions.

For cowboys, it all meant long hours in the saddle "riding line"—patrolling an outfit's upper, lower, and outside boundaries to keep cattle from straying.[10]

"In those days, mighty few cattle watered away from the river," noted James P. Jones, who worked for the John Chisum spread in New Mexico in 1871 and 1872. "Therefore, the outside line camp men had very little work. Those on the south side were the ones that had the battle."[11]

Not all outfits were conscientious about keeping their cattle in check, thereby increasing the work for line riders of bordering ranches. The Mule Shoe and TX operations were noted offenders in the late 1880s and early 1890s. "They were two of the biggest outfits," recalled F. S. Millard, who cowboyed out of a line camp at Tunis Springs twenty miles east of Fort Stockton, "and they would do nothing to help keep their cattle from eating us out."[12]

The threat to an outfit's range did not always come from other Pecos operations; sometimes it came from afar. In the winter of 1883, cowmen in the Panhandle and Southern Plains devised a system which they hoped would discourage their blizzard-driven cattle from drifting south to the river and elsewhere. Setting up twenty-five-man camps near the fledgling settlements of Colorado City, Big Spring, and Midland, respectively, the outfits rode line along the Texas and Pacific Railroad as far west as the Pecos.[13]

Although Pecos cattle ranged far from the river for forage, they trailed in regularly for water. Cliff Newland, cowboying along the mid-Texas stretch about 1900, could look across the flats every clear morning and find dust rising against the distant hills. "That's when them old-time cattle would start in and get a drink of water . . . ," he recalled in 1964. "It'd kill these cows [of today]—they couldn't take it."[14]

Indeed, with the later introduction of high-grade cattle to the Southwest, cowmen had to ensure that the animals never had to graze more than two or three miles from a water source, as they required water daily.[15] Longhorns, however, were not bound to such a schedule—an essential attribute along the Pecos, considering the prohibitive distances to and from forage. In fact, Pecos cattle would trail in for water only every other day—or a mere two times a week, in some instances.[16]

With the passage of years, cattle seeking water brought about two physiographic changes to the river—they may have contributed to the sloughing of the once-uniformly sheer banks,[17] and they tramped out the reeds which had thrived at water's edge.[18] In turn, the Pecos wreaked havoc with many of those same thirsty cattle, miring them in its quicksand or "black-looking mud," as 1920s cowhand Jim Witt described it.[19]

Whether in the 1870s or the 1920s, the situation required reliable cowhands to pair up and "ride bog," which may have spawned the saying, *He'll do to ride the river with.*[20] One of their tasks was to push cattle away from the river in late evening[21]; otherwise, the animals might get trapped overnight, chill, and die.[22] But bog riders faced their biggest challenge in dealing with cattle already hopelessly mired though very much alive.

About 1919, Hudson "Bud" Mayes witnessed the effects of the Pecos muck during a cattle drive from a ranch north of present Rankin, Texas, to a spread below Sheffield. One night he and his fellow drovers held their 600 to 700 cows and calves in Hickox Jog, a "trap" or fenced area on the Pecos about ten miles north of Sheffield.

"The next morning, we was throwing those out of that trap and starting on down the river with them," recalled Mayes seven decades later.

"And I looked over the bank, and there was three ol' cows in there that had gotten into quicksand—just see the top of their back and their horns sticking up. We just rode off and left them there. I guess they washed away whenever it rained."[23]

Riding bog was especially important not only in late winter and spring, when cattle were gaunt and weak, but after floods, which softened the earthen banks and deposited fresh quicksand. Extricating a mired animal proved a test of resolve regardless of the occasion, for cowhands learned that a horse and rope were not enough. Recalled nineteenth-century Pecos hand B. A. Oden: "You would pull a cow's head off, if you had power enough, before you could pull their legs out of the sand."[24]

To accomplish the task, a bog rider had to dismount and resort to what was known as "trompin' them out."

"It was a SOB," recalled Witt, who cowboyed on the Cross C east of the city of Pecos. "One would have to be down with the cow trompin' [tramping] around her legs. That ol' mud had a helluva suction, and you could tromp down beside their leg and break that suction. The guy on his horse, with his rope around their horns, would give a pull, and the guy down with the cow would tell him when and how much to pull."[25]

Added Oden: "You tromp one leg at a time out and tie it up, and when you have all the legs out of the sand tied up, you roll them out to hard ground."[26]

Even as he assisted the cow to its feet, the muddy cowhand had to guard against the animal's quick temper and wicked horns. "The cowboy's defense . . . ," said 1890s bog rider Robert M. Dudley, "is to catch it by the tail and pull to whichever side the animal tries to turn, so as to keep the animal's head and horns away from him. And usually a few back and forth turns like that and the animal is ready to go straight away."[27]

All too often, cowhands rode upon a bogged cow too late. "The Pecos was a graveyard for cattle," observed Barney Hubbs, who emigrated to a Pecos River ranch thirty-seven miles north of the city of Pecos in 1908.[28]

J. T. McElroy, a noteworthy rancher on the Pecos in the 1890s, was especially hard-hit by bog losses. "He told me one time," related Fount Armstrong, who began cowboying about 1901 near present Crane, Texas, "[that] he'd lost more cattle in the Pecos River than Mr. Buchanan [of

W. B. Oates, Roy E. Bar, and Paul Platter "tromping" a steer out of the Pecos on the W Ranch in the early twentieth century. COURTESY OF WEST OF THE PECOS MUSEUM, PECOS, TEXAS

the Miles G. Buchanan Ranch twelve to fifteen miles west of Crane] ever owned, and Mr. Buchanan had about 3,000 head of cattle at that time [the early 1900s]."[29]

On at least one occasion, the Pecos graveyard resulted in a moment of levity. Working cattle along the southern New Mexico stretch in the 1890s, Bob Dow of the S Cross watched cowhand George Nelson sprawl at water's edge and drink his fill.

"When George got up," related Dow, "he looked just above where he had been drinking and saw an old dead cow lying there in the water. He broke and ran for about 50 yards and then stopped and started back as though he was stepping off the distance."

When another cowhand asked him why he had run, George pointed to the carcass and exclaimed, "We've drank right under that old dead cow! . . . They say that running water purifies every 50 yards and I wasn't going to leave that stuff lying in my stomach without purifyin' it!"[30]

By the close of the nineteenth century, cowmen tried to minimize their monetary loss by assigning cowboys the unpleasant chore of skinning the bogged carcasses.[31] Meanwhile, the animals' calves were left to roam the bank and fend for themselves as "dogies." One story has it that a lady from back East heard the term in the song "Git Along Little Dogies" and asked a cowboy, "Will you please tell me something about these little dogies, and whether they ever grow to be fine-looking dogs?"

"Why lady, they're not dogs at all," said the cowhand. "A little dogie is a poor little calf whose mother has bogged in the quicksand, and whose father has run off with another cow."[32]

For Pecos Dogies, the situation was anything but humorous. Dow recalled their plight:

Pecos Dogies . . . are just different from any other kind of animal. When their mothers die, leaving them to make their own way, they naturally have to stay near the river [because] . . . they become poor and weak and are not able to get out far enough to where the grass is good. Their hair becomes long and their legs and hams are tiny—in fact, just skin and bones. They have . . . a huge stomach which often almost drags the ground. Where the range is good for several years, though, Pecos Dogies will grow and make fairly good-size cattle.[33]

To cowhands, a Pecos Dogie was also known as a maverick, a general term for an unbranded and unclaimed bovine. The indiscriminate branding of such an animal, done so without regard for who its owner might be, was called mavericking. "It was the unwritten law of the open range that where a man drove in an unbranded yearling that was not following a cow, and claimed it, he got it," said 1890s Pecos hand Julius D. Henderson.[34]

When a cowboy found a maverick, he branded it on the spot. "We'd just catch him and brand him with a [metal] ring," recalled Jim Witt of his days with the Cross C in the 1920s. "We carried a ring on our saddle, and built a fire and put that ring in there [to heat]. Get you two green sticks [to hold it with] and you could brand him with that."[35]

Fearing an abuse of the practice in the 1880s and 1890s, New Mexico cowmen took appropriate steps.

"During the nine years [1884 to 1893] I was on that [Pecos] River work . . . ," recalled B. A. Oden, "there was a gentleman's agreement to brand no mavericks except on roundup, each outfit having certain points on the river which they claimed as their ranges, and all mavericks in the roundup [of a particular point] were considered as belonging to that [particular] outfit."[36]

Sometimes, however, the matter of ownership became complicated. A Pecos Dogie might survive only by stealing milk from a free-ranging cow—without regard, of course, to whether the two of them belonged to the same outfit. If the calf already bore a brand, it created a situation in which a cow and its adopted calf might carry separate brands. By the 1880s, Pecos cowmen in Texas had devised a system to cope with the problem.

"It was customary then," said cowhand F. S. Millard, "when you found somebody's else [branded] calf following your cow, to stripe its [the calf's] legs with a hot iron and brand one [unmarked calf] of theirs."[37]

Sometimes, a cowhand might resort to mavericking if a neighboring outfit failed to confine its cattle to its own range. "When we first came . . . [to Tunis Springs in fall 1889], we rode a line to throw the Mule Shoe cattle back off of us," said Millard. "But the Mule Shoe outfit would do nothing [to help], so we quit after the first winter and would brand all the Mule Shoe mavericks we could after that. . . . I never bothered anybody's calves but the Mule Shoe's and the TX."[38]

Millard did not consider his actions unethical, only customary. In fact, he noted in retrospect, "I can count all the men on my fingers that never branded anything but what they knew was theirs and probably have a finger or two left."[39]

While many instances of mavericking were justified, the fact that motherless Pecos Dogies were free-for-the-branding invited some cowmen into a devious form of thievery. "The ranchers across the river," recalled Barney Hubbs, who lived on a west-side spread in 1908,

Jim Witt on the Cross C about 1931. COURTESY OF JIM WITT

"sometimes would encourage [other outfits'] cattle into these quicksand areas, because they would pay their cowboys 50 cents if they would brand a [dogie] calf for them."[40]

Furthermore, an unscrupulous cowhand, yearning to build a herd of his own, might target any unbranded calf for pilfering, even though it was obviously not a dogie. A roundup drive presented an ideal opportunity. Riding alone through an isolated area, he could burn his own brand across an unmarked calf, tie it down, and push the cow on to the rendezvous point. Later, he could return and release the calf, or *sleeper*, and plan to claim it for his own at the next roundup.[41]

Additionally, some thieves practiced outright "brand-burning"—the altering of brands with a running iron. The resulting mark, never legally recorded for obvious reasons, was known as a "slow brand."[42] Billy Rankin, a cowboy of the 1920s, related an incident in which a Pecos cowhand of poor reputation sat doodling on the riverbank with a stick. "What are you doing?" an acquaintance of Rankin's asked.

"Oh," replied the cowhand, studying his art work, "I'm just a-thinkin' of the brands that can be run."[43]

If bogged animals and cow thieves weren't enough to watch for, every flood would leave plenty of cattle in need of a cowboy's attention.

"Those big floods would get completely across that flat, a mile wide and three or four feet deep," recalled Witt, who cowboyed from the present U.S. Highway 80 bridge to a point seventeen miles downriver. "If there was an island out there somewhere and you had some cows out there, you had to get them off, move them out. You'd ride along [through the floodwaters] and you'd fall off in a draw or something—your horse would swim for 30 or 40 feet and then he'd get his feet back on the [submerged] ground. I guess it might've been a little dangerous, but I never did know anybody that drowned."[44]

In all phases of his work, a Pecos cowhand demanded much of his horse, even as it demanded much of him. Owned by the outfit, his "mount," or string of geldings cut out specifically for him, generally consisted of broncs, broken but still resistant to a man in the saddle. As none were tame enough for a cowboy to walk up to in the pasture and bridle, the hands resorted to penning the remuda in a makeshift corral.

Roping out horses on the W Ranch on the Pecos. COURTESY OF WEST OF THE PECOS MUSEUM, PECOS, TEXAS

Early on, a horse learned fear of a rope, and even though each side of the corral consisted of but a single catch-rope stretched between men afoot, the animals usually would not break through. Looking over the bunch, a cowhand would call out the name of the horse he wanted, and the boss, afoot, would "rope out" the animal for saddling.[45]

"We used to name bad horses after bad men," recalled 1890s Pecos hand Julius D. Henderson. "I rode a bay horse that had been real bad and had killed one man. We called him Red Tom after a boy that lived here [on the Pecos], Tom Yost (red-headed). He had gone to Arizona and turned train robber."[46]

In "roping out," it was important for a cowhand to be able to identify the horses in his mount. Otherwise, he might select another man's horse, perhaps an outlaw bronc from the "rough string"—the mount of vicious horses assigned to the outfit's best rider.

"One time we had an ol' boy who kept saying, 'Oh, catch me anything,'" recalled Bill Eddins, who began cowboying on Sid Kyle's 150-section Pecos spread astride the Texas–New Mexico line in 1918. "And [the boss] kept saying, 'Well, I told you his name.' So the next time the ol' boy said, 'Oh, catch me anything,' he *caught* him anything, and [the hand] couldn't saddle him—he was a bronc. He fired him right there."[47]

Saddling a Pecos bronc seldom was easy. Often, a cowboy would have to subdue the animal by "earing it down"—biting its ear—in order for another hand to throw a saddle on. At the most extreme, he would have to rope the bronc from horseback, "choke it down," and tie up one of its feet before the animal would take a saddle.[48] Even after pulling the cinches tight, a cowboy seeking to mount had to "cheek" the horse—pull its head around to its side by means of the bridle.

Despite such efforts, some broncs still proved troublesome, as Julius D. Henderson found out in dealing with an animal known as Muskhog on the TX range.

"It would take an hour or more to get your saddle on him," recalled Henderson. "When we would rope him in the remuda, he would rear up and paw at the rope and walk out on his hind feet with his mouth open. Once . . . [a hand] got a bridle on him, he would not let you come near him with a saddle. He would just back around and keep his head toward you, and he would paw you sure if you got close. After we got our saddle on him, we had to pull his mane down and blind his eye, cheek him, and stand just as far as we could in front to put our foot in the stirrup, and he nearly always kicked when we started to mount. He was sure enough a bad horse."[49]

Once a cowboy gained the saddle, it was no easy chore to stay on through a half-day's work, for a Pecos bronc rarely was gentle enough for even roping purposes before age five.[50] At any time, a bronc might suddenly "swallow his head" and "break in two"—a cowboy's way of saying *pitch*—with little provocation and no warning except an abrupt tightness in its shoulders. The situation demanded not only a good rider, but the proper saddle.

"You could not," recalled Henderson, "set up on one like he was a rocking chair, like these men who ride cutting horses at these rodeos. You had to get down deep in a big, roomy saddle with a good, high cantle, then sometimes the best riders would go over their [the horses'] heads."[51]

To increase the depth of the saddle, a cowhand sometimes tied a rolled-up blanket behind the saddle horn. Still, there never was a cowboy "who couldn't be throwed," as the saying goes, and Pecos hands tasted the alkali ground more times than they cared to remember. Sometimes, the very name of a horse served as a warning to new hands. Green Mankin, who cowboyed in the lower Pecos country in the 1920s, recalled a horse named *Regular Mi Cuenta*—Spanish for "Regulate My Account" or "Figure Up My Time"—as one disgusted cowboy told the boss after the animal had pitched him off on one occasion too many.[52]

Sometimes a cowboy met with serious injury or death at the hooves of a bronc. Tom Jones, cow-hunting alone far from any line camp on Christmas Day, 1888, suffered a broken leg when his horse threw him and ran away. Unable to walk, Jones could only lie on the frozen prairie and fight a raging fever and frostbite for the next four days. When searchers found him, said the *San Angelo Standard*, his frozen feet were "a terrible sight to behold," the flesh "having dropped from his toes." Finally, on December 31, he gained medical attention in Pecos City.[53]

Even in good weather and in the company of other cowhands, falls could be dangerous. Although they might not result in immediate injury, their cumulative effect invariably left an old cowboy "stove-up," or hobbled. Sometimes, a fall not only disabled, but disfigured. In 1926 Ollie Brown, running his horse across a mesquite grass flat on the Blackstone-Slaughter Ranch near Sheffield, suddenly went down hard when the animal found an unexpected prairie dog hole.

"When I got to him," related cowhand Gid Reding, "he sat up and his . . . lower lip was down under his chin. It was the dangedest-looking thing, that ol' chin sticking out there. . . . I had to put my knee against his chest and pull it back. He got well, but his ol' lip always hung out."[54]

One of a cowboy's greatest fears was of getting hung to a runaway horse and dragged. On November 25, 1887, Mule Shoe cowhand Maximo Alvarez narrowly escaped death when his bolting horse fell with him, breaking his collarbone and knocking him unconscious. Only after searchers rescued him did he learn that his foot had lodged in the stirrup and that the horse had dragged him for eight hours.[55]

Cowhand Jim Witt fortunately avoided such a prolonged ordeal on the Cross C Ranch near Emigrant Crossing in 1927 or 1928. Running his horse after a bolting calf, he felt his mount's leg give way to a gopher or rabbit hole. He fell with the horse, and as the animal's momentum rolled 1,100 pounds of horse flesh over him, Witt got caught up in the rope on the saddle. "He drug me just a little ways," he recalled, "but I had somebody with me and they stopped him. It . . . just skinned me a little bit. Hell, he didn't drag me a hundred feet, two hundred feet, [but] I didn't want to go any further."[56]

The Pecos terrain offered unforeseen pitfalls for riders. One blazing summer day in 1921 or 1922 found cowboy Bill Eddins loping his horse up a draw after a runaway steer on the Kyle Ranch on the river's east side. Here, runoff had created a pair of two-foot-deep ditches, snaking side-by-side in the arroyo's bed. Suddenly his horse went down, pinning him in one of the channels.

"It caught my right leg . . . and I knew . . . my foot was in the stirrup," related Eddins. "I held him down for a minute, afraid he'd get up and drag me. Then I saw he *couldn't* get up—he kept kicking and all four feet was up in the air. That's when I began to get scared; nobody knew where I was. Then I was trying to get him up—I didn't care if my foot *was* in the stirrup."

The animal finally exhausted itself, leaving Eddins still pinned under the broiling sun. Calling on all his wits, he managed to reach across, unbuckle the cinches, and free the saddle. Again, he desperately urged the horse to rise, and now, unburdened by the extra weight, the animal began to kick and finally freed the two of them.[57]

If a bronc's temperament and horse wrecks weren't enough with which to contend, a Pecos hand also had to watch his mount for signs of "alkaliing," a condition especially troublesome to hard-worked saddle horses which either had drunk from the river or had grazed alkali-rich plants such as goldenrod.[58] John C. Reid, writing of his 1857 trip to the Pecos, noted that "unless an animal is thoroughly used to it, he should

L. B. "Bill" Eddins in 1989. COURTESY OF THE AUTHOR

not be permitted to appropriate more of this grass or water than will allay hunger or thirst. Riding animals . . . are often seriously injured—sometimes killed—by being suffered to drink and eat heartily after having been ridden hard."[59]

Andrew Young learned of the dangers firsthand when he began ranching northeast of Bakersfield in 1883. During his first winter on the Pecos, sixty-five of his saddle horses inexplicably died, although not a single unridden horse perished. Cesario Torres, who had farmed along the river since 1870, told Young that the animals had fallen prey to alkali poisoning, and that he should herd his saddle horses away from the flood plain and its alkali-rich plants. Thereafter, Young lost no more animals.[60]

Still, with most remudas ranging free (as far as twenty-five miles back from the river prior to fencing),[61] every Pecos cowhand came to recognize the symptoms of a horse that had alkalied. "It messes up his coordination and messes up his strength," noted Paul Patterson, who cowboyed on the Pecos in the early 1930s. "And when he gets hot, he doesn't have any endurance anymore. He just starts trembling, his legs will give way with you, and he's no good anymore."[62]

Pecos cowhands quickly learned never to press horses or cattle unnecessarily in hot weather. "If you choused them and they had alkali, they'd just fall out . . . ," said Bill Townsend, a Pecos cowboy of the late 1920s. "If they got hot enough, bad enough, they'd just keel over. If you'd go off and leave him alone there a while and not bother him, why, he'd get straightened up. But once in a while, one would die."[63]

In 1928 or 1929 Jim Witt was riding along near Barstow when he suddenly realized that his horse had alkalied. "This horse started trembling," he recalled, "and I got off of him and he just laid over. I pulled my saddle off of him and he died."[64]

By 1931 a section of fenced land along the river near Girvin had become known as the "death trap," due to the proliferation of alkali-poisoned dandelion. Driving almost five hundred horses from Mertzon and Rankin to Orla that year, Patterson and three other cowboys held the animals overnight at the site. By morning, several of the horses had alkalied, including one which they later left at a ranch upriver near Buena Vista.

"You could ride him four or five miles and he'd get hot, then his hind legs would give way on him . . . ," recalled Patterson. "But they traded him to a rodeo company, and . . . since he didn't have to work over ten seconds a day, he'd throw people coming and going."[65]

With "snaky" broncs and alkalied animals so commonplace, a Pecos cowhand had high regard for a good cow pony, especially one with the endurance to tolerate a ride that would give it the *thumps*. "It takes an awful good horse to run hard and long enough to take the thumps," said Julius D. Henderson. "They jerk and their sides sound like you were pounding on an old barrel."[66]

One such animal was a small, iron-gray horse named Nick, which proved its mettle in a blizzard in a March 1900 cattle drive up the Pecos from southwest of present McCamey.

"I was the largest man in the outfit and had the youngest and smallest horse . . . ," recalled Henderson in the 1950s. "I rode him [on guard] all night. We had 60 cows dead the next morning, and had to help about 100 up. The snow had been very wet and slushy and a hard crust froze on top of it, and the going was just awful the next day."

Nevertheless, Henderson stayed astride the gray throughout those long hours of daylight.

"By night, every horse in the outfit but mine was give out completely. So I held the cattle all that night by myself. And next morning, that pony was still good. I had rode him steadily for 50 hours."

Through Henderson's long years of cowboying, Nick the gray was the animal for which he held the most esteem.

> *I rode that horse 12 years and he never pitched, run off and left me, never fell down, and was never jerked down, never gave out. A polo man offered me $500 for him. I asked him $1,000 and rode off—I was afraid he might take me up [on the offer].*
>
> *He [the horse] has been dead more than 40 years, [but] I still dream I am riding him and talk to him in my sleep. Joe Evans of El Paso said, 'A good dog is my first love.' Not for me—of the animal kingdom, I'll take a good horse.*[67]

Pecos cowman Sid Kyle developed his own special attachment to a cutting horse named Charlie. When the animal took sick, evidently from mesquite beans, he dispatched a rider for Pecos City for medicine. The hand made the forty-mile round trip in four and one-half hours, only to find Charlie already dead.

"We dug a grave and buried him," recalled Henderson. "Sid cried like [a] little boy and said, 'If it would make that horse live as long as I do, I

Julius D. Henderson and best friend. COURTESY OF PERMIAN HISTORICAL ARCHIVES, UNIVERSITY OF TEXAS OF THE PERMIAN BASIN, ODESSA, TEXAS

would willingly give every one of my cattle [away] and start over again.' He had three hundred and fifty head."[68]

Some cowboys, however, considered horses as mere tools of the trade and treated them as such. Such a hand might bloody or even cripple an unruly bronc by spurring it in the shoulders, or perhaps he would work the iron-loaded butt of a quirt between its ears. In most outfits, such mistreatment was a firing offense, for a sizable operation required scores of saddle horses and each animal was vital, especially during roundup.[69]

On the open range Pecos, roundups were often massive affairs, conducted jointly by many outfits working long stretches of river. During spring roundup, which usually began in May after the cattle had shed their winter hair and left the brands easily identifiable, cowhands would brand the new calves (and castrate the bull calves), separate the different brands, and return the cattle to their home ranges after the winter drift. Outfits also rounded up in order to cut out animals for trailing to market or to northern ranges.

A general roundup actually consisted of many small roundups, conducted in logistical fashion. A boss, selected by the outfits, would set up a main camp on the Pecos near the southernmost point to be worked. From there, cowhands would conduct several roundups, then the camp would move north along the river and the hands would repeat the process. For each individual roundup, the boss would designate a rendezvous point (or roundup ground) on the Pecos, often in a pronounced bend (with a gap perhaps only thirty feet wide) in which hands could easily hold a herd.

With each day demanding long, hard hours in the saddle, every cowboy required about seven animals: two "drive" horses, two "round up" horses, two "evening" horses, and one "night" horse. As each of the four phases demanded particular qualities in an animal, a cowhand carefully matched horse with task, based on the gelding's level of maturity, temperament, endurance, and skill.

A roundup hand's day began about 4 a.m. when he would ease out of his bedroll and eat breakfast at the chuck wagon. He would then swing astride his drive horse—generally a temperamental bronc—and ride away from the river a predetermined distance before turning back to work a specific, designated lane.[70]

Cowboys and remuda on the W Ranch on the Pecos. COURTESY OF J. EVETTS HALEY COLLECTION, N. S. HALEY MEMORIAL LIBRARY, MIDLAND, TEXAS

"The Pecos boys . . . ," related Pecos cowhand F. S. Millard, "would dash out, round up about 7 or 8 miles of the river, brand out, and go again, mak[ing] about 4 round ups a day getting the cattle that were close to the water."[71]

With the stronger cattle venturing far from the Pecos, however, roundup demanded even more of some cowboys. "As the outside cattle would go 20 miles from the river," noted cowhand B. A. Oden, "the drive would mean a circle of 45 to 55 miles for the leaders of the drive."[72]

The Pecos was not always cooperative, however. In large bends prone to flooding, mesquite brush was so thick even by the late nineteenth century that no cowhand dared take his horse inside, much less attempt a roundup drive. Julius D. Henderson recalled one such twenty-section bend which, in 1899, held scores of unbranded cattle, including "cows three and four years old with calves that had never seen a man." As Henderson and Sid Kyle bore upstream with a herd, the river flooded and flushed the wild cattle from the brush. Only then did cowhands from the W Ranch round up the animals and burn a brand across their hides.[73]

Where rare flowing tributaries extended the longhorn's grazing range beyond a distance feasible for a cowboy to ride out from the Pecos and drive back in a single day, a hand would undertake a "moonshine." In the evening, he would ride for the head of a particular creek in order to be ready at daybreak for the long drive back. Although the boss would dispatch only a top hand for such duty, as it required expertise to locate the young hidden calves, a calf sometimes would escape even the most diligent search. In such a case, the mother cow would refuse to leave the area, forcing the cowboy to "neck" the animal, or secure it by rope to a free-marching cow which would urge its sister on.[74]

Under conditions not requiring a moonshine, a drive leader would complete his forty-five- to fifty-five-mile round trip and throw his cattle into the roundup herd about two or three o'clock in the afternoon. He would break long enough to down a hearty dinner of perhaps frijoles, fried beef with flour gravy, sourdough biscuits, canned tomatoes or corn, and Arbuckles coffee strong enough to "float a horseshoe." Saddling up a roundup horse, he then would help cut out the cattle as necessary, perhaps the unbranded calves or the older animals brand by brand.[75] This demanded a good cow horse with the intelligence and skill to study a particular bovine's actions and immediately respond with little or no rein.[76] In the 1880s A. T. Windham of the Seven Rivers Cattle Company had such confidence in his roundup horse that he bet his boss, John Harris, that he could cut 100 dry cows from the herd in an hour without using the bridle.

"I cut [for] 25 minutes and had five cows over my average for that time when a rain came up and stopped us," related Windham. "This horse was a dapple gray 15 hands high and would have weighed from 950 to 1,100 pounds. He was a Spanish horse and we called him Bullet. . . . I rode [him] for nine years and there never was another man on him."[77]

After cutting out an unbranded calf, the cowboy would rope and drag it to the branding fire, where flankers waited to throw and hold the animal down while another hand applied the brand with a red-hot iron. With the calf bellowing and the maternal instincts of the mother cow strong, the men would have to take precautions.

"They would keep a good man on a good horse between the round up [herd] and branding fire with a bull whip to keep those old cows off the flankers . . . ," recalled Henderson. "Those calf flankers really worked. . . . The calves . . . were of all sizes, often yearlings with horns three or four inches long. And they would be on the peck when we got them branded and chase the branders. Some of those brands were monsters and it took half an hour to brand a calf."[78]

With mature longhorn cows, flanking was dangerous, no matter the occasion.

"When one of them old-time longhorns was caught, thrown, and then turned loose so they had a chance at you," recalled cowhand M. H. Loy, "it meant have a horse ready for the man on the ground that loosed the rope, so he could put his foot in the stirrup, swing onto his horse, and go mighty quick, as they seldom failed to make a run at your horse."[79]

After helping brand perhaps 400 to 500 calves, the cowhand might switch to an evening horse—another skittish bronc—and drive the "cut" ten or fifteen miles to main camp and arrive in time for a sunset supper.[80] But before he could even consider falling exhausted on his bedroll (returned via chuck wagon), he would have to saddle his night horse and stake it in a grassy area fifty or so yards from the wagon. On this animal, he would ride guard around the herd for about two hours during the night. Potentially, this was the most dangerous duty of a roundup hand, for a herd could spook easily and lead him on a blind ride into unexpected pitfalls. For the task—which demanded complete trust in a horse's innate night vision, balance, and instincts—a cowhand would choose his gentlest and most dependable animal. Furthermore, he would look for an animal smart enough not to entangle itself in the stake rope and burn its feet.[81]

Every cowhand knew these as the traits of a horse worthy of taking a saddle at dusk. Nevertheless, in his 1899 drive upriver from the Horsehead Crossing vicinity to the Kyle Ranch, Henderson bucked tradition in setting up a practical joke on a couple of new hands.

"We boys liked our fun, so we told them a lot of wild stories," related Henderson. "They said, 'You boys are fooling no one but yourselves—we weren't born yesterday.'"

Cowhands and cook at chuck wagon in the Pecos country about 1895. COURTESY OF SOUTHEASTERN NEW MEXICO HISTORICAL SOCIETY, CARLSBAD, NEW MEXICO

Neither had Henderson been, and his thoughts turned to the remuda and a young bronc that was as vicious as they came.

"He would fight a man anytime he saw one afoot," he recalled, "and we always run him off from the wagon and did not put him in the corral ropes when we went to catch horses. No one rode him."

One evening, however, Henderson announced that he intended to ride the outlaw on night guard.

"[Sid Kyle] hit the ceiling and said, 'I won't sleep a bit all night! ... You know what he'll do—he'll run right into camp and jump on any man he sees!'"

Nevertheless, when evening came, Henderson set his sights on the outlaw. "I roped him horseback and choked him down and tied him, put a hackamore on him, tied his foot up, let him up, and put my saddle on him. I never saw a horse pitch worse than he did."

As ordered by Kyle, Henderson staked the animal well away from the wagon, near which the cowhands would unroll their bedding. Recalled Henderson: "I was to go on guard at midnight. . . . All the boys went to bed with their boots on except those two strangers. . . . After they [the strangers] went to sleep, I went out and got on Sid's [gentle] night horse and took a saddle in my hands and come tearing into camp. Sid jumped up and yelled, 'Hold him, Julius! Hold him!' An old boy jumped up and said, 'Run, boys! Here he comes!'

"That was all those fellows wanted to know—they took off like old Satan was after them."[82]

Wild broncs and wilder cattle were common fare on the Pecos, but the sudden staccato of *maracas* underfoot or an abrupt chorus of howls in the night would quickly remind a cowboy that this country held other creatures also worthy of attention.

NOTES

Unless otherwise indicated, all towns, counties, and map quadrangles throughout notes are in Texas.

1. *The Fort Stockton Pioneer*, 17 September 1908 (reprint of *Texas Sun* article, November–December 1880).
2. *San Angelo Standard*, 12 June 1886, 2, col. 3 (originating at *Dallas News*).
3. Dobie, *Longhorns*, 169.
4. Windham, interview.
5. Report of Edward Fitzgerald Beale, in Lewis Burt Lesley, ed., *Uncle Sam's Camels: The Journal of May Humphreys Stacey* (Cambridge: Harvard University Press, 1929), 158 (entry for 11 July 1857).
6. 1990–91 *Texas Almanac*, 167, 218, 234, 239, 260; and "1933 Driest Year Save One Since Rain Records Have Been Kept in Reeves County," *The Pecos Enterprise and Gusher*, 27 July 1934.
7. Armes to AA general, 8 September 1879.
8. Carl M. Eddins, taped interview with Paul Patterson, place not recorded, 8 June 1968, Southwest Collection, Texas Tech University, Lubbock; John C. Reid, *Reid's Tramp, or a Journal of the Incidents of Ten Months Travel Through Texas, New Mexico, Arizona, Sonora, and California* (Austin: Steck Company, reprint, 1935, originally published in 1858), 115–117; and W. R. Baggett, "Early Day Irrigation Ditches On the Pecos," *Frontier Times* Vol. 19, No. 10 (July 1942), 365.
9. Windham, interview.
10. W. R. Owen, interview, 24 June 1937.
11. Jones, interview.

12. Millard, *Cowpuncher*, 31.
13. Don H. Biggers, *From Cattle Range to Cotton Patch* (Bandera: Frontier Times, 1944, originally published in 1904), 59.
14. Newland, interview.
15. Dobie, *Longhorns*, 186.
16. Newland, interview; and Dobie, *Longhorns*, 186.
17. Author's inspection (by foot and canoe) of various stretches of the river.
18. Notation by Haley of an oral statement given Hervey Chesley and him by an unspecified person, on typescript of Charles Ballard, interview with Haley and Chesley, Luna, New Mexico, 9 January 1939, Haley Collection, Haley Library, Midland.
19. Witt, interview, 22 July 1995.
20. Hubbs, interview with Cox.
21. M. Huffman, interview with Haley, Junction, 30 November 1927, Haley Collection, Haley Library, Midland. Huffman rode bog with the XIT in the Panhandle, not on the Pecos, but the necessity of pushing cattle away from the river in late evening would have been equally important on the Pecos.
22. Hubbs, interview with Cox.
23. Hudson "Bud" Mayes, composite of statements in interview, 30 April 1991, and in taped interview with author, Ozona, 22 February 1990.
24. Oden, "Cowboy Standards of 50 Years Ago."
25. Jim Witt, composite of statements, taped telephone interview with author, Loving, New Mexico, 17 July 1993, and interview, 22 July 1995. Although Witt cowboyed in the fenced era, not in open range days, the method of "tromping out" would have been the same. Throughout this discussion of the open range cowboy, I have included such examples of later incidents if the methods remained unchanged from the earlier era.
26. Oden, "Cowboy Standards of 50 Years Ago."
27. Written statement by Robert M. "Bob" Dudley in Mrs. Bob Duke file, J. Evetts Haley Collection, Haley Library. Dudley, who signed on with the XIT outfit in the Panhandle in 1893, rode bog on the Canadian River.
28. Hubbs, interview with Cox; and Barney Hubbs, taped telephone interview with author, Pecos, 19 March 1992.
29. Armstrong, interview. Buchanan's initials are from Cochran, "Walter C. Cochran's Memoirs," 38.
30. Bob Dow, "Daybreak All Over the World," typescript, Haley Collection, Haley Library, Midland, 9–10.
31. Hubbs, interview with Cox.
32. Dow, "Daybreak All Over," 12.
33. Ibid., 11–12.
34. Henderson, "Memories of an Old Cowboy," 23.
35. Witt, interview, 22 July 1995.
36. Oden, "Early Cowboy Days."
37. Millard, *Cowpuncher*, 31, 33.
38. Ibid., 31.
39. Ibid., 41.

40. Hubbs, interview with Cox.

41. Clayton Williams, *Last Frontier*, 312.

42. Millard, *Cowpuncher*, 41; and Adams, *Western Words*, 287–288. By law, a brand had to be recorded in the county of origin.

43. Rankin, interview, 29 April 1991.

44. Composite of statements, Witt, interview, 22 July 1995.

45. L. B. Eddins, interview.

46. Henderson, "Memories of an Old Cowboy," 71.

47. L. B. Eddins, interview. Number of sections from Clayton Williams, *Last Frontier*, 320.

48. Henderson, "Life of an Oldtimer," book one, 7.

49. Henderson, "Life of an Oldtimer," book six, 6.

50. Ibid., prologue, 14.

51. Ibid.

52. Green Mankin, interview with author, Mills County, 14 September 1989.

53. *San Angelo Standard*, 14 January 1888, 2, col. l.

54. Gid Reding, interview with author, Fort Stockton, 1 September 1989.

55. Clayton Williams, *Last Frontier*, 309.

56. Witt, interview, 22 July 1995.

57. L. B. Eddins, interview.

58. Baggett, "Early Day Irrigation," 365; Witt, interview, 22 July 1995; Bill Townsend, interview with author, Odessa, 3 August 1995; Patterson, interview, 29 April 1991; and Reid, *Reid's Tramp*, 115–117.

59. Reid, *Reid's Tramp*, 117.

60. Baggett, "Early Day Irrigation," 364–365. Information on Torres is from Clayton Williams, "The First Two Irrigation Projects on the Pecos River in Texas," *The Permian Historical Annual* 15 (December 1975), 2.

61. Notation by Haley (in the form of a question that was not denied) on typescript of Ballard interview.

62. Patterson, interview, 29 April 1991.

63. Townsend, interview.

64. Witt, interview, 22 July 1995.

65. Patterson, interview, 29 April 1991.

66. Henderson, "Memories of an Old Cowboy," 72.

67. Henderson, "Life of an Oldtimer," book one, 3–4.

68. Ibid., book two, 2.

69. L. B. Eddins, interview.

70. This study of roundup on the Pecos is based on: *San Angelo Standard*, 21 February 1885, 2, col. 2, and 24 April 1886, 2, col. 2; Oden, "Cowboy Standards;" Clayton Williams, *Last Frontier*, 311–312, 321–322; Newland, interview; Millard, *Cowpuncher*, 36; and L. B. Eddins, interview.

71. Millard, *Cowpuncher*, 36.

72. Oden, "Cowboy Standards."

73. Henderson, "Life of an Oldtimer," book two, 1–2.

74. Loy, manuscript; and Dobie, *Longhorns*, 252.
75. Oden, "Cowboy Standards."
76. L. B. Eddins, interview.
77. Windham, interview.
78. Henderson, "Life of an Oldtimer," book four, 16.
79. Loy, manuscript.
80. Oden, "Cowboy Standards;" and L. B. Eddins, interview.
81. L. B. Eddins, interview.
82. Henderson, "Life of an Oldtimer," book one, 6–7. According to Henderson, the two strangers, Howard L. Royston and George J. Abshire, were hanged after participating in a bank robbery (evidently in or near Denver, Colorado) during which two men were killed. In Henderson, "Memories of an Old Cowboy," 71–72, Henderson says the cattle drive occurred in the spring of 1898.

CHAPTER NINE

Loafers, Diamondbacks, and Wild Horses

LONG BEFORE COWMEN TURNED THE FIRST HERDS LOOSE IN THE region, explorers recognized that a predator prowled the Pecos.

"The antelope and wolf alone," wrote U.S. Army Captain S. G. French in 1849, "visit its dreary, silent, and desolate shores."[1]

With the advent of open range ranching along the river, the lobo or "loafer" wolf no longer had to subsist on mere native game—suddenly, just beyond the horns of the cows and hooves of the mares, there were helpless, young calves and colts on which to prey.

"[Wolves] was worse up and down this Pecos than any place in existence . . . ," noted M. L. "Mike" Liles, who cowboyed along the New Mexico stretch beginning in the 1880s. "They liked to have ruined this country."[2]

Downriver in Texas, loafers did their greatest damage along and south of a line from Horsehead Crossing to the Glass Mountains near present Alpine.[3] Running in packs of five to ten animals, they were a threat even to mature cows and horses.

"In killing an animal," noted H. M. Hill, who worked cattle on the lower Pecos in 1885, "they tore first one flank out and then the other flank, which would let the guts fall out, and then they ran up and grabbed the guts and pulled them on out. Then the animal would fall down. I've seen them pull cows down and they'd lie there and bawl while the loafers were eating on them. I never saw them hamstring one. I've seen them kill grown mustangs, ripping out first one side and then another."[4]

Even cowhands were not immune to the danger. "One-Armed Bill" Wilson, staggering on foot down the Pecos to get help for the wounded Oliver Loving in 1867, found wolves at his heels throughout a long, desperate night.

"I would give out, just like a horse, and lay down in the road and drop off to sleep," he related, "and when I would awaken, the wolves would be all around me, snapping and snarling. I would take up that stick [part of a tepee pole], knock the wolves away, get started again and the wolves would follow behind. I kept that up until daylight, when the wolves quit me."[5]

By the 1890s loafers had become such a problem that some newly organized counties, as well as certain cattle outfits, paid bounties for their scalps. For a cowboy making a dollar or so a day, wolf-hunting could be lucrative, netting him $5 a scalp in Crockett County[6] and $25 from big outfits north of the T&P Railroad.[7] Often, he could collect multiple bounties on a single kill. Liles, cowboying on the Bar V in southern New Mexico, killed thirteen loafers in a two-day span about 1900 and pocketed $2.50 per scalp from the Bar V and $20 per scalp from the county—in all, almost a year's pay at cowhand wages.[8]

About the same time, a ranch ten miles from Fort Stockton paid $50 for the scalp of a single notorious lobo. Pecos County pioneer O. W. Williams, in noting the typical $20 bounty offered in 1908 by area outfits, believed it a small price to pay in order to minimize calf losses.

"I have heard of a lobo about five years ago [i.e., 1903] killing nine calves on nine successive days on a ranch not far from [Fort Stockton] ...," he related. "If these calves were worth only $5 each, that lobo destroyed $45 worth of property in a little over a week and may have done damage during its lifetime that would run up into hundreds of dollars."[9]

To rid the country of the menace, the HAT outfit in New Mexico even imported nine Russian wolfhounds in the 1890s.

"They had not been at the ranch long," reported Julius D. Henderson, who cowboyed nearby at the time, "until the whole outfit went off to town to a big Fourth of July celebration and left the dogs alone. And those wolves come in and killed and ate the whole bunch. They then gave their men orders to quit any job they were on and run any wolf they saw, and they paid $25 for scalps too."[10]

Hunting wolves was a challenge, for they were swift, cunning, and wary. "You . . . never could even get a shot at one of them," noted Liles. "They'd get off half a mile."

They were equally difficult to ride down, as Liles learned while cowboying with the VOX outfit in 1896. "One morning I was catching saddle horses early and I heard a calf bawl," he related. "The boss says, 'That's a loafer getting his breakfast.' We thought we'd catch a horse right quick and saddle up and go over there and see if we couldn't catch one of them. While we were saddling up, they ate that one up and caught another one. I think there was thirteen loafers in the bunch and we caught five."[11]

Such rare success at overtaking a wolf generally came only with extenuating circumstances. Around the turn of the twentieth century, cowboys with the Gibson and Baldridge Ranch sighted a pack near Horsehead Crossing and gave chase. Although not mounted on swift horses, the cowhands managed to ride down and rope three of the wolves. Williams, reporting the incident in 1908, attributed their success to the fact that the chase occurred on a flat (rather than among hills unsuited to an all-out gallop), and that the loafers were not fully mature and had just fed and watered heavily.[12]

Wolf hunters generally resorted to trailing the animals to their dens (usually in burrows or shallow caves) in the spring and summer and then digging them out.[13] Some men, such as Will Elliott and Lem Boren in southern New Mexico, found it so profitable that they reportedly took steps to ensure that the animals continued to breed.

"They'd trail them afoot," related Liles, an acquaintance. "You'd get a location on one and get close to a den and the tracks would be there just like a herd of sheep had been there. . . . They never bothered the old ones. They'd just get the young ones. They was making too much money out of them. They didn't want to stop the breed."[14]

By the 1920s, however, the hated loafer was a rarity on the Pecos. Jim Witt, who took up residence on the Cross C Ranch just downstream of the T&P Railroad about 1924, saw but a single animal during his ten years on the river.[15] Bill Townsend, cowboying on the Pecos near Pyote, Texas, in the late 1920s, also encountered but a lone wolf. He first realized that there was an unusual animal about when its howl stirred him from his bedroll during a two-day cattle drive along the river with veteran cowhand Eric King in late 1928 or 1929.

"I knew it was something strange," Townsend recalled almost seven decades later. "I laid my tarp back and lay there and it howled again. I never had heard nothing like that. The next morning, Eric King . . . said that was a lobo." A day or two later, Townsend rode over a ridge and sighted a large canine 200 or more yards away.

"That ol' white grass was high—16, 18 inches—and I could see light under his belly above that grass, so he was a *big* rascal. He [King] said that was a wolf."

Upon completing the drive, Townsend and King scouted back downstream for strays. Riding through a salt cedar thicket on the flood plain, the two cowboys suddenly came face-to-face with an old Mexican rider with a double-barreled shotgun across his saddle; the stranger was part of a "wolf drive" undertaken by several cowboys attempting to flush the calf-killer from the brush. Townsend never again heard the howl of a Pecos lobo.[16]

Bill Townsend in 1995. COURTESY OF THE AUTHOR

Wolves were not the only predators with which Pecos cowboys had to contend. Down in the broken country below present Girvin, mountain lions were so troublesome that Crockett County levied a bounty of $5 per scalp in the 1890s,[17] and coyotes were as thick as jackrabbits throughout the river's coils and threatened not only sheep but small calves.

"We had a lot of bob-tailed calves," noted Bill Eddins, who cowboyed on Sid Kyle's Pecos River spread beginning in 1918. "They'd grab them by the tails and cut its tail off. The calf would get away."[18]

Although threats to cowhands by predators were not unknown, rattlesnakes (generally diamondbacks) posed a much greater danger on the Pecos, which cowhand Witt described as a "rattlesnake den."[19] In fact, far-ranging Charles Goodnight observed that "the lower Pecos country was infested with rattlesnakes, more snakes per mile than anywhere I ever traveled, and good-sized ones too."

On the first Goodnight and Loving drive up the Pecos in 1866, drover Nath Brauner shot seventy-two rattlesnakes. Nevertheless, the hands found little reason to feel more at ease on the return trip. Traveling downriver by night to avoid Indians, the staccato of rattlers seemed to greet them with almost every stride of their mules. Goodnight, who had a sensory impairment, could not hear the snakes and became unnerved by his drovers' repeated warnings of yet another rattler. "After this had gone on for a while," Goodnight related, "I told the boys to let me and the rattlers alone; I'd just take my chances as I could not tell which way to dodge, and they could look out for themselves if they wished. Fortunately, we finished the trip without any mule getting bitten."[20]

Sometimes, a Pecos cowboy found himself closer to a rattlesnake than he ever wanted.

"One night we got in kind of late," recalled Witt, "and I unsaddled my horse, and I didn't take my leggings off. I guess I was just so damned tired. And I headed for the bunkhouse, and I guess I stepped on one or something; it was dark. Anyhow, he struck and hit my leggings. He'd've got my leg if I hadn't had my leggings on. I don't know why I had them on even—that was the first and only time I ever wore them to the house."[21]

Some cowhands were not as lucky in escaping the fangs, and in an era before antivenin serum, they could only look to folk medicine for

J. Evetts Haley with diamondback rattlesnake during cattle drive through the sands east of the Pecos about 1923. COURTESY OF J. EVETTS HALEY COLLECTION, N. S. HALEY MEMORIAL LIBRARY, MIDLAND, TEXAS

treatment. A common method was to submerge the victim's wounded limb in a bucket of kerosene and pour whiskey down him[22]; another involved the use of a common food additive carried on every chuck wagon.

"I know of no relief more instantaneous and complete than common salt," noted Goodnight, a onetime Texas Ranger. "Scarify the place as deep as the fangs went and apply the salt freely. The finer the salt, the better. It won't lame the animal or person, and the next day they will be as good as ever. . . . In the Ranger days, we ate what meat we could get, usually without salt, but we always kept enough salt for snakebite emergencies."[23]

Two other denizens of the Pecos country also occasionally occupied the attention of some cowhands. One was a wild animal turned domestic, the other a domesticated animal turned wild.

In 1879 the last significant buffalo kill in Texas occurred at Mustang Springs, seventy miles northeast of Horsehead Crossing and the TX headquarters.[24] Soon, however, a remnant herd—a buffalo bull and a few buffalo cows—drifted to the Pecos and the TX range. On through the 1880s, the animals endured as stubborn reminders of the great, wild herds which for millennia had thundered across the South Plains.[25]

By the time J. Arthur Johnson became manager of the TX in 1887, the outfit had drilled a water well east of the river at a point seventeen miles upstream from Horsehead.

"We had about 400 horses and . . . we had one well there and a reservoir, and I kept a man out there all the time," recalled Johnson. "Never allowed a cow around that. The only brute outside the horses [that was permitted to water] was . . . a buffalo bull. . . . There was a buffalo cow that stayed down there between the ranch and the salt lake [Juan Cardona Lake]. The other cow stayed 10 or 15 miles down the river. . . . I put them together a dozen times, put them in the horse pasture, and they just went right through it [the fence]. Never did breed, and I don't know why."[26]

At times, the buffalo would respond to instinct and wander afar, sometimes sixty miles northeast to the young town of Midland. Townspeople, however, believed them wild and eventually hunted this last Pecos herd to extinction.[27]

Another dying breed was the mustang, whose roots on the upper Pecos dated to the sixteenth century when Spaniards introduced thousands of horses to the Southwest. By the latter 1700s, when Comanches from the Arkansas and Red rivers began raiding haciendas in Mexico, mustangs probably roamed up and down the river.[28]

As war parties drove stolen Mexican horses back across the Pecos country, strays and runaways probably fell in with the mustangs and became outlaws—a fate which likely befell many emigrant and cow ponies in the nineteenth century.[29]

By the era of open range ranching, only a few mustangs trod the Texas stretch. In 1884 a small herd ran free on the west side near Horsehead Crossing,[30] and the late 1890s found two bunches ranging on the east side near Horsehead and its upstream counterpart, Salt Crossing, situated five miles east of present Imperial.[31] One herd consisted of dark bays, stocking-footed and bald-faced, while very small light bays composed the second herd.[32] A third bunch, all paints, ran along the river in Pecos County, while other mustangs ranged near Narbo's Crossing and on the W outfit range north of the city of Pecos.[33]

The Pecos mustangs generally ran in groups of fifteen to twenty mature animals and raised only a few colts, almost always fillies. The mares stood twelve to thirteen hands high and the stallions—of which Henderson knew of but three in all the Pecos country—measured thirteen and one-half to fourteen hands.[34]

With a demand in the 1890s for small horses to work the cotton fields of East Texas, Louisiana, and Arkansas, some cowboys took to "mustanging" on the Pecos.

"It was the dream of every cowpoke to catch a mustang," observed Henderson.[35]

Cowhands used two methods to capture these wild horses—"walking down" and penning. To walk a herd down, a mustang outfit would station men at nearby watering places on the river to deny the animals water. Then riders would follow the wary mustangs day and night, never allowing them rest or forage. At first, the horses might maintain a distance of more than a mile, but the gap would close little by little as the days dragged on. By the fourth or fifth day, the constant "chousing" would take such a toll that the riders could loose several tame horses into the herd and trail the mixed group to a corral.[36]

The alternate method, penning, required considerable preparation. First, an outfit would study the river and identify a mustang watering place by the approaching trails. In a brushy area nearby, hands would stretch wire from mesquite to mesquite and form a closed horseshoe against the river's sharp, impassable bank. Clearing the brush from the center of the pen, they would pile it along the perimeter to obscure the wire, and then they would construct a pole gate and camouflage it. From that opening, they would stretch a lengthy, brush-covered wire back into the flat, leaving a gap for the advancing horse paths. When the ponies would trail to the river, the hands would seal the gap and drive them down the single-strand fence to the waiting pen.[37]

Although without the physical demands of walking down, penning proved every bit as stressful on mustangs.

"The things just seemed to have the ability to lay down and die when they were caught . . . ," noted Henderson. "They could not stand confinement. The older horse[s] would die in just a little while."[38]

Once, after walking down and corralling about twenty mustangs, Henderson and his fellow cowhands were chagrined to find that more than half died almost immediately. Furthermore, he noted that he knew of five bunches which had been penned—not walked down—and that every animal more than one year old had died within a matter of hours. The five included a herd trapped by brothers Jack and Bill Jolly, who turned their saddle horses in with the penned animals and made plans to drive the herd to Pecos City the next day. By morning, every mustang was dead although the tame horses continued healthy.[39]

While a colt younger than one year could be raised on cow's milk and gentled,[40] any older animal—even if it survived—already was so habituated to the wild that it would always remain an outlaw. In the early 1900s, Young Bell and Billy Gibbons captured a small herd near Narbo's Crossing and sold the animals for $10 a head to Bill Ross across the territorial line in New Mexico. Ross believed he could gentle the mustangs by turning them in with his 200 to 300 head of saddle horses. After six months of running with the remuda, not only were the mustangs as wild as ever, but they had induced many of the saddle horses to turn outlaw. Ross had no choice but to have the mustangs shot.[41]

The era of the wild horse on the Pecos soon came to a close. By 1908 only about fifteen mustangs, all of them inferior animals due to inbreeding, roamed Pecos County.[42] One by one, the mustangs fell by the wayside, until finally, sometime after May of 1923, a single bald-faced, bay stallion trod the river's east side as the last of a breed. An oilman, not versed in the ways of untameable mustangs, told Henderson he had offered a cowboy $150 to capture the horse. Henderson replied, "I hope he catches him—you'll give me $300 to help you turn him loose."[43]

Like a mustang, a Pecos cowboy knew only one way to live, but the trials of the Big Drift of 1884-1885 may have given some saddle-sore cowhands cause for second thoughts.

NOTES

Unless otherwise indicated, all towns, counties, and map quadrangles throughout notes are in Texas.

1. Report of S. G. French, *Reports of the Secretary of War*, 65.
2. M. L. "Mike" Liles, interview with Haley, Kenna, New Mexico, 4 August 1937, Haley Collection, Haley Library, Midland.
3. O. W. Williams, "Something About the Plants and Animals of Pecos County: The Lobo," *The Fort Stockton Pioneer*, 23 July 1908.
4. H. M. Hill, interview with Haley, Midland, 9 September 1931. The incidents which Hill describes evidently occurred in the Panhandle rather than on the Pecos.
5. Wilson's narrative in Hunter, *Trail Drivers of Texas*, 911–912.
6. *A History of Crockett County* (San Angelo: Crockett County Historical Society, Anchor Publishing Company, 1976), 57.
7. Henderson, "Life of an Oldtimer," prologue, 15–16.
8. Liles, interview.
9. O. W. Williams, "Something About the Plants and Animals of Pecos County: The Lobo," *The Fort Stockton Pioneer*, 23 July 1908.
10. Henderson, "Life of an Oldtimer," prologue, 15.
11. Liles, interview.
12. O. W. Williams, "Something About the Plants and Animals of Pecos County: The Lobo," *The Fort Stockton Pioneer*, 23 July 1908.
13. Liles, interview; and Henderson, "Life of an Oldtimer," 15–16.
14. Liles, interview.
15. Witt, interview, 22 July 1995.
16. Townsend, interview.

17. *History of Crockett County*, 57.

18. L. B. Eddins, interview.

19. Witt, interview, 22 July 1995.

20. Goodnight, "Recollections II," 74–75.

21. Witt, interview, 22 July 1995.

22. Ethel Pitt Harris, taped telephone interview with author, Albuquerque, New Mexico, 23 May 1985.

23. Goodnight, "Recollections II, 47–48.

24. Joe S. McCombs in Ben O. Grant and J. R. Webb, "On the Cattle Trail and Buffalo Range, Joe S. McCombs," *WTHA Year Book* 2 (November 1935), 100. For information on Mustang Springs, situated near present Stanton, see Patrick Dearen, *Portraits of the Pecos Frontier* (Lubbock: Texas Tech University Press, 1993), 106–114.

25. J. A. Johnson, interview; and H. Knowles, interview with Haley, place not recorded, 21 November 1936, Haley Collection, Haley Library, Midland.

26. J. A. Johnson, interview.

27. Knowles, interview.

28. Newcomb, *Indians of Texas*, 86–88, 107–109, 114, 156–157, 233; Wallace and Hoebel, *The Comanches*, 12, 38, 39, 288, 289; and O. W. Williams, *Pioneer Surveyor-Frontier Lawyer*, 278.

29. For an account of the capture of a "fine Kentucky saddle horse" which had run off with a mustang herd about 1899, see Henderson, "Life of an Oldtimer," book 1, 6.

30. O. W. Williams, "Something About the Plants and Animals of Pecos County: Wild Horses," *The Fort Stockton Pioneer*, 7 May 1908.

31. Henderson, "Memories of an Old Cowboy," 70–71; and Henderson, "Life of an Oldtimer," book one, 5–6. For a study of Salt Crossing, see Dearen, *Crossing Rio Pecos*, 109–111.

32. Henderson, "Memories of an Old Cowboy," 70.

33. Henderson, "Life of an Oldtimer," book four, 15; and Bell, *Seventy Years in the Cow Business*, 29–31.

34. Henderson, "Life of an Oldtimer," book 1, 6; and Henderson, "Memories of an Old Cowboy," 16, 71. Henderson indicated that stallions likely killed the young male colts. Young Bell told of one mustang herd with mature horses 14 to 16 hands high. See Bell, *Seventy Years in the Cow Business*, 30.

35. Henderson, "Life of an Oldtimer," book one, 4, 5 (quote); and Henderson, "Memories of an Old Cowboy," 70.

36. Henderson, "Memories of an Old Cowboy," 70–71; Henderson, "Life of an Oldtimer," book one, 5–6; and Bell, *Seventy Years in the Cow Business*, 29–31.

37. Henderson, "Life of an Oldtimer," book one, 5.

38. Henderson, "Memories of an Old Cowboy," 15.

39. Henderson, ibid., 15–16, 70–71.

40. Henderson, ibid., 71.

41. Bell, *Seventy Years in the Cow Business*, 29–31.

42. O. W. Williams, "Something About the Plants and Animals of Pecos County: Wild Horses," *The Fort Stockton Pioneer*, 7 May 1908.

43. Henderson, "Memories of an Old Cowboy," 16. The mention of an oilman indicates that the incident occurred after Santa Rita # 1 blew in on May 28, 1923 near Texon (28 miles northeast of the Pecos) and ushered in the West Texas oil boom. See *New Handbook of Texas* Vol. 5, 890.

CHAPTER TEN

The Big Drift

BY THE WINTER OF 1884–1885, COWHANDS RODE RAMROD OVER GREAT herds of cattle not only up and down the Pecos, but throughout the vast, unfenced stretches of the Texas Panhandle and South Plains. Even so, some observers already grumbled that imprudent owners had set themselves up for a fall.

"The open range was glorious, is still glorious when there is more grass than stock," observed cowmen in the January 10, 1885, *Texas Live Stock Journal.* "But it has a weakness when there are two cows to feed and only grass can be found for one. Today as we write, the ranges in Texas are, in some instances, overstocked."[1]

To prevent Kansas herds and other Great Plains cattle from drifting south into Texas in search of winter forage, stockmen built an east-west fence north of the Canadian River in the early 1880s. Spanning the Panhandle from New Mexico to Indian Territory,[2] it was a monumental undertaking, but it did nothing to prevent drift problems for outfits on the Pecos side of the barbs. Smaller-scale fences to the south, such as between the Canadian and Sweetwater Creek of Wheeler County,[3] still might hinder a longhorn which was fleeing its home range with a norther nipping at its flanks. But if the wire snapped or if the animal bore south-southwest from the overstocked Canadian, scarcely a lone, scrub mesquite would bar its course the entire 300 to 400 miles to the Pecos.

With the onslaught of severe weather late in 1884,[4] the result was inevitable—cowhands would witness such an incredible migration of cattle that they would call it simply the "Big Drift."

With suddenness, the storm came howling across the South Plains from the northeast,[5] a terrifying blizzard that set cattle marching, hour after hour, day after day. For a week, the fierce, wind-driven snow swept through the barbed wire of the Panhandle fence,[6] and as bawling cattle from the Cimarron and Arkansas rivers struck it, they piled against it and died, one atop another, until the thousands of cattle behind them bridged it by their carcasses and kept going. From the Canadian ranges and the Pease, great herds fled, carried along by animals from the north, until the South Plains was a seething mass of bellowing cattle.[7] Soon, 100,000 head crowded against the fences near Sweetwater in Nolan County,[8] and another 100,000 were striding free across the T&P track between Midland and Monahans, bound for the Pecos.[9] Still others drifted toward the Devils, Frio, and other south-lying rivers.[10]

Jim Cook, manager of the Two-Circle Bar in Fisher County, watched the drift herds carry his outfit's cattle away like an all-consuming flood on an unyielding course. "The storm was coming from the northeast to the southwest," he related. "When they got on the plains, the cattle kept their tails to the wind."[11]

Watching the herds thunder past Sand Creek near the Garza-Borden county line, cowhand H. D. "Nick" Beal of the Jumbo Cattle Company, or Buckle B, could only shake his head. "It was impossible," he said, "to think of holding them back."[12]

At the Henderson Ranch eight miles north of Odessa, Julius D. Henderson watched Pecos-bound herds trample a great trail through an eighteen-inch snow.

"They came by there in a run," related Henderson, who was a child at the time. "The herd was a mile wide at times. Some cattle that gave out and stopped, froze to death standing up."

A Henderson milk cow, the only animal carrying an AX brand, left its calf to join the stampeding mass. "The next day at noon," recalled Henderson, "she was at J. M. Keithley's ranch about fifteen miles southeast of Monahans, a distance of about forty miles. The storm broke then and she turned back. She came in home about sunup the next morning. She had made the round trip of about eighty miles in thirty-six hours."[13]

Down in the Middle Concho country, meanwhile, cowhand Bill Carr awoke to an incredible sight. "It was night and was a very warm one . . . ," related Carr, who had unrolled his bedding under the open sky at a sheep camp. "Way along in the night I got awfully hot. I threw the cover back and I was just buried in snow. About daylight, cattle commenced to coming, and by ten [o'clock] they were really bawling. As far as you could see them, the whole world was just covered with cattle, trailing right in front of that blizzard."[14]

A Fort Worth publication of the day put it all in perspective, labeling the mass drift the worst in "the history of Texas."[15]

Not only did the storm exact a terrible toll on livestock, but on ranch hands as well. Trudging through the chill to save his sheep, a sheepherder south of the Middle Concho lost his way in the dark. The sharp, icy ground shredded his shoes, rendering him virtually barefoot by the time he found his camp.

"Those feet was the awfullest sight I ever saw," recalled Carr. "They were just in terrible shape, terrible. Caught cold in them, you know, inflamed."[16]

Thousands of southwest-bound cattle, meanwhile, pushed on relentlessly, never stopping until they reached the barrier Pecos. Mad with thirst, many plunged over the sheer bank and drowned, or bogged hopelessly in the unforgiving mire. Upstream and downstream, from above Pecos City to below Pontoon Bridge, the surviving cattle flooded the range.[17] Soon the blizzard faded into memory, but as winter wore on, the animals joined the native stock in grazing the ground bare. Weakened by the frenzied push down from their home ranges, and now deprived of forage, the migratory cattle, especially, fell by the thousands.[18] Suddenly, the Big Drift had become the Big Die-Up.

Pat Wilson, who soon rode the country, found the flood plain so concentrated with carcasses that a man could have walked for five miles, he said, without stepping on the ground.[19] Below the bank, meanwhile, lay a festering mass of maggot-infested carrion unlike anything cowhands had ever seen.

"I saw so many dead cattle in the Pecos that the river was absolutely dammed with them in the spring of 1885," recalled cowhand H. M. Hill.[20]

Even as the Big Die-Up claimed their beeves, Panhandle and South Plains outfits could only tough it out and hope they still would have cattle left when conditions finally would permit them to set out in search. As it was, plains ranches such as the Square and Compass already had their hands full with their own "graze-out," for their ranges were filled throughout winter with cattle not their own.[21]

In late winter the outfits met at Colorado (now Colorado City) on the T&P and organized the largest roundup in the history of the Pecos. Representatives selected C. A. "Gus" O'Keefe, manager of the C. C. Slaughter spread, as ramrod, and he quickly set out by train to assess the situation on the river.[22]

Meanwhile, on February 17, 1885, 300 Pecos cowmen and hands gathered at a Pecos Valley Stock Association meeting in Toyah, a railroad stop twenty miles west of the Pecos, and planned their own roundup. Set for May 20, it was to commence at Pontoon Bridge.[23]

O'Keefe, returning from his scout, decided to conduct the massive drift operation in carefully devised stages. From a pool of thirty or so ranches, he dispatched at least twenty-seven wagon outfits, each including as many as twenty cowboys.[24] Earlier, the Big Drift had launched the greatest cattle migration to the Pecos in history; now, in February, it spawned the greatest influx of cowhands ever.[25] Down the old Goodnight-Loving Trail they came, hundreds of cowboys and 1,000 saddle horses,[26] veering southwest at abandoned Centralia Mail Station to trace the rerouted Upper Road to the Pontoon Bridge region. Others, meanwhile, may have headed straight for points upstream.

"I came out . . . in February 1885 and went to the JALs [in southeastern New Mexico] and the whole world was working with cattle," remembered Lod Calohan.[27]

Some outfits sent two or more wagons apiece: the C. C. Slaughter, Spur, Matador, Cross Tie of Deep Creek in Mitchell County, Two-Circle Bar, Shoe Bar, and OX. Other wagons represented the M Cross of Mitchell County, Mallet (situated thirty miles west of the upper Colorado River), High Webb, Jumbo Cattle Company's Buckle B, St. Louis Cattle Company, L Upside-down V NC, Kidwell, LX, NUN, T Bar, IO Upside-down V, Square and Compass, and Bar 96.[28] Cattle bearing the brands of many smaller outfits also had drifted to the Pecos, but, in a classic example of "neighboring," larger ranches such as the Bar 96 volunteered to return the animals along with their own.[29]

Striking the river, the consolidated crews immediately encountered problems, for, with the arrival of eight cowhands "repping" for outfits that did not send wagons, there were more cowboys than the cooks could feed.[30]

With so many thousands of mixed-ownership cattle ranging along the Pecos, O'Keefe directed cowhands to round up without regard to brand. On the first day alone, cowboys threw together a herd of 8,000 animals on the lower Pecos. While other hands continued the process upriver and downriver, a contingent took charge of the herd and began pushing it back toward the Middle Concho. As the days wore on, cowhands gathered more and more cattle to turn them toward their home

Chuck wagon scene at the W Ranch on the Pecos. COURTESY OF J. EVETTS HALEY COLLECTION, N. S. HALEY MEMORIAL LIBRARY, MIDLAND, TEXAS

ranges, frequently in herds so large that they could only be drifted, not driven. The animals, gaunt and weak, dropped by the hundreds, marking every mile of the way with their carcasses. Fully half of that first herd of 8,000 never reached the Middle Concho.

From the Horsehead Crossing area, drovers pointed herd after herd for the head of the Colorado River by way of Odessa and Midland. Along the way, O'Keefe had stationed other outfits—the Tom Love bunch near Odessa, H. D. "Nick" Beal and the Buckle B at the Chicago Ranch northwest of Midland—to receive the herds and take up the drive on to the Colorado. There in the breaks, they would loose the animals for later reworking and separating by brand for the trek on to their respective home ranges.[31]

Even at its height, the Goodnight-Loving Trail had never witnessed such a mass drive through the Pecos country.

"There was a solid herd of cattle from Horsehead Crossing to the Colorado River," noted Julius D. Henderson.[32]

But, as in all routes leading from the Pecos, a major problem faced herds bound for the Colorado—a dearth of water. Some drovers cut a trail to Ward's Wells, approximately seventy-five miles northwest of Midland, only to find that the wells could not accommodate large numbers of animals. Fortunately for herds bearing straight for Monahans or Odessa, and on through Midland, O'Keefe had arranged with the T&P for cattle to water at hastily dug earthen tanks at railroad wells in the respective communities.[33]

H. M. Hill, in charge of the St. Louis Cattle Company wagon outfit, was among the drovers trailing herds away from the Pecos in February. He recalled:

"They cut me out a herd of about 7,000, and with my 20 men, I started it across from below Carlsbad [New Mexico] to Rich Lake, which was 20 miles southwest of Double Lakes, and then turned them loose on the head of the Brazos in the Post country [where other cowhands later would rework the animals]. I rigged up a red lantern and put a boy in the lead of the herd to carry this lantern. . . . We did a pretty long stretch without water, I guess about 60 miles, but there was still snow on the ground and the cattle got through all right."[34]

By late March, cowhands had returned 25,000 cattle to their home ranges.[35] Yet, some observers already expressed concern that their efforts would not be enough.

"It is the opinion of those at work there that many cattle have even crossed the Pecos," noted the March 28 *Texas Live Stock Journal*. "A large trail has been discovered west of the pastures bordering the plains, and this trail crosses the plains in a southwesterly direction and would land the cattle on the Pecos below where the present outfits are at work or will work." The publication further noted that "it will require the combined efforts of the entire western country to get the cows home to their respective ranges."[36]

Meanwhile, the Pecos outfits below Pecos City were suffering the consequences of not only the Big Drift, but the unprecedented roundup.

"Besides having their ranches eaten out," said A. T. Windham, who was with the Seven Rivers Cattle Company in 1885, "lots of their cattle were carried off in the herds of men who ranched to the north. The cattle had long hair and they could not help carrying off some."[37]

On May 20 the Pecos outfits presumably met as planned at Pontoon Bridge and began their own roundup. As they moved up the river and overlapped the efforts of the South Plains and Panhandle cowboys, the Pecos hands found their own brands so greatly outnumbered that they undertook the culling process in unheard-of fashion. Noted Jim Cook, manager of the Two-Circle Bar of the lower plains: "They cut out the Pecos cattle from ours, instead of the other way about."[38]

By July the roundup for the Big Drift finally was over.[39] By the estimate of participating cowhand H. M. Hill, drovers had shoved an incredible 120,000 to 150,000 cattle back up to their home ranges.[40] Nevertheless, the losses were staggering.

"There were more of these cattle drowned and died in the Pecos than ever were brought back home," said cowhand Walter C. Cochran.[41]

Furthermore, the calf tally for the Panhandle and South Plains outfits dropped by at least one-third that year,[42] with ranches such as the Square and Compass suffering even greater declines. "The calves were practically all lost," lamented Square and Compass ramrod Rollie Burns.[43]

Beyond the immediate loss in mature animals and calves, and the expense in seeing the surviving animals home, the Big Drift wrought a dire change in ranching for the outfits to the north and northeast of the Pecos. More than any other event, it brought an end to open-range grazing on the plains.

"The winter of 1884–5, now about over, will have taught many men who are running stock on the open range that it is necessary that they should adjust their cattle to their lands, or adjust their lands to their cattle, which is one and the same thing," said the *Texas Live Stock Journal* of February 28, 1885. "In short, all Texas must get under fence."

Some cowmen still would oppose the action, said the publication, "but these will be a minority, and the minority will be smaller every year. It is just dawning on the intellect of some ranchmen who have considered the fence an unmixed evil that there is something in being under the lee side . . . of a fence, and there is good by being protected from the drifts [of cattle]."[44]

Along the Pecos, meanwhile, fences were still a decade or more away, but the multitude of carcasses left to rot on its barren, east-lying flat portended the pestilence that would begin creeping across the land within a matter of weeks.

NOTES

Unless otherwise indicated, all towns, counties, and map quadrangles throughout notes are in Texas.

1. "The Signs of the Times," *Texas Live Stock Journal*, 10 January 1885.
2. Nelson, "Judge O. H. Nelson;" and Haley, *Charles Goodnight*, 321.
3. Mose Hayes, interview with Haley, San Antonio, 3 March 1935.
4. Dobie (*The Longhorns*, 197) says the blizzard struck late in December, while Rollie Burns ("Reminiscence of 56 Years," 66, manuscript, Haley Collection, Haley Library, Midland) gives a date of late fall. Henderson ("Memories of an Old Cowboy," 27) says it occurred early in November, although he incorrectly gives the year as 1888.
5. Direction of the storm is from Jim Cook, "Jim Cook's Dictation," typescript, Haley Collection, Haley Library, Midland. Cook's Two-Circle Bar cowhands helped recover the drift cattle on the Pecos.
6. Duration of the storm is from H. D. "Nick" Beal, interview with Haley, Gail, 11 September 1931, Haley Collection, Haley Library, Midland.
7. Lod Calohan, interview with Haley, Kansas City, Missouri, 1 January 1926, in "South Plains Interviews," bound volume, Haley Library, Midland; Cochran, "Walter

C. Cochran's Memoirs," 38; Henderson, "Memories of an Old Cowboy," 27; *San Angelo Standard*, 9 May 1885, 3, col. 2; "Cattle Badly Drifted," *Texas Live Stock Journal*, 28 March 1885, 4; Nelson, "Judge O. H. Nelson;" and Dobie, *The Longhorns*, 197.

8. *Fort Worth Gazette*, 16 January 1885.

9. Cochran, "Walter C. Cochran's Memoirs," 38; and Henderson, "Memories of an Old Cowboy," 27. Cochran was relating information told him by George Cowden, while Henderson (who was born in 1881) was a very young eyewitness to the drift.

10. *San Angelo Standard*, 9 May 1885, p. 2, col. 3; and Biggers, *From Cattle Range*, 60.

11. Cook, "Cook's Dictation."

12. Beal, interview.

13. Henderson, "Memories of an Old Cowboy," 26, 27.

14. W. J. D. "Bill" Carr, interview with Haley, place not recorded, 1947, Haley Collection, Haley Library, Midland. At the time, Carr was working on the E. T. Comer Ranch, which had headquarters twelve miles upstream of Arden. There is a possibility that Carr is describing the cattle drift of the previous winter, rather than that of late 1884.

15. "Cattle Badly Drifted," *Texas Live Stock Journal*, 28 March 1885.

16. Carr, interview. The sheep camp (the same at which Carr awoke to see the drift cattle) may have been located on the divide south of Spring Creek. Again, it is possible that this event occurred during the previous winter, rather than that of late 1884.

17. Cook, "Cook's Dictation;" *San Angelo Standard*, 21 February 1885; Hill, interview; Cochran, "Walter C. Cochran's Memoirs," 38; and Biggers, *From Cattle Range*, 32–33.

18. Hill, interview; and Cochran, "Walter C. Cochran's Memoirs," 38.

19. *Ward County 1887–1977* (The Ward County Historical Commission, place and date not indicated), 69.

20. Hill, interview.

21. Burns, "Reminiscence of 56 Years."

22. Ibid.; Beal, interview; Windham, interview; Biggers, *From Cattle Range*, 32; and Hill, interview.

23. *San Angelo Standard*, 21 February 1885.

24. The number of hands per wagon is from Hill, interview. I have drawn the figures for the wagons and ranches from various sources cited in the notes for this chapter. One source (Henderson, "Memories of an Old Cowboy," 27) says there were 100 wagons involved.

25. Date is from "Cattle Badly Drifted," *Texas Live Stock Journal*, 28 March 1885; Hill, interview; and various other interviews or manuscripts cited in the notes for this chapter.

26. Number of horses is from Henderson, "Memories of an Old Cowboy," 27.

27. Calohan, interview.

28. I have drawn these names from the various interviews and manuscripts cited in the notes for this chapter. I also drew upon O. B. Holt Sr., interview with Haley, Midland, 3 January 1927, Haley Collection, Haley Library, Midland. I am presuming that the LX sent wagon[s], as Calohan, interview, indicates that LX cattle were in the drift herd. Some outfits listed by name may be duplicated by brand.

29. Nelson, "Judge O. N. Nelson."

30. Burns, "Reminiscence of 56 Years." To "rep" was to represent an outside outfit's brand at another ranch's roundup. The cowhands who did such were sometimes called "stray men" or "outside men."

31. This description of the roundup and return of the drift animals is based on: D. H. "Bob" McNairy, interview with Haley, Mineral Wells, 22 January 1932, Haley Collection, Haley Library, Midland; Nelson, "Judge O. N. Nelson;" Burns, "Reminiscence of 56 Years;" Beal, interview; Cook, "Cook's Dictation;" Henderson, "Memories of an Old Cowboy," 27; and Biggers, *From Cattle Range*, 60–62.

32. Henderson, "Memories of an Old Cowboy," 27.

33. Burns, "Reminiscence of 56 Years;" Cook, "Cook's Dictation;" Windham, interview; Calohan, interview; Dobie, *The Longhorns*, 200; and Biggers, *From Cattle Range*, 60. For a photo of a returning herd of drift cattle near Odessa, see Patrick Dearen, *Bitter Waters: The Struggles of the Pecos River*, 37.

34. Hill, interview.

35. "Cattle Badly Drifted," *Texas Live Stock Journal*, 28 March 1885.

36. Ibid.

37. Windham, interview.

38. Cook, "Cook's Dictation."

39. Cochran, "Walter C. Cochran's Memoirs," 38.

40. Hill, interview. Rollie Burns of the Square and Compass Ranch, who dispatched a wagon to the roundup but did not personally participate, placed the figure at a much more conservative "nearly 30,000" head. (Burns, "Reminiscence of 56 Years.")

41. Cochran, "Walter C. Cochran's Memoirs," 38.

42. Cook, "Cook's Dictation."

43. Burns, "Reminiscence of 56 Years."

44. "Range and Pasture," *Texas Live Stock Journal*, 28 February 1885, 4.

CHAPTER ELEVEN

The Big Dry

THROUGHOUT THE SUMMER OF 1885, PECOS COWBOYS RODE UNDER A swollen sun that burned with a quiet fury.

It was yet another extreme in a time of extremes. In the last several months, cowhands had felt the bite of an unprecedented blizzard. They had seen more cattle, alive and dead, along the Pecos than ever before. Now, a Big Dry had taken hold, a drouth worse than any of them had ever seen, and they could only watch as the hot-as-blazes sun parched the west-side range and disintegrated the grass nubs in the ravaged country across the river.

Typically in this unpredictable land, spring had given no hint of the coming blight. Eastward 120 miles, 2.80 inches of rain had greened Fort Concho's parade ground in May[1], and similarly good showers had lifted settlers' spirits in the Midland region.

"The year of 1885 was a wonderful year," related Mrs. J. H. Barron, who followed her husband to Midland that year. "All the lakes [playas] were full of water. The farmers of Marienfield [present Stanton] made a wonderful crop. Lots of people visited them, saw what they had grown, and then came and filed on land, expecting to farm."[2]

In late August or early September, one last rain teased the Pecos,[3] and then there was only the wind sweeping the alkali barer by the day. For cattle, it was all but a death sentence. Weakened by the past brutal winter and the scarcity of forage during the graze-out of spring, the surviving animals had scarcely begun to regain their strength before they had to face this new pestilence.

Insidiously, it crept across not only much of Texas, but northern Mexico, extreme southern Arizona, and the part of New Mexico lying south of Fort Sumner and east of the mountains.[4] Soon, a homesteader in Blanco County, Texas, would flee his stake and leave a note scrawled on his door:

"250 miles to nearest post office; 100 miles to wood; 20 miles to water; 6 inches to hell."[5]

Riding the Big Dry for the next two years, Pecos cowhands would probably have sworn that hell was right there on the river, just as the buffalo hunters always had said.[6]

Midland settlers shared their vision of perdition.

"I thought my eyes would go out from the glare," recalled Mrs. Barron. "There was not a cloud to be seen, nothing but the broiling sun. Everything was parched, and only the bear grass was green."[7]

Of Texas' seven million cattle, one-third ranged in the drouth-stricken area.[8] In 1884 they had been worth $30 a head. Three years later, a cowman would be lucky to find a taker at $4.[9]

On through the Big Dry's first autumn, the sky continued cloudless over the Pecos. Still, the gaunt, bony animals held on until the onslaught of bitter cold, when the weaker cattle sank to the frozen turf and never got up. Then came January 1886 and mass losses, wrought by a brutal storm that plummeted the mercury sixty-four degrees in a mere twelve hours along the normally mild Texas Gulf Coast.[10]

By the still-rainless spring, the situation on the Pecos had become critical. Many of the cattle which had survived winter were little more than buzzard bait now, too weak to range in search of forage. Up in New Mexico, the scarcity of grass had set the stronger animals to drifting, as far downriver as old Fort Lancaster and below.[11] Now, weakened by the push, they died by the hundreds.[12]

Earlier, the Pecos Valley Cattle Association had set the general roundup in Pecos County for May 1 at Leon Holes (eight miles west of Fort Stockton), from which it was to proceed to the Great Falls of the Pecos. In late April, however, organizers postponed the roundup indefinitely, "owing to the drouth and bad condition of cattle," reported the *San Angelo Standard*.[13] A month later, *Texas Live Stock Journal* reported that the roundup would not be scheduled again until fall.[14]

As the cattle grew weaker, the bog problem intensified. A Dodge City, Kansas, newspaper reported on April 27 that one man, in traveling several miles along the Pecos in southern New Mexico, counted 200 to 300 head of mired carcasses.[15]

"You could go . . . [a considerable distance] and never get off a cow in the bog—the cow bogged and the calf out on the bank dead," recalled M. L. "Mike" Liles, who cowboyed in southern New Mexico during the blight.[16]

In places, the carcasses grew so thick down inside the banks that they became a grotesque barricade.

"I have seen the men have teams to haul the [dead] cattle out of the river so that the others could get in to drink," recalled W. E. McLendon, who also rode the southern New Mexico stretch during the drouth.[17]

With the snowmelt of spring in the Sangre de Cristos at the river's head, the rising waters swept the carcasses downstream in a gruesome spectacle. One cowhand, J. V. Stokes, stood on the bank that year and counted forty dead cattle an hour float past.[18]

Most cowboys tried to avoid the repulsive banks. Indeed, recalled McLendon, "the water smelled terrible and was full of hair and maggots"[19]—a condition which also plagued the carrion-ridden Black River and the natural lakes of southeastern New Mexico.[20]

"Just imagine," said cowhand Walter C. Cochran, "what a time we had working that [Pecos] country and drinking that water off those dead cattle."[21]

To mask the water's taste and appearance, cowhands turned to coffee, black and hot, from water strained "through a gunny sack to get the maggots out of it," remembered cowhand Frank Lloyd.

On one occasion during the drouth, Lloyd rode into an LFD cow camp at Cave Lake in New Mexico and started to drink from the chuck wagon barrel, only to be warned by the cook to wait until he boiled the water for coffee.

"He showed me where he had strained out a lot of maggots," recalled Lloyd. "I waited until they'd cooked it a while and got a cup of coffee, and it was stronger than I could stand. That was all I had to drink."[22]

By early May of 1886, reports of disastrous cattle losses on the Pecos began to filter back across the Staked Plains to newspaper writers in San Angelo and Big Spring, and from there to locales throughout the Midwest.[23]

Horses, as well, fell by the score, especially to the unforgiving overflow ponds, which, with the flats bare of alkali-absorbing vegetation, had grown even deadlier.[24]

As the spring and summer wore on—not merely rainless in most locales, but cloudless[25]—the entire Pecos country became a mass of carcasses, rotting under a relentless, broiling sun.

"The plains west of here," reported a Big Spring correspondent on May 18, "are parched and dry, and the carcasses of thousands of cattle are to be seen in every direction. . . . There is very little grass anywhere near the water, and that little so dry and dead that it does not contain enough substance to do the cattle any good. . . . A rough estimate places the rate of mortality by thirst and starvation at 900 head per day. Fully 20,000 carcasses cover the plains. The stench as one passes along the Texas Pacific west of here is terrible."[26]

A week later, an El Paso correspondent penned a letter to the *Texas Live Stock Journal.* "From the Pecos River for 100 miles below and 200 miles above the Texas and Pacific Railroad," he wrote, "cattle are reported as dying daily by the hundreds, and if all reports be true, I may say by the thousands."[27]

For cowhands, whose very job demanded a certain kinship with cattle, it was a frustrating and troubling time. "You could have gone up the Pecos River on both sides and it was four feet high with dead cattle," recalled Lloyd.[28]

The Horsehead Crossing stretch was especially unforgiving. Related Julius D. Henderson, "You could walk a mile . . . on either side of the river . . . at Horsehead Crossing without getting off a dead TX cow."[29]

Toyah Creek, a northeast-trending tributary in what by then was Reeves County, was equally revolting, as cowman W. D. Cowan learned. "He and one of his boys," noted Henderson, "rode six miles of the creek and counted 3,000 dead cows."[30]

However, cattle along at least one stretch of the Pecos in Texas fared better, at least initially. The Nub Pulliam, Frank Culbertson, Day, and Childress outfits found their animals strong enough to round up in May 1886. "Of the 30,000 head which they calculated they had worked," reported the *San Angelo Standard* on May 29, "only about 50 head that belonged on the range had been seen dead. . . . All the [other] dead cattle seen there belong up in New Mexico and are drifting down the river and dying."

Evidently an optimist—as Pecos cowmen had to be—Pulliam estimated that the four outfits combined would lose no more than 300 of their 17,000 animals, even if the Big Dry endured until September.[31]

Cutting out 1,300 yearlings, Pulliam cowhands pushed the herd toward market.[32] The Seven Rivers Cattle Company, meanwhile, shipped 6,000 head by rail from Pecos City.[33] Other outfits, choosing to point their stronger animals up the Goodnight-Loving Trail, may have met with disaster. On July 24, the *Weekly Yellowstone Journal and Livestock Reporter* of Miles City, Montana, reported that trail losses in the driving season were already "without parallel" in history.

"The range [along the trails] is strewn with carcasses," said the writer. "This has resulted from several causes. The herds were, as a rule, in poor condition for starting. The drouth made grass and water short along the trail."

Furthermore, noted the writer, "the occupants [i.e., cattlemen] of the range along the trail have thrown every obstacle in the way, and the owners of herds have found difficulty in crossing every political boundary line."[34]

The right-of-way situation bedeviled drovers along other routes as well. As early as April 27, the *Globe Livestock Journal* of Dodge City, Kansas, reported that "large herds of cattle are said to be coming up the Texas–New Mexico line, and it is thought some of these herds will attempt to drive through New Mexico, which the cattlemen of that Territory say must not be done, or trouble will surely follow. They say that their ranges are fully stocked and that there is neither grass nor water for transient stock."[35]

Nevertheless, by July 3, 180,000 cattle from the drouth districts of western Texas were en route north through New Mexico.

"They are headed for the Trechera [Trinchera] Pass [east of present Raton], which has been forced by the local stockmen and is being defended by a large armed force," a Fort Worth correspondent reported on July 3. "These immense herds must get through the pass or die, as they are too weak to be driven back into Texas."[36]

Beyond the human threat was that of nature, for regardless of the route, the Big Dry seemed to creep alongside every herd that pushed up out of Texas.

"Just now," reported the *Weekly Yellowstone Journal and Livestock Reporter* on June 29, "there are more than 100,000 head of cattle en route to the north from Texas on the old Dodge Trail. . . . The trail over which these thirsting cattle pass is lined with the dead bodies of the animals which have been unable to endure the torture. The ground is dry and parched, and the bellowing of the suffering herds can be heard for miles. All through the cattle country to the west and south of here, the same condition of affairs exists."[37]

Even as the desperate drives up the Pecos were getting under way, the skies teased with the promise that the drouth was breaking. On June 2 a "good rain" fell on the TX, reported the *San Angelo Standard*,[38] and a few days later more "soaking rains" reportedly fell through much of the Pecos valley.[39] Buoyed by false hope, TX co-owner J. T. Word told the newspaper that, with the grass now starting to grow, cattle would "rapidly recover and be in fine condition for winter."[40]

It was not to be. As the skies turned barren again, on through the long hot summer, on into fall, and through another hard winter, the high-grade animals, especially, fell by the thousands.

"That was where I fell out with those fine cattle," recalled Frank Lloyd, who saw the die-up for himself along the Pecos in New Mexico. "[LFD foreman J. Phelps] White had these Texas cattle [longhorns] and he never lost one-third as many as [James or Pittser] Chisum did. Chisum had his bred up to Durhams and . . . they just died like sheep."[41]

With little forage for their animals, outfits sought supplemental feed, including the bean of an indigenous scrub tree which heretofore had been regarded as a nuisance.

"Mesquite beans are eagerly sought by stock," reported *The Staked Plain* of Midland on July 22. "Horses prefer them to oats. They are very nutritious and during the present scarcity of grass, the bounteous crop of them are a great help to stockmen."[42]

By late summer, alfalfa hay was worth $10 per ton along the Pecos,[43] while in the west-lying Davis Mountains, outfits were burning the serrated outer leaves from sotol plants and feeding the hearts to their starving cattle.[44]

Meanwhile, the farmers who had been lured to the Midland-Marienfield area by the bountiful harvest of 1885 were watching their own crops wither and die under the pitiless sun.

"After the drought came, nearly everyone had to leave . . . ," recalled Mrs. J. H. Barron, a Midland resident at the time. "Even the mesquite trees were brown."[45]

The Chisum outfit—likely that of Pittser and James Chisum—at a general roundup in probably the 1880s. COURTESY OF ROBERT N. MULLIN COLLECTION, N. S. HALEY MEMORIAL LIBRARY, MIDLAND, TEXAS

As the blight lingered, the coveted few springs in the Pecos country dried up,[46] and with the river virtually unfit for man or beast, some outfits turned to digging wells. On the fringe of the plains about fifty miles north of Pecos City, A. T. Windham of the Seven Rivers Cattle Company drilled one of the first.[47] Initially, some ranches pumped with horsepower,[48] but by the fall of 1886, a few windmills had begun to sentinel the river and take advantage of the ever-present winds.[49]

Although the Pecos country of Texas and southern New Mexico continued dry, runoff far upstream ironically set the river on a rise in late September and early October. Roaring out of its banks—"higher than has been known for years," reported a newspaper correspondent[50]—it swept through the heart of the Big Dry, carrying away "fences, windmills, tanks and other improvements," said the October 2 *San Angelo Standard*.[51]

While it may have cleared the flood plain of carcasses, the flood did nothing to prevent the continued loss of livestock. W. D. Hudson, who boasted that a man could not ride a good horse across his giant spread (south of Pecos City) in a full day, lost "everything," according to Julius D. Henderson.[52] The Seven Rivers Cattle Company fared little better. Although the outfit had branded 12,000 calves the preceding two years, its calf crop was virtually zero in 1886, as most of the mature cows fell prey to the circling vultures.[53]

With the universal loss of cattle came financial disaster, especially for smaller outfits.

"The two years drouth of 1886 and 1887 broke all the little cowmen on the Pecos," said cowhand Walter C. Cochran.[54] Of the few who chose to remain, most were forced to hire on with larger outfits.[55]

The most striking departure during the Big Dry was that of the enormous Hash Knife outfit, which Aztec Cattle Company of Holbrook, Arizona, purchased in 1885.[56] The exodus of its cattle was less attributable to drouth, however, than to the fact that the Hash Knife had no legal claim to its range, as well as to taxation and overstocking.[57] Pushing up the Pecos and veering west through Albuquerque, the first 7,500 Hash Knife steers reached Arizona in July 1885. Four droves, including three herds of breeding cows, followed in the fall, while 1886 would see an additional 26,000 head depart the carcass-ridden Pecos range. Finally, in 1887, another two or three Arizona-bound drives carried away the last of the Hash Knife animals.[58]

By May 1887, only a couple of weeks after cowboys had found the Pecos lower than anyone had ever seen it,[59] the consensus of cowmen was that the drouth had claimed fully 50 percent of the cattle in the Pecos country.[60] Then finally, after twenty-one devastating months in which "it never rained a drop" in some sections, remembered cowhand F. S. Millard, rains again peppered the Pecos country.[61] Still, the range was so bare and the surviving animals so weak that it would be almost another full year before the cattle industry would thrive again.[62]

Ironically, the heavy rains in the spring of 1888,[63] while breaking the drouth once and for all, brought heartache to Midland store owner J. H. Barron, who had supplied many a cowhand with dry goods and tobacco. Throughout the lingering pestilence, Barron had steadfastly clung to his mercantile business and to his belief that "It'll rain sometime." Making sacrifices in order to stay, he rented out his two-room house and moved his family to the rear quarters of his store, which occupied the first floor of a newly constructed two-story adobe building on a dusty Midland street.

Untested throughout the dry spell, the adobe brick withstood a week of slow, steady rain in April 1888 before the clouds yawned wide one night and deluged the young cow town. Awakened, Barron found the plaster beginning to fall. "Get out!" he cried to his wife. Without hesitation, she snatched up their baby and the three of them fled, reaching the back door simultaneously. Suddenly, the front wall fell, sparing them only because it collapsed outward. They managed to make it outside, a bankrupt man and his family, struggling across a long-dry prairie that now swirled knee-deep with water.[64]

The Big Dry was over, but its effects would linger a lifetime for cowhands and townspeople alike.

Notes

Unless otherwise indicated, all towns, counties, and map quadrangles throughout notes are in Texas.

1. *San Angelo Standard*, 29 May 1886, 3, col. 1.

2. Composite of statements, Mrs. J. H. Barron, interview with Haley, Midland, date not recorded, Haley Collection, Haley Library, Midland.

3. *Rocky Mountain News* (Denver, Colorado), 29 January 1886; "Thousands of Cattle Dying," *Globe Livestock Journal* (Dodge City, Kansas), 25 May 1886; and Millard, *Cowpuncher*, 40.

4. "From El Paso" (letter to the editor dated 25 May 1886), *Texas Live Stock Journal*, 29 May 1886, 1; "News Item," *Texas Live Stock Journal*, 10 July 1886, 5, 8; *Weekly Yellowstone Journal and Livestock Reporter* (Miles City, Montana), 17 July 1886; "Thousands," *Globe Livestock Journal*, 25 May 1886; and Carr, interview.

5. W. C. Holden, "The Great Drouth of '86," *Frontier Times* Vol. 19, No. 10 (July 1942), 356. (Originally published in *Southwestern Sheep and Goat Raiser*, 1936).

6. As stated earlier, the buffalo hunters used to say that "when a bad man dies, he goes either to hell or the Pecos." See Dobie, *Vaquero*, 274.

7. Mrs. Barron, interview.

8. "Thousands," *Globe Livestock Journal*, 25 May 1886.

9. Henderson, "Memories of an Old Cowboy," 21.

10. "Texas Cattle Losses," *Rocky Mountain News*, 29 January 1886; and "Fear for Cattle," *Times* (Fort Morgan, Colorado), 15 January 1886.

11. *San Angelo Standard*, 29 May 1886; and Holmsley, interview.

12. *San Angelo Standard*, 29 May 1886.

13. *San Angelo Standard*, 24 April 1886, 2, col. 2 (originating at *El Paso Live Stock Journal*). Location of Leon Holes, which consisted of three large springs averaging thirty feet in diameter and twenty feet deep, is from Clayton Williams, *Last Frontier*, 132. The Great Falls of the Pecos earlier had been known as Pecos Falls.

14. "From El Paso," *Texas Live Stock Journal*, 29 May 1886.

15. "Stockings," *Globe Livestock Journal*, 27 April 1886.

16. Liles, interview.

17. W. E. McLendon, interview with Haley, Clovis, New Mexico, 16 January 1927, Haley Collection, Haley Library, Midland.

18. Cochran, "Walter C. Cochran's Memoirs," 41.

19. McLendon, interview.

20. Ibid.; and Lloyd, interview.

21. Cochran, "Walter C. Cochran's Memoirs," 41.

22. Lloyd, interview. The LFD was situated along the Pecos in the Bosque Grande region. See Moses, "Some Texas Cattlemen," 16.

23. "A Welcome Rain," *Texas Live Stock Journal*, 8 May 1886; *San Angelo Standard*, 29 May 1886; "From El Paso," *Texas Live Stock Journal*, 29 May 1886; and "Thousands," *Globe Livestock Journal* (Dodge City, Kansas), 25 May 1886. Dateline for the latter article is "Big Springs, Texas, May 18."

24. Oden, "Early Cowboy Days."

25. "Thousands," *Globe Livestock Journal*, 25 May 1886; Millard, *Cowpuncher*, 40; and Mrs. Barron, interview.

26. "Thousands," *Globe Livestock Journal*, 25 May 1886.

27. "From El Paso," *Texas Live Stock Journal*, 29 May 1886.

28. Lloyd, Interview.

29. Henderson, "Life of an Oldtimer," book four, 8, augmented by Henderson, "Memories of an Old Cowboy," 21.

30. Henderson, "Life of an Oldtimer," book four, 8.

31. *San Angelo Standard*, 29 May 1886. Pulliam held range from below Fort Lancaster upriver for a considerable distance. See Holmsley, interview.

32. *San Angelo Standard*, 29 May 1886. Whether the drovers trailed the yearlings all the way to market, or drove them to the railroad for shipping, is not clear.

33. Windham, interview.

34. *Weekly Yellowstone Journal and Livestock Reporter*, 24 July 1886. The writer attributes the information to *El Paso International Livestock Journal*.

35. *Globe Livestock Journal*, 27 April 1886.

36. *Weekly Yellowstone Journal and Livestock Reporter*, 17 July 1886.

37. *Weekly Yellowstone Journal and Livestock Reporter*, 29 June 1886.

38. *San Angelo Standard*, 12 June 1886, 3, col. 3.

39. *San Angelo Standard*, 12 June 1886, 2, col. 3. Despite the report, *Texas Live Stock Journal* of July 10 reported that the "country west to the Pecos where the drouth has been most severe has not had any general rain."

40. *San Angelo Standard*, 12 June 1886, 2 col. 3.

41. Lloyd, interview. The ranch of James and Pittser Chisum, who were brothers to John Chisum, was managed at the time by William Robert. (Hinton, interview).

42. *The Staked Plain* (Midland), 22 July 1886.

43. *San Angelo Standard*, 18 September 1886, 2, col. 2.

44. Henderson, "Memories of an Old Cowboy," 21.

45. Mrs. Barron, interview.

46. Henderson, "Memories of an Old Cowboy," 33.

47. Windham, interview.

48. Oden, "Early Cowboy Days."

49. *San Angelo Standard*, 2 October 1886, 2, col. 2.

50. *San Angelo Standard*, 16 October 1886, 1, col. 6.

51. *San Angelo Standard*, 2 October 1886.

52. Henderson, "Memories of an Old Cowboy," 21.

53. Windham, interview.

54. Cochran, "Walter C. Cochran's Memoirs," 41.

55. McLendon, interview.

56. Moses, "Some Texas Cattlemen," 63; and *New Handbook of Texas* Vol. 3, 499.

57. Windham, interview.

58. Tom Rainey, interview with Haley and Hervey Chesley, Willcox, Arizona, 1 March 1945, Haley Collection, Haley Library, Midland. Rainey began cowboying for the Hash Knife outfit in the spring of 1887. Some of these herds evidently were shipped by rail from Albuquerque to Arizona, while the 1886 herds evidently were shipped by rail from Pecos City.

59. *San Angelo Standard*, 16 April 1887, 3, col. 5. Nub Pulliam said the Pecos "could be crossed almost anywhere."

60. Lloyd, interview; Holmsley, interview; Henderson, "Memories of an Old Cowboy," 21; Biggers, *From Cattle Range*, 62; and Millard, *Cowpuncher*, 30–31.

61. Millard, *Cowpuncher*, 40; Holden, "Great Drouth," 361; and J. A. Johnson, interview.

62. *San Angelo Standard*, 28 April 1888, 3, col. 3.

63. Ibid.

64. Mrs. Barron, interview.

Chapter Twelve

The Pecos Comes Under Fence

As cowboys rode out of the big dry and into the 1890s, changes were astir along the Pecos.

For one thing, sheep had begun to graze alongside cattle in the lower stretches. Initially, sheepherders (often Mexican nationals) took care of the flocks, but eventually cowboys would become involved, rounding up and working the animals much as they did cattle.[1]

Also, as the skeletons of windmills began to rise over the bordering plains, cattle no longer had to depend exclusively on the Pecos for water. Not only could cowmen finally turn herds loose beyond the narrow band split by the river, they also realized that the animals might never need to forage more than two or three miles from one windmill or another. Before, the longhorn's ability to graze back twenty or more miles from water had made it the breed of necessity along much of the Pecos; now, cowmen opted for breeds of choice, introducing more and more blooded stock (such as Herefords) and "breeding up" their herds.[2]

The most striking change, however, came in approximately 1896, when outfits began stretching barbed wire across the country. Built with mesquite posts and stays,[3] the two- and three-strand fences[4] created pastures as large as 100 sections.[5] The "big pasture" philosophy would endure for decades, but the days when a cowboy rode free across a sprawling land finally were over. The consequences for the ranching industry were not always good.

"I heard some men talking about that time [the 1890s]," related cowhand Julius D. Henderson. "One man said, 'If we can fence our land, it will

Hereford cattle on the W Ranch on the Pecos. COURTESY OF J. EVETTS HALEY COLLECTION, N. S. HALEY MEMORIAL LIBRARY, MIDLAND, TEXAS

be like a National Bank.' But it did not work out that way. This country would not stand overgrazing, and everyone overstocked. And each time we have had a drouth, the land has run a few less cattle afterwards, until now [in the 1950s] it only runs about 10 per cent of what it once carried."[6]

At the same time that the Pecos country began to come under fence, barbed wire was springing up along the old Goodnight-Loving Trail up out of Texas. Even if open range abided along a particular stretch, New Mexico or Colorado cattle outfits likely had laid claim to the all-essential forage and water holes. As a result, even though portions of the trace would continue to carry droves for another two decades, the 1890s marked the end of the route as a major thoroughfare. Faced with uncertain passage up through New Mexico, Texas outfits increasingly pointed their herds to Lubbock and Amarillo in the Texas Panhandle, from which they shipped the animals by rail on to the maturing ranges of Kansas or the northwest.[7]

"The cattle from west of the Pecos crossed the river at Horsehead and traveled what was then called the Horsehead-Midland Road," recalled Henderson, who helped drive several herds to the Panhandle in the late 1890s. "There were some water wells along this route, and the men charged 10 cents per head for water."[8]

Often, however, the wells and earthen tanks on the Horsehead-Midland Road could not accommodate a succession of herds, leading some Panhandle-bound droves to cross at Salt Crossing and push up past the Henderson family ranch, situated nine miles southeast of Monahans. Negotiating with the boss of one such trail outfit, Henderson took in $170 in gold—six months' pay at cowhand wages—for watering 500 steers and rounding up another 100 animals and 20 horses which had strayed along the Pecos.[9]

While the Pecos cowboy was facing transition on the range and trail, the country around him was beginning to settle up, at least to a limited extent. No longer was it a raw wilderness fraught with the threat of marauding Comanches or Apaches; the military post of Fort Stockton, in fact, had become a ghost in 1886.[10] The land was still rugged, all right, and could never be fully tamed, but now towns and new railroad lines were appearing, and where big outfits once had grazed cattle on the open range, nesters were digging in. Furthermore, reported the *Dallas Morning News* on February 16, 1896, the potential for irrigation from the Pecos had lured "a good farming class" to the region, which held the promise of becoming the most populous in the Southwest.

"It has been wholly changed . . . from the days when we rode through that region in squads and kept perpetually on the watch for redskins and bandits," ex–Texas Ranger J. L. Richards told the newspaper after a trip to the Pecos. "I found some of the old battlefields and there were schools and laughing children playing in groves, some of the trees of which bear the marks of both arrows and bullets."[11]

Cowhands witnessed yet another transition along the river in the 1890s, for the departure of the Hash Knife outfit during the Big Dry had presaged the eventual demise of the cattle kings. Most closed their Pecos operations for much the same reasons as the Hash Knife—taxation, overstocking, and the trend toward deeded or leased land, rather than range occupied on a priority claim basis.[12]

Cattle losses, both on the range and on drives, also took a toll, especially on the Mule Shoe outfit. Owners Hart Mussey and Jesse H. Presnall, with their credit at rock bottom after losing 1,611 cattle on separate drives to Missouri and Montana, closed out the Mule Shoe at the very time that the Hash Knife herds were striding for Arizona.[13] Negotiating for the Mule Shoe brand, the Western Union Beef and Land Company (which branded a 7D) organized a roundup for the free-ranging cattle. Repping were hands from the TX, the JM, the S, Dunn Houston's NA, Pecos Land and Cattle Company, and F. W. Young's Diamond Y. Rounding up 14,000 to 15,000 Mule Shoe cattle, the Western Union Company paid Mussey and Presnall $12 a head. The outfit also burned the 7D across 355 horses, 180 of them saddle animals.[14]

But even as the Hash Knife and Mule Shoe brands vanished along the Pecos, the W Ranch stepped in with its own large-scale operation. Three opportunistic brothers—W. D., Lee, and F. "Woody" Johnson of Washington County (and later Brown and Nolan counties)—ventured to the Pecos toward the close of the Big Dry in 1887 and began buying the brands of smaller outfits which had "gone under"—the RUD, the Bill Birchfield, and the Allen Gibson. From Continental Land and Cattle Company; the Johnsons acquired the W cattle, which had originated with Jim and Lish Carter at Adobe Walls. Leasing land in present Winkler, Ward, and Loving counties, the W Ranch eventually controlled 1,200 sections, including thirty miles of river, and grazed thousands of cattle burned with its trademark W or a slash left and right. Lee Johnson soon left the outfit and W. D. moved into Pecos City to manage the Johnson Brothers general store, but F. "Woody" stayed on at the ranch to oversee the operation.[15]

Meanwhile, the TX, which now owned twenty alternate sections on the Pecos and controlled twenty to twenty-five miles of range along each side, ran into legal troubles, even as it branded 9,000 calves in 1888 under new foreman J. Arthur "TX" Johnson.[16] Delinquent in paying its Pecos County taxes, the TX almost lost 1,027 cattle in an auction which would have netted the county $174.59, or a mere 17 cents per head. However,

F. "Woody" Johnson. COURTESY OF BARNEY HUBBS COLLECTION, PECOS, TEXAS

W. D. Johnson. COURTESY OF BARNEY HUBBS COLLECTION, PECOS, TEXAS

Pecos County Sheriff John Edgar had failed to hold the herd the required twenty days before the auction, and the buyers had to return the animals to the TX.[17] Nevertheless, the outfit continued to be careless about paying its taxes, for on April 1, 1890, future sheriff A. J. Royal purchased sixty TX cattle for only $11.84 in a legally binding auction.[18]

The woes continued for the big cow outfits. In 1889 the Quien Sabe pulled back from the river and took up range near Midland.[19] By the end of 1891, the Seven Rivers Cattle Company—with its range playing out along the Pecos—had driven many of its cattle to a ranch near Pike's Peak, Colorado, and had relocated another 4,000 head to a 200-section spread on Toyah Creek near present Saragosa.[20] Up at Bosque Grande, New Mexico, cowhands for the giant Littlefield outfit pushed the last LFD herd off the Pecos in 1894.[21] The following year, the legendary TX Ranch finally yielded to changing times and closed out, selling its cattle to a cowman in southeastern New Mexico.[22]

Then on December 15, 1898, the huge Western Union Beef Company transferred its 7D brand for $16 a head to John T. McElroy, who also acquired the outfit's 400 sections of Pecos country range.[23] There would still be other noteworthy cowmen who would make their marks along the river—William P. Hoover, Arthur Hoover, Sid Kyle, and more—but the true cattle kings of the Pecos had gone the way of the open range.

Although the advent of the windmill had created an environment suitable for the small rancher or nester (who no longer had to compete with the big outfits for river frontage and water), the four-section act of 1903 assured his place in the Pecos country. Now, a person could file on and homestead up to four sections (2,560 acres) of state-owned land. In order to "prove it up," he had to live on it six months out of the year for three years, during which he had to make $350 in improvements—perhaps fences and a shed and a box house of one-by-twelve planks with strips over the cracks. Thereafter, he had forty years to pay for the homestead, at a mere $1 per acre with very low interest rate.[24]

For a cowhand settling down to the life of a small rancher, it was back-breaking and sometimes heartbreaking.

"These little ranchers would try to raise a little feed, and it was all walk and plow, cut the sorghum by hand, no machinery at all," recalled Cliff Newland, a Pecos cowhand of the early 1900s. "You'd try to break broncs and work cattle and farm with a walking plow, and chop [sorghum] . . . in armfuls . . . [with] sheep shears. . . . That's a devil of a job, and then that sorghum was hot and the ol' wind would hit you in there cutting that stuff."[25]

Seeking wilder country, some cowpunchers drifted to New Mexico or Arizona,[26] territories far removed from the farms, fences, and homesteaders of the Pecos. Still, the sparsely settled river was hardly obliging to a cowboy starved for romance and family life. Indeed, a cowhand always had to look far and wide for a good woman with whom to settle down.

"There were about three men to every woman in that country when I was growing up," recalled Henderson, who was born December 5, 1880, "and when a couple married, they married for keeps."[27]

Even on into the 1910s, pickings stayed mighty slim for a lonely cowboy. When Walter Boren signed on with a Crane County ranch a few miles east of Horsehead Crossing about 1916, there were only six women, married or single, in the entire 782-square-mile county.

"Wasn't no *place* for a woman out there in that country," noted Boren. "Nothing out there but just cows and cowboys."[28]

Generally, a Pecos cowhand had the utmost respect for women, even while perhaps paying a visit to the nearest bawdy house.

"I heard one old cowboy say, 'Be respectful—even if she's a whore, you ought to respect her, because she's a woman,'" recalled Ted Powers, who punched cattle in the lower Pecos country in the 1920s.[29]

Indeed, despite trysts with soiled doves, vocabularies rich in curse words (except around women), and a disregard for church-going, the typical Pecos range cowboys were men of high character, not unlike the trail hands of the 1800s.

"They had courage, they had optimism, they had a sense of humor, and they also had a sense of honor," noted folklorist Paul Patterson, a Pecos cowhand in the 1920s and 1930s.[30]

"Most of them were good people, rough and ready," amplified 1910s ranch hand Bill Eddins. "They were trustworthy and honest [and would] look after the neighbors."[31]

Added 1920s cowpuncher Bill Townsend: "They knew what they were doing and they were truthful. Now, once in a while you'd find some ol' boy [who'd] spout off and tell you lots of these big bear stories, and you knew he was lying. But he didn't mean anything by it; he was just entertaining."[32]

Jim Witt, who rode the Pecos in the 1920s, cut to the heart of the matter: "They was a little salty, but they was damned good men."[33]

As ranchers continued to expand their range away from the Pecos, livestock numbers swelled in the region. By 1906 Crockett County (which looked to the Pecos for its west boundary) grazed 75,313 cattle, 86,819 sheep, 3,896 goats, and 3,082 horses and mules.[34] Sheep and goats, particularly, required good fences.

Naturally, a young fellow who aspired to be a cowhand did so out of his love for horses and for the challenge of working cattle in the backcountry. No tenderfoot ever came out to the Pecos, "a cowboy for to be,"[35] out of a yearning to dig post holes and stretch barbed wire. Increasingly, however, many cowboys found themselves doing just that, at the expense of blisters and swollen hands. By the mid-1910s, most of the Pecos country was crisscrossed with fences,[36] although many ranches so neglected their upkeep that, even in the late 1920s and early 1930s, a steer could roam the west bank from below Horsehead Crossing to the city of Pecos.[37]

With water available at windmills and earthen tanks, some ranches fenced off their entire river frontage to avoid bog problems.[38] Others saw fit to fence only certain stretches, perhaps 50 or 100 feet, where the banks had sloughed sufficiently to lure cattle into the mire.[39] On ranches which did not deny access, such as the Homer Tippitt west-side spread above present Iraan, cattle developed an uncanny knowledge of the Pecos.

"There'd be springs running into the river where the water was pretty good," said Patterson, who cowboyed across the river from the Tippitt Ranch in 1934. "They might even be under the surface. Those ol' cattle

Eclipse windmills at the W Ranch on the Pecos. COURTESY OF J. EVETTS HALEY COLLECTION, N. S. HALEY MEMORIAL LIBRARY, MIDLAND, TEXAS

would know exactly what parts of the river that they could drink the water."

Wild river cattle, he noted, posed a special problem for cowboys during roundup.

"Tippitt's cattle . . . were a lot smarter than we were about that river. They knew where to cross. . . . When you'd try to gather them on that side, they'd cross to the other side. And if you didn't cross where they did, you might be a goner; you might bog up."[40]

Although the basics of cowboying on the Pecos remained unchanged from the days of the open range, the era of big fenced pastures brought subtle modifications, as well as additional chores. For one thing, with the demise of longhorns and the increased dominance of higher grade (but less hardy) breeds, cowboys undertook an aggressive campaign against cattle parasites. In 1906 Crockett County ranch hands began dipping cattle for ticks. With a sizable herd, it was a major operation, for cowboys had to round up each animal and drive it through a dipping vat every twenty-five days for more than three months before the bovine might be tick-free. Crockett County ranches intensified their efforts in 1913, but it was another seven years before they ridded their herds of ticks.[41]

Increasingly, too, Pecos cowhands spent much of their time doctoring "wormies," or cattle suffering from screwworms. Deposited as eggs by the blowfly Lucilia macellaria in sores such as a recent brand or the navel of a young animal, these maggots long had plagued Texas stock. As early as 1886, Zenas Bliss—who as a U.S. Army officer had first crossed the Pecos in 1855—cursed them as "an awful scourge," for they threatened the health of not only cattle and horses, but sometimes people. Visiting a stock ranch at an unspecified location in Texas, he once observed cowhands treating wormy horses:

"The horses were lassoed, and thrown, and a liniment poured into the wound. As soon as it touched the worms, they would pour out of the hole. Sometimes as much as a quart [of worms] would be taken from a wound that, at the surface, was not much more than a quarter of an inch in diameter. As soon as the wound was free of them, it was covered with pine tar and the animals turned loose."[42]

On the open-range Pecos with its vigorous longhorns, screwworms evidently were not the problem that they became in the early twentieth century, when a cowhand's main chore in a rainy spring was to rope and doctor young calves with worm-infested navels.

"When they shed that navel, there's a little raw place there, and they'd get screwworms every damned time," recalled Jim Witt. "Many a day I've ridden all day doctoring screwworms. We used Martin screwworm killer, a dark-looking fluid. A lot of times, you'd doctor one and, a week or two later, you'd see him and you'd have to doctor him again."[43] To avoid repeated treatment, cowhands sometimes packed the wound with cotton in the hope of smothering the larvae.

Ranches soon learned to avoid branding during blowfly season, which began about May 1 and extended to October. Nevertheless, during rainy years, blowflies were so abundant that even the prick of a mesquite thorn would create an inviting wound.[44]

"In '32 we had a lot of rain down there," recalled cowhand Bill Townsend. "And some of those ranches got to where they didn't ride and pick up a few wormies here and there—they'd just round up the pasture [for doctoring]."[45]

Roundups in the fence era generally involved "neighboring," the equivalent of repping in open range times, although an outside outfit now did it more as a reciprocal courtesy than out of a need to pick up its strays. In making a roundup drive, the new breed of cowhand had to take into account the thickets of salt cedar, which had taken root down inside the river's once-bare banks and had spread across many lowland bends. Suddenly, a ride through the sharp snags of a cedary horseshoe— or across flats swelling with scrub mesquites—necessitated leggings and careful maneuvering.[46]

"Those cattle were pretty wild in those days [the 1920s]," recalled Witt, "and they'd head for that brush on the river when you started working them. When they got in those damned salt cedars, they was just *in* there. You know, a dog couldn't hardly get through there."[47]

To avoid the problem, cowhands took to making the roundup drive very early in the day, when the cattle generally were too far from the river to gain the cedars.[48] The ensuing rendezvous usually would be at a watering place—now more likely a windmill or earthen tank than the river—from which cowhands might drive the herd on to a corral for branding and castrating.[49]

As ranches spread east from the Pecos, cowhands learned the special demands of working cattle in the sands, which stretched from the Horsehead country on up to a point near Roswell, New Mexico. A dwarf oak, commonly called shinnery, hugged the dunes throughout much of the region, wreaking havoc with cattle's digestive tracts at certain times of year. Cowhand Lonnie Griffith, wintering about 1920 in a sandhills line shack on the Texas–New Mexico line east of Seminole, Texas, saw the consequences for himself.

"I never saw as poor a bunch of cows in my life, and a lot of them was dying," he recalled. "They was eating shinnery stalks. They was eating so much of that wood, [they'd] get it wound up in their stomachs and it'd kill them. That's what we called shinnery colic."[50]

With the danger greatest when the shinnery began to bud,[51] ranches took to driving their cattle to other forage in early spring. Negotiating

Branding a yearling on the 69 Ranch at Pope's Crossing on the Pecos about 1910.
COURTESY OF J. EVETTS HALEY COLLECTION, N. S. HALEY MEMORIAL LIBRARY, MIDLAND, TEXAS

the loose, grasping sand with a herd required patience and plenty of cowboys.

"In that sandhill country you couldn't drive a cow over seven or eight miles 'cause she'd give out," recalled Walter Boren, who worked on the Adobe Ranch a few miles from Horsehead Crossing in the late 1910s. "If they were raised in the sand, their feet would be flat.... We'd throw them down there close to the Pecos River, what they called the V Rocker, a hard-land country.... We'd come back [in a safe season] and throw 'em back on the shinnery and brand the calves. Pretty hard to flank calves in the sandy country."[52]

Cattle drives remained an essential part of a Pecos cowhand's life through the 1920s and, in some instances, on into the 1940s. If a cowpuncher wasn't throwing a herd on or off the shinnery, he was pushing sale beeves to some ranch or to the nearest railroad shipping point. Whatever the destination, drovers at times still faced the Pecos, which remained unpredictable and dangerous.

In 1921 Bill Eddins, pointing 500 to 600 steers from the east-lying Sid Kyle spread for the railroad pens at Riverton in northern Reeves County, reached Narbo's Crossing to find the Pecos on a rise.

"That ol' river was swift," related Eddins. "We got some horses in there and some of them come out on this side and some on the other side. . . . [Drover Young Bell] tried it first, but his horse quit swimming. He quit his horse and he swum out on the other side, and his horse come back on this side."

With the river impassable, Eddins and the remaining cowhands had no choice but to push upriver a few miles and hold the steers overnight in a half-section trap. The next day, they regained the crossing to find that the river had subsided. Nevertheless, as they paused on the east bank for lunch, they suddenly saw their opportunity fast slipping away. Recalled Eddins:

"At that time, there was a lot of rain up in New Mexico; they was releasing a lot of dams up there, and it'd go down and up nearly every day. . . . The river started rising just as we were getting ready to eat dinner. We got through quick then, and it had rose about two feet."

In a frenzied, hour-long push, they crossed the herd, but the river had risen so dramatically that the horses had to swim with their riders.[53]

Sometimes the Pecos currents still led to tragedy. In 1917 or 1918 Hudson "Bud" Mayes and other Blackstone-Slaughter Ranch hands held an eastbound herd overnight two miles shy of swift-running Four-mile Crossing, situated under an imposing rock bluff four miles north of Sheffield. The next morning, the boss sent Mayes on ahead with the chuck wagon. Mayes crossed the river without mishap, but as the drovers brought up the herd, a Mexican hand drowned when his horse failed to swim and the current swept them into a bank.[54]

Because of such mishaps, drovers began turning to the truss bridges erected in the 1910s at points such as Salt Crossing and Girvin. Finally, they could avoid the river's direct dangers, although the structures offered their own pitfalls for spooked cattle and boogered horses and teams. Hoover Ranch hand Bill Townsend, driving 400 cows and calves from the Buena Vista area to a spread northwest of Rankin in 1929, feared the worst as the herd neared the Girvin bridge.

Bill Townsend in 1923. COURTESY OF BILL TOWNSEND

"I was just flat scared to death," he recalled. 'I'd crossed cattle across a bridge back [upriver] . . . , and they didn't like to cross it. But Mr. [Arthur] Hoover knew how. He got the horses . . . right up at the mouth of the bridge, and he had a boy go up there to stop the traffic. And he said, 'When we get them cattle up [to the bridge], cross the horses.' And when them cattle went across, [there] wasn't a one of them turned back. They just trailed right across."[55]

Things didn't always work so smoothly, however, as Mayes learned when he received a herd at Girvin from the EL trail outfit and the two parties pushed on east to the bridge.

"Those steers was kind of hungry and dry for water, and five or six of them jumped off of the bridge into the river—went around the side kinda-like," he recalled. "They got in there and bogged down in quicksand. The boss of the other outfit had a Mexican boy he'd raised, and he just threw this boy out in there right with those cows and told him, 'Tromp 'em out of there!' Sometimes you couldn't even see the Mexican, but he kept sloshing around in there until it got soft enough till he got them out."[56]

Three shipping points in particular were prime destinations for regional trail drives. Foremost for droves originating at east-side ranches in the lower Pecos country was the Irion County community of Barnhart. Situated on the Kansas City, Mexico, and Orient Railway at a point forty-five miles northeast of the river, Barnhart gained an unparalleled reputation in the 1920s.

"More head of livestock was loaded out there than any other place in the world," noted Green Mankin, who drove herds to the site in the early 1920s.[57]

More-northerly ranches pointed their herds for Pecos (as Pecos City became known) and Odessa, through both of which passed the T&P Railroad.[58] No matter the site, wild cattle not only resisted penning, they balked at even crossing a track to reach the stockyards.

"Those cattle would mill," recalled Julius D. Henderson, who faced the problem on drives up to Odessa. "They would form a center, get their heads over each other's neck in the center of the herd, and the others would just wedge in around them like sardines in a can and go around in a circle. You could not ride into them or move them."[59]

With a small herd, a cowboy might rope and drag every animal across the track, as Henderson had to do in 1893 in driving fifty cattle back to his home ranch after repping at a B 5 roundup north of Odessa.[60] With a big herd, however, hard work alone wouldn't suffice. Indeed, it took an experienced hand and a skilled horse to cut out a couple of beeves and run them across the track or into the pen, thereby inducing more and more cattle to follow and eventually breaking the mill.[61]

Cowmen no doubt wished that their cowboys had the wherewithal to break drouths and cold snaps as skillfully, for weather extremes continued to bedevil the Pecos. A drouth in 1910 severely impacted smaller ranches, including the Hubbs spread thirty-seven miles upriver from the town of Pecos.

"Cattle prices went to nothing, practically," recalled Barney Hubbs, a teenager at the time. "So we went broke in the cow business and we moved to Pecos."[62]

Meanwhile, the W Ranch, wise to the ways of the Pecos desert, added a seemingly innocuous clause to a contract to deliver 10,000 cattle: the ranch would fulfill it "thirty days after the first general rain." Years passed before nature decreed that the ranch meet its obligation.[63]

The intense dry spell not only precluded a decent calf crop in 1910, but also wrenched the strength from mature cattle.[64] When a heavy rainstorm struck on a cold Valentine's Day 1911, the result was inevitable.

"Along in the evening it started snowing and froze hard that night," recalled Henderson. "Every low place was full of water; the country just could not absorb it. Cattle walked onto the ice and slipped down, broke legs, and could not get up. It was so cold we just could not get water for them. All lead pipes [in windmills] were frozen [and] troughs froze solid and bursted open."[65]

Cattle losses were heavy,[66] leading to yet another poor calf crop, but timely spring rains lifted the spirits of cowmen.

"The country never had a brighter prospect for good grass and good crops than it has now . . . ," observed *The Pecos Daily Times* on June 13,

1911. "Cattle are getting in fine shape and a large increase is looked for next year."[67]

Ranches in Reeves County, which averaged about 12 inches of precipitation annually,[68] were blessed again in 1914, when 17.27 inches fell, and no one complained about the 11.24 inches which greened pastures in 1915.[69] Still, a smart cowman knew to prepare in the good years for the lean ones to come, for on the Pecos, a drouth or killer blizzard were only as far away as the horizon.

And the two which lay in wait this time were, as a cowboy would have put it, *tough enough to take the hide off.*

NOTES

Unless otherwise indicated, all towns, counties, and map quadrangles throughout notes are in Texas.

1. Townsend, interview.
2. As stated earlier, L. Paxton introduced Durham bulls to the Pecos by 1880. See *The Fort Stockton Pioneer*, 17 September 1908 (reprint of *Texas Sun*, November–December 1880).
3. Henderson, "Life of an Oldtimer," book four, 10.
4. Patterson, interview, 1 July 1993.
5. Mankin, interview. Mankin began cowboying on the lower Pecos in 1921.
6. Henderson, "Life of an Oldtimer," book two, 8.
7. Henderson, "Memories of an Old Cowboy," 35; and Henderson, "Life of an Oldtimer," book two, 10.
8. Henderson, "Life of an Oldtimer," book two, 10; and Henderson, "Memories of an Old Cowboy," 29.
9. Henderson, "Memories of an Old Cowboy," 35–36; and Henderson, "Life of an Oldtimer," book two, 10. In the latter account, Henderson says he received $175.
10. *New Handbook of Texas* Vol. 2, 1119.
11. "Pecos River Region," *Dallas Morning News*, 16 February 1896. The prediction that the Pecos country would one day become heavily populated has yet to be realized.
12. Windham, interview.
13. Hunter, *Trail Drivers*, 388; and Clayton Williams, *Last Frontier*, 321.
14. Clayton Williams, *Last Frontier*, 321–322.
15. This study of the W Ranch is based on: Mrs. Woody Johnson, interview with Haley, Pecos, 9 January 1927, Haley Collection, Haley Library, Midland; W. R. Owen, interviews, 12 January 1927 and 2 March 1933; Moses, "Some Texas Cattlemen," 5, 10; Henderson, "Memories of an Old Cowboy," 21; Cochran, "Walter C. Cochran's Memoirs," 41; Dobie, *The Longhorns*, 169; and Marj Carpenter, "Early Brands in Area Held Local History for Cowpokes," *The Pecos Independent and Enterprise*, 16 November

1961. Continental Cattle Company became known as Continental Land and Cattle Company in 1884. See *New Handbook of Texas* Vol. 2, 295.

16. J. A. Johnson, interview.

17. Millard, *Cowpuncher*, 38–39.

18. Clayton Williams, *Last Frontier*, 341.

19. Patrick Dearen, *Halff of Texas*, 98.

20. Windham, interview.

21. Haley, *George W. Littlefield*, 164.

22. Patterson, "A Forgotten Empire," 25.

23. Marsha Lea Daggett, ed., *Pecos County History* (Canyon: Pecos County Historical Commission, Staked Plains Press, 1984), 159; and Moses, "Some Texas Cattlemen," 8.

24. Newland, interview; and Henderson, "Life of an Oldtimer," book four, 9.

25. Newland, interview.

26. Ibid.

27. Composite of statements in Henderson, "Memories of an Old Cowboy," 22, and Henderson, "Life of an Oldtimer," book four, 17. Henderson's birth date is from Carlysle Graham Raht, *Reveries of a Fiddlefoot* (Odessa: The Rahtbooks Company, 1970), 255.

28. Walter Boren, interview with author, Post, 8 August 1990. Boren worked on W. N. Waddell's Adobe Ranch, with headquarters 20 miles south of present Crane.

29. Ted Powers, interview with author, San Angelo, 23 August 1989.

30. Patterson, interview, 29 April 1991.

31. Eddins, interview.

32. Townsend, interview.

33. Witt, interview, 22 July 1995.

34. *History of Crockett County*, 61, citing the *Ozona Kicker* of 1906.

35. From the song, "Sam Bass," in Jules Verne Allen, *Cowboy Lore* (San Antonio: The Naylor Company, 1943, 6th printing), 112. The full phrase is: "Sam first came out to Texas, a cowboy for to be. . . ."

36. Patterson, interview, 1 July 1993.

37. Rankin, interview, 9 August 1989.

38. Patterson, interview, 1 July 1993.

39. Witt, interview, 17 July 1993.

40. Patterson, interview, 1 July 1993.

41. *History of Crockett County*, 58.

42. Zenas R. Bliss, "Reminiscences Vol. 1," 48–50, Williams Collection, Haley Library, Midland.

43. Witt, interview, 22 July 1995.

44. Townsend, interview.

45. Ibid. In 1932 the city of Pecos received 28.15 inches of precipitation, more than 16 inches above its average annual rainfall. See "1933 Driest Year Save One," *The Pecos Enterprise and Gusher*, 27 July 1934; and 1990–91 *Texas Almanac*, 239.

46. Leggings were little used in open range days, as there was generally little brush along the river. See Ballard, interview.

47. Witt, interview, 22 July 1995.

48. Ibid.

49. L. B. Eddins, interview.

50. Lonnie Griffith, taped interview with author, Big Spring, 30 March 1983.

51. Ralph Davis, taped interview with author, Sterling City, 4 March 1989; J. E. Fairweather, taped interview with author, Midland, 1 March 1989; Leonard Proctor, taped interview with author, 2 March 1989; and Boren, interview.

52. Boren, interview.

53. L. B. Eddins, interview. Eddins did not call the crossing by name, but his description of its location identifies it with Narbo's Crossing.

54. Mayes, interview, 30 April 1991.

55. Townsend, interview.

56. Composite of statements in Mayes, interviews, 22 February 1990 and 30 April 1991.

57. Mankin, interview. Other cowhands who claimed Barnhart was the largest shipping point in the world (or in the United States or Texas) were Gid Reding (interview), Claude Owens (taped interview with author, Fort Stockton, 2 March 1990), Louis Baker (taped interview with author, 14 February 1990, Coke County), and Steve Armentrout (taped interview with author, Fort Stockton, 1 September 1989).

58. Henderson, "Memories of an Old Cowboy," 28, 41.

59. Ibid., 41.

60. Henderson, "Life of an Oldtimer," prologue, 10.

61. Henderson, "Memories of an Old Cowboy," 41.

62. Hubbs, interview, 21 October 1991. Date of the drouth is from Henderson, "Life of an Oldtimer," book four, 9.

63. Dobie, *The Longhorns*, 194.

64. Henderson, "Life of an Oldtimer," book four, 9; and "And Still It Rains," *The Pecos Daily Times*, 13 June 1911.

65. Henderson, "Life of an Oldtimer," book four, 9.

66. Ibid.

67. "And Still It Rains," *The Pecos Daily Times*, 13 June 1911.

68. 1990–1991 *Texas Almanac*, 239.

69. "1933 Driest Year Save One," *The Pecos Enterprise and Gusher*, 27 July 1934.

CHAPTER THIRTEEN

The Big Thirst

IF ADVERSITY BUILDS CHARACTER, THEN COWHANDS HAD PLENTY OF opportunity for personal growth beginning in the fall of 1916, for a drouth even more withering than the Big Dry of 1885–1887 took a strangle hold on the Pecos.

The summer of '16 gave cowmen no hint of the coming blight. Indeed, the range was in ideal shape, thanks to general rains which included a typical 4.55 inches in July, August, and September in Reeves County.[1]

"This country was a paradise," recalled Julius D. Henderson. "Up until the drouth you could put up a fine hay most anywhere around Odessa. I have seen the sand country when the grass covered the ground knee high (with big blue stem five or six feet high), sunflowers so thick you could hardly ride through them and seven or eight [feet] high, and the mesquite bushes just loaded down with ripe beans and blooming at the same time."[2]

During such times of luxuriant pasturage, a section of sand country could accommodate thirty-five to fifty cows, as well as abundant wild-life—deer, musk hogs, feral domesticated hogs, blue quail, and prairie chickens.[3] Nor was forage limited to the river's east-lying country.

"We have always had drouths," acknowledged early 1900s Pecos cowhand Cliff Newland in 1964, "but up until the '17 drouth, I never seen a time you couldn't go fifty or sixty miles in some direction and get all the grass you wanted [for your cattle]. You couldn't do it in '17 and

Cliff Newland in the 1960s. COURTESY OF JACK AND BONNELL NEWLAND

you can't do it now. You could stake an ol' horse [before the drouth] and go two or three hundred miles [and] he'd do all right."[4]

In early October 1916, widespread rains—"the soaking, wetting kind," described one newspaper—encouraged cattlemen.

"Many ranchmen believe this will put a filaree crop well on its way," said *The Enterprise* of Pecos, where 1.79 inches fell, "and that would make the West Texas ranchmen as happy and bright as a big sunflower."[5]

But the smiles would soon fade, wilting under a branding fire sun along with those very flowers of comparison.

Still, unsuspecting cattlemen continued to stock their ranches on through the end of 1916. In late November (a month in which Reeves County recorded a mere .05 inch of precipitation), rancher W. W. Camp received the balance of a shipment of 308 Mexican cattle, and *The Enterprise* reported on December 8 that E. A. Humphries of Toyah had recently purchased a herd of young cattle to add to his fine "white faces" or Herefords.[6] But after a minuscule .01 inch of moisture teased Reeves County in December—and the new year of 1917 ushered in what old settlers termed "the hardest winter" on the Pecos in twenty-five or thirty years—experienced cowmen may have had second thoughts. After all, the benefits to the range from .08 of January snow and freezing rain or sleet were far outweighed by the cold snap's detrimental effect on cattle.[7]

With only a trace of moisture falling on the city of Pecos in February and just .06 inch in March, Julius D. Henderson was forced to begin feeding his herd of 125 cows. Initially, he could purchase cottonseed cake for $20 a ton, but within eight months, demand would balloon the price threefold.[8]

Still, few cowmen were panicking in late winter of 1917, for spring was on its way with its promise of good showers. Even after a disappointing .02 of precipitation in Pecos in April, spirits remained generally high. On May 4, *The Enterprise* reported that the outlook for the range between the New Mexico line and a point twelve miles north of Toyah was "encouraging,"[9] and a week later the newspaper reported similarly promising conditions in Pecos County.[10] Nevertheless, even when a cold front swept through the region on May 6 and plunged temperatures 30 degrees, it brought only enough drizzle to lay the dust for a day.[11]

In late May, with only .05 inch of rain recorded for the month in Reeves County and just .27 since the previous October, area ranchers inspected their withering ranges and finally began shipping their cattle elsewhere. G. B. Finley and L. W. Anderson took five rail cars of cattle from Pecos to the Fort Worth market, while E. P. Stuckler of the U Ranch shipped the first 300 of an expected herd of 1,800 from Saragosa, thirty miles south-southeast of the Pecos River, to alfalfa fields at Barstow, immediately east of the waterway.[12]

By June, a few Pecos country cowmen already were selling significant portions of their herds. W. D. Hudson, whose ranch had suffered severe losses during the Big Dry of 1885–1887, sold 2,500 head to the Finley and Anderson outfit and made the first of three deliveries to Dalhart in the Panhandle in mid-June. Marcus Snyder, meanwhile, disposed of 1,000 cattle by likewise shipping them to Dalhart and a waiting buyer.[13]

Still, most cattlemen held on, teased by skies that threatened to break the drouth. Soon after an anonymous individual advertised in the Pecos newspaper for a good rain—"a ground-soaker and chunk-mover"[14]—thunderstorms roamed the Pecos. Nevertheless, these late-June showers were too isolated to have significant impact on the range; the rains had peppered certain locales, all right, but areas such as the town of Pecos (with .06 inch) were not as blessed. "Many [stockmen]," lamented *The Enterprise and Pecos Times* of Pecos on June 29, "have as yet had no rain and the stock are getting in bad shape."[15]

The drouth did not limit itself to the Pecos. Indeed, it gripped 100 counties in Texas,[16] where the average rainfall in 1917 was an incredible 29 percent less than what it had been even in 1886, the height of the Big Dry.[17] The range along the Colorado River in Borden County, 115 miles northeast of Horsehead Crossing, was a typical casualty of this latest pestilence.

"There was a termite on every blade of grass, and everything laying on the ground was covered with termites," recalled Lonnie Griffith, then a young cowhand on the fifty-three-section Bar N Ranch twelve miles south of Gail. "They just cleaned the country—there wasn't no grass, there wasn't nothing. Mesquite beans would fall off the tree, [and] you had to hurry up and get them or they'd cover them up. I never saw that before in my life. It didn't rain, period, for about eighteen months."[18]

Billy Rankin, who lived on his family's ranch astride the Midland-Upton county line about forty-five miles northeast of the Pecos, saw similar devastation.

"In '16, '17, '18, altogether in the two years and eight months [of drouth], it did not rain enough on that property to wet you one time in a light summer shirt," he remembered.[19]

The Enterprise and Pecos Times, overly optimistic, boldly proclaimed the drouth "broken" in early August 1917, when "splendid" but isolated showers struck Reeves County.[20] After ensuing, widespread downpours (reportedly the best in ten months) on August 14, the newspaper observed that, should another rain come soon, the Pecos country would have fine winter range and ranchers would be "on easy street by spring."[21] Despite the jubilation, the woes for stockmen were far from over, for the official .77 inch of August precipitation in Reeves County only bent—not broke—the Big Thirst.

Meanwhile, the search for grass intensified. In early August, W. D. Hudson purchased a large ranch in northern New Mexico and made plans to pasture some of his remaining cattle on its ample grasses.[22] About the same time, Tom Wheat traded his Saragosa ranch for a spread near Deming, New Mexico.[23]

As fall approached, signaling the start of the second year of drouth, cowhands were driving herd after herd to the nearest railroad stop. There, they loaded the bellowing animals onto cattle cars by the hundreds for the long ride out of this searing land. In a three-day span in mid-September, twenty-four cars of cattle and four cars of sheep rolled out of the Pecos country of Texas, most of them bound upriver for Artesia and Roswell, New Mexico. Another twenty cars of cattle headed out from Riverton en route west to Clint and fields irrigated from the Rio Grande. Already, wise observers recognized the writing on the wall. "These movements, it is thought," said *The Enterprise and Pecos Times* of September 21, "will continue until most of the stock in West Texas have been placed on better ranges."[24]

Nevertheless, that same edition of the newspaper—for the second time in seven weeks—reported the drouth broken, thanks to what it termed the "finest rains . . . for fully a year." Reeves County's 1.57 inches, in fact, constituted more than one-third of the 4.46 inches recorded in the county the preceding twelve months. The development was promising enough for the newspaper to proclaim that "winter grass is assured."[25] Little could anyone have realized, however, that the skies would yield only a trace of precipitation the rest of the year, and a mere .23 inch the next seven months.

It indeed was a Big Thirst, unlike any that cowhands had ever seen on the Pecos.

Saragosa rancher A. J. Carpenter, when asked how things were in his sector, answered with a bluntness shared by many: "We're gradually starving to death."[26] Nevertheless, a few cattlemen were able to maintain a measure of levity. Lee Windham quipped that the only thing he had raised on his southern New Mexico ranch during the year was his new mustache, but that he intended to "stay and see how long they could do without rain before starving out."[27]

Never were perseverance and optimism more important to the Pecos cattle industry. Seeking a taker for barren range land, the F. P. Richburg Land and Rental Company of Reeves County noted on October 19 that "it is not going to stay dry always."[28] On the same day, *The Enterprise and Pecos Times* observed that, "regardless of [the drouth] . . . there is no better stock country in Texas than this section. . . . The older cowmen of the country . . . have all made and lost money, but those who have stayed with the game are all satisfied and growing steadily in wealth."[29]

Few stockmen shipped cattle in October 1917,[30] but it wasn't due to stubbornness or because they had seen improvement in isolated sections of the range, though that was true of the Davis Mountains, Kent, upper Toyah Creek, Orla, and the Reeves-Culberson county line west of Toyah.[31] There was also the difficulty of locating suitable pasturage and securing the necessary rail cars.[32] Rancher Elmer Wadley, upon returning in early October from a search for grazing land in the Southwest, reported that pasturage was scarce in New Mexico and that landowners in grass-rich Arizona were waiting to take advantage of cowmen from drouth-stricken territories.[33]

Late in October, with the Great War raging in Europe, the federal government finally recognized the grave consequences of potentially losing 1.5 million Texas cattle to the drouth.[34] "Their loss," said one contemporary news report, "would [be] . . . serious . . . to the country at large." Not only did the United States Food Administration need to eke out enough food for U.S. forces in Europe and for their allies, they had to do so without upsetting the supply at home.[35]

With virtually no cattle cars available on the T&P or the Kansas City, Mexico, and Orient Railway—and an estimated 6,000 cars needed to remove 150,000 animals from Texas and southern New Mexico—the United States Food Administration requisitioned 1,500 cars from the Illinois Central; the Chicago, Burlington & Quincy; and the Missouri Pacific lines. Two weeks later, the government commandeered an additional 3,500 cars.[36] Nevertheless, even as they arrived in Texas, regulations hindered their immediate use. Because the cars had passed through quarantine sections to the east, they were shunted to a side track at Baird, 250 miles shy of the Pecos, for cleaning and disinfecting. As workers could treat but twenty-five to thirty cars per day, Pecos stockmen were still handicapped in moving their ever-weakening herds.[37]

With cottonseed cake selling at $56 to $60 per ton—a price unaffordable for many ranchers with starving animals—cottonseed crushers and cattlemen conferred in mid-November in Houston. There, they decided on a price of $45.50 per ton for 30 percent protein cake, and $53.50 for the 43 percent variety.[38] About the same time, the Food Administration seized 15,000 tons of cottonseed cake and meal, originally intended for export to neutral countries, and advised cattlemen that the feed would be ready to ship to drouth areas (to which it was limited) from Galveston on November 19.[39] The government also ordered railway companies to give the feed priority in car supply and in transportation to all points in Texas and New Mexico.[40]

With ranchers in dire need of ready cash, national banks determined that, as of November 20, more than $50 million was available for loan throughout the 100-county drouth district of Texas.[41] Still, for outfits with large herds, feeding was a "heartbreaking and pocket-breaking business," reported the *El Paso Times*.[42]

As cattle cars finally rolled into the Pecos country in late November and December, many ranches chose to ship rather than feed. Numerous outfits found alfalfa pasturage in the Clint region, the destination of dozens of cars of cattle from Reeves County alone. Other stockmen had no choice but to load their herds on cars bound for the Fort Worth or Kansas City markets, where rock-bottom prices prevailed.[43] Even if a bony animal survived the march to the nearest rail stop, however, there was no guarantee it would endure the cramped, jostling ride to the sale ring. On November 27, for example, workers at Big Spring removed seventy-two dead cows from east- bound shipments on the T&P.[44]

Many horses, as well, rode the weaving cars, en route to East Texas farms where they would wear the harness the rest of their lives.[45] As yet another drouthy winter blew in, other horses—such as the remuda on the Sam Brown–Bill Tucker spread twenty-five miles southeast of Midland—seemed destined for the vultures. In late December, it fell upon Dewitt "Shag" Ethridge and twenty-year-old Tyson Midkiff to drive the Brown-Tucker animals west for the Pecos and the promise of better grass beyond.

"I think we had about thirty or forty head," Midkiff recalled more than seven decades later. "They was pretty poor, too—they was about to starve to death. And we drove them across to meet these other boys at the Horsehead Crossing. I think it took us about four and a half days to get over there. We just turned them loose [at night]. If there was a water trough some place, they wouldn't go very far. We met them boys that we was delivering the horses to there on the other side, right at the river."

At legendary Horsehead, Midkiff saw for himself the drouth's devastating impact on the once-raging Pecos.

"The river had gone down a lot . . . on account of it being so dry—it hadn't rained in a long time. I don't think the river was much over a foot, foot and a half deep. [The horses] just went right on across; it wasn't no trouble. I remember riding my horse across it and then turned around and rode back."[46]

Spending two days on the return ride, Midkiff reached his family's ranch in south Midland County in early January 1918 and undertook a cattle-feeding operation[47] under sunny, spring-like skies. On January 9, the mercury climbed to a balmy 73 degrees along the banks of the Pecos in the Barstow region. As the sun rose the next morning, quickly warming the east-lying cow town of Midland to a promising 56 degrees by 9 a.m.[48] or so, only seasoned cowmen may have guessed by the deep indigo sky to the north that trouble was on the way. Midkiff was among those caught unawares.

"We had one pasture about three miles to the southeast of the house," he remembered. "Me and my brother had a good ol' span of mules and a little old hack. So we put some cake on that, and that spell hit about 9 or 10 o'clock in the morning—little ol' dry snow and it was blowing hard. There was a fence on the prairie, and six cows balled up against that and froze to death. Down in the corner, there was a mesquite and greasewood thicket, and we went down there and set an old rat's nest two or three feet high on fire. Them cows would come up around it. We fed them cake and started back to the house."[49]

Wagoning into the teeth of a snowstorm driven by forty- to sixty-mile-per-hour winds,[50] Midkiff and his brother soon realized that their lives were in danger.

"We'd get off behind that buggy and trot a little piece, then we'd get in it and ride a little piece. And we got back to the house three miles, but dat-gum, we liked to not made it."

As the day wore on, conditions worsened on the Midkiff homestead.

"It got to about 12 degrees below zero," recalled Midkiff. "We had a dirt tank there, and you could ride a horse across it. That ice got nearly a foot thick on that thing."[51]

Meanwhile, the winter storm roared through the city of Pecos with a vengeance. With the morning breaking warm, school children left home without wraps, but by 9:30 a.m., reported *The Enterprise and Pecos Times*, "a north wind began its whining whistle, accompanied by snow." By noon, a blizzard blinded the area, eventually depositing almost a foot of snow and rendering the T&P rails impassable for trains.[52]

On to the north on Sid Kyle's Pecos River spread, sixteen-year-old cowhand Bill Eddins felt the bite of a chill factor estimated at 50 degrees below zero.

"Gosh, it was cold," he remembered seventy-one years later. "But it was colder north of us [reportedly 30 below zero in southeastern New Mexico].... There was two or three people ... froze to death up there in New Mexico."[53]

The storm was especially intense downriver in the Castle Gap–King Mountain vicinity.

"I lived over at Upland [east of Castle Gap in Upton County]," recalled Paul Patterson, who would later cowboy in the region. "... At the courthouse square, the snow drifted over the [five-foot-high] fence and stayed on the ground for about three weeks. It was a sixteen-inch snow. ... Two sheepherders froze to death on King Mountain ... and a bunch of cattle froze over there standing on their feet."[54]

Weakened by the protracted drouth, many other cattle perished as well, some after losing their hooves to frostbite. For a considerable number of ranchers, losses were devastating.[55]

"An old fellow, Bill Underwood, that had country leased from my granddaddy, lost damn near all that he had," recalled Billy Rankin.[56]

Stockmen in the sheltered Davis Mountains fortunately escaped significant loss,[57] but the Collier-Love Ranch and other outfits in the Guadalupe Mountains foothills were hit hard. Reported *The Enterprise and Pecos Times*: "Many of the old sisters [cows], enfeebled by age and the long drouth, cashed in their checks and passed on to additional usefulness in furnishing leather for soldiers' shoes, and fertilizer for the cotton planters."[58]

Nevertheless, a few Reeves County cattlemen—desperate for precipitation of any kind—took encouragement in the .16 inch or less of snow-melt which had moistened the ground in the area. Said one cowman, "If the drouth continued, they [the cattle] would have all died after we went broke feeding them. This is a lifesaver."[59]

Still, hard times were far from over. Legislator and newspaperman Don H. Biggers of Lubbock soon proclaimed the West "bankrupt" and in need of federal aid, prompting a defensive January editorial in the *Abilene Reporter*. "It is not so," said the newspaper. "True, we have been pretty hard hit by the drouth, but the West has ever been able to withstand hard knocks. ... We don't want federal financial aid. ... Give us plenty of rain and the people will do everything else that needs to be done."[60]

But rain, or the lack thereof, remained the problem. February brought a mere .07 inch to the city of Pecos, and March and April only a trace. While the Davis Mountains and its foothills were recovering,[61] the Pecos range abided as barren as ever, except in isolated sections.[62] In an attempt to relieve ranchers of the expense of cottonseed meal and cake, the Food Administration considered soliciting bids on Louisiana rice straw.[63] Meanwhile, A. B. Cooksey of Reeves County cut his feed costs in half by supplementing cake with shredded bear grass. After a fifty-day trial on a herd of 300 purebred Herefords, he reported that the native plant was as nutritious as dry silage or sorghum fodder.[64]

Nevertheless, cowmen continued depleting the region of cattle in January and early February, dispatching the animals to the Fort Worth market or, occasionally, to spreads as distant as Arizona.[65] Finally on February 12, with the range improving in northern Reeves County after snow and local rains, Thomas B. Jones imported the first significant numbers of cattle to the region in fourteen months. On the west bank of the Pecos at Arno, near the old Hash Knife headquarters southwest of present Mentone, cowhands unloaded seven cars of Pecos cattle which Jones had wintered in Clint.[66]

As cowhands bedded down for the night of May 2, however, the Big Thirst reigned as intense as ever. In the previous eighteen months, dating all the way back to October 1916, the city of Pecos had recorded a mere 2.90 inches of precipitation, while rainfall on the east-lying range had been all but nonexistent. Twice after rains in the summer of 1917, many Reeves County cowmen had believed the drouth broken, only to face a fall, winter, and spring as dry as the hell to which buffalo hunters had once compared the Pecos. There was little hint that this night would be any different.

Then, a drop at a time, it came—rain. It fell slowly, from Roswell southward to the lower Pecos and from El Paso eastward to Stanton, and, said *The Enterprise and Pecos Times*, "the dry and parched earth drank it up . . . , letting none get away."[67] Finally, cowhands would awaken to a clouded sun rising over a land in which there was again hope.

"The stockmen . . . are elated," the newspaper reported on May 3, "and are . . . wearing the broadest smiles in many months. . . . [The rain] will do a world of good towards boosting the morale of our stockmen, who have suffered the heaviest losses . . . at any time in the history of the country."[68]

Still, one good soaking rain would not immediately bring grass, but at least the downpour was a start. So encouraged was Reeves County rancher Clay Slack, who had been in Colorado seeking range when the showers had come, that he decided against moving his cattle.[69]

Nevertheless, many ranchers continued sending their herds elsewhere, even with the official .97 inch of rain in Pecos in May, and the .81 inch in June and July. The Midland-Odessa range was the first to bounce back, prompting numerous Pecos country ranchers to ship cattle to the region in late June and July.[70] Then in late August, with 2.05 inches of rain muddying Reeves County and the flats up and down the Pecos, massive herds finally began to return to the river which had nurtured them.[71]

For many cowmen, however, the moisture had come too late.

"[West Texas ranchers] lost [from] one-half of our cattle to all of them," noted Julius D. Henderson. "I did not lose but four cows, but I only got one calf out of 125 cows in 1918. I got 95 percent calf crop in 1917, but . . . I got very little for them. . . . When the rain come in 1918, I was $13,000 in debt. That is the way it has always been in this country. Every time we get on easy street, a drouth has hit us."[72]

The Big Thirst also had exacted a severe toll on the land.

"It ruined a lot of this West Texas country—it never was as good afterwards," observed cowhand Billy Rankin seven decades later.[73]

At times, the devastation manifested itself in dramatic ways before the relentless Pecos winds.

"After 1917 we often had sandstorms that lasted twenty-four hours, some thirty-six, and a few went forty-eight hours," noted Henderson. "They were hard enough to wreck windmills. . . . In 1919 one bowled over forty windmills in Odessa. Sometimes there was electricity in those winds, and it just popped and cracked. . . . Wagon cooks often could not cook a meal when they [the sandstorms] were bad. I have seen them so bad, we had to turn roundup loose. We could not see how to work cattle after we rounded them up."[74]

But at least, for a while, there was still a need for a cowboy of the Pecos. All too soon, his golden moment in history would pass.

NOTES

Unless otherwise indicated, all towns, counties, and map quadrangles throughout notes
are in Texas.

1. "1933 Driest Year Save One," The *Pecos Enterprise and Gusher*, 27 July 1934.
2. Composite of statements in Henderson, "Life of an Oldtimer," book two, 6–7, and
book four, 8.
3. Henderson, "Life of an Oldtimer," book two, 7.
4. Newland, interview.
5. "West Texas Gets Fine Rain," *The Enterprise*, 13 October 1916. The rainfall total,
which was for the entire month of October, is from "1933 Driest Year Save One," *The
Pecos Enterprise and Gusher*, 27 July 1934. Unless otherwise stated, all precipitation totals
in this chapter are from that same article.
6. *The Enterprise*, 1 and 8 December 1916.
7. "Reeves County in Severe Storm Clutches," *The Enterprise*, 19 January 1917.
8. Henderson, "Life of an Oldtimer," book 2, 6; and "25,000 Tons of Cake Sent West
to Save Cattle," *The Enterprise*, 11 January 1918.
9. *The Enterprise*, 4 May 1917.
10. *The Enterprise*, 11 May 1917.
11. "Some Weather," *The Enterprise*, 11 May 1917.
12. "Sold Five Carloads of Cattle at Fort Worth" and "Took 300 Cows to Barstow," *The
Enterprise*, 1 June 1917.
13. *The Enterprise*, 22 June and 10 August 1917.
14. *The Enterprise and Pecos Times* (hereinafter, *E&PT*), 15 June 1917.
15. "Fine Rains Fall in Various Sections," *E&PT*, 29 June 1917.
16. "Texas Banks Able to Give Drouth Relief," *E&PT*, 11 January 1918.
17. J. W. Williams, "A Statistical Study of the Drouth of 1886," *WTHA Year Book* Vol.
21 (October 1945), 108.
18. Griffith, interview.
19. Rankin, interview, 9 August 1989.
20. "Long Drouth in This Section Is Broken," *E&PT*, 3 August 1917.
21. "West Texas Comes Into Its Own," *E&PT*, 17 August 1917.
22. "Purchases Large Ranch," *E&PT*, 17 August 1917.
23. *E&PT*, 17 August 1917.
24. "Cattle Shipments During the Past Week," *E&PT*, 21 September 1921.
25. "Fine Rains in This Vicinity Past Week," *E&PT*, 21 September 1917.
26. "Toyah Valley Items," *E&PT*, 12 October 1917.
27. *E&PT*, 12 October 1917.
28. *E&PT*, 19 October 1917.
29. "Biggest Cattle and Ranch Sale in Years," *E&PT*, 19 October 1917.
30. Based on my study of *E&PT* for October 1917.
31. "Range Conditions Improved," *E&PT*, 28 September 1917; *E&PT*, 5 October
1917; *E&PT*, 12 October 1917; and "Biggest Cattle and Ranch Sale," *E&PT*, 19
October 1917.

32. "Back from New Mexico," *E&PT*, 12 October 1917; and "Rushing Cars to Texas and New Mexico," 2 November 1917.

33. "Back from New Mexico," *E&PT*, 12 October 1917.

34. "Rushing Cars to Texas and New Mexico," *E&PT*, 2 November 1917; and "25,000 Tons of Cake Sent West to Save Cattle," *E&PT*, 11 January 1918.

35. "25,000 Tons," *E&PT*, 11 January 1918.

36. "Rushing Cars," *E&PT*, 2 November 1917; "Cars for Drouth Area," *E&PT*, 16 November 1917; and "25,000 Tons," *E&PT*, 11 January 1918.

37. "Rushing Cars," *E&PT*, 2 November 1917.

38. "25,000 Tons," *E&PT*, 11 January 1918.

39. "Seized Cottonseed Cake Ready for Cars," *E&PT*, 23 November 1917. By January 11, 1918, the U.S. Food Administration had made 25,000 tons of cotton seed meal and cake available to drouth-stricken areas. See "25,000 Tons," *E&PT*, 11 January 1918.

40. "25,000 Tons," *E&PT*, 11 January 1918.

41. "Texas Banks Able to Give Drouth Relief," *E&PT*, 11 January 1918.

42. "U.S. Commissioner at Pecos Says Rain Needed," *E&PT* (originating at *El Paso Times*), 30 November 1917.

43. *E&PT*, 9, 16, 23, and 30 November, and 7 and 21 December 1917.

44. "Toll of the Drouth," *E&PT* (originating at *Big Spring Herald*), 30 November 1917.

45. E&PT, 2, 16, and 30 November and 28 December 1917.

46. Composite of statements, Tyson Midkiff, taped interviews with author, Rankin, 9 August 1989, 11 December 1990, and 29 April 1991.

47. Midkiff, interviews, 9 August 1989 and 29 April 1991.

48. Susan G. Denney, "Oral Recollections of the January 1918 Blizzard," *WTHA Year Book* Vol. 65 (1989), 115–116.

49. Composite of statements, Midkiff, interview, 9 August 1989.

50. Estimate of wind speed is from Denney, "Oral Recollections," 113.

51. Midkiff, interview, 9 August 1989.

52. *E&PT*, 11 January 1918.

53. L. B. Eddins, interview. The reported temperature in New Mexico is from Patterson, interview, 13 November 1989, Crane County.

54. Patterson, interview, 13 November 1989.

55. Denney, "Oral Recollections," 119–120.

56. Rankin, interview, 9 August 1989.

57. "Mountain Ranges in Fine Shape from Snow," *E&PT*, 18 January 1918.

58. *E&PT*, 25 January 1918.

59. *E&PT*, 11 January 1918.

60. "Stockmen of the West Not Bankrupt," *E&PT* (originating at *Abilene Reporter*), 25 January 1918.

61. *E&PT*, 15 and 29 March 1918.

62. *E&PT* reported on 15 February 1918 that range conditions in Reeves County had improved "considerably" after recent snows and showers.

63. "25,000 Tons," *E&PT*, 11 January 1918.

64. "Shredded Bear Grass as a Future Feed," *E&PT*, 31 May 1918.

65. *E&PT*, 11, 18, and 25 January, and 1, 8, and 15 February 1918; and L. B. Eddins, interview.

66. "Stock Shipments Light During This Week," *E&PT*, 15 February 1918.

67. "Copious Rain Breaks Our Two-Year Drouth," *E&PT*, 3 May 1918.

68. Ibid.

69. *E&PT*, 10 May 1918.

70. *E&PT*, 28 June, and 5 and 12 July 1918.

71. "Cattle Movements During the Past Week," *E&PT*, 30 August 1918.

72. Henderson, "Life of an Oldtimer," book two, 6–7.

73. Rankin, interview, 9 August 1989.

74. Henderson, "Life of an Oldtimer," book four, 9.

Epilogue

In 1928 twenty-eight-year-old Chon Villalba and four other Scharbauer Cattle Company drovers pointed 100 bald-face cattle down into Horsehead Crossing on a drive from a Fort Stockton area ranch to Midland. As they splashed their horses across the Pecos, which rose belly-deep on their animals,[1] the men no doubt considered it just another weary day in the saddle, not a moment of significance. After all, they were cowboys, not soothsayers or historians. They could not have realized that they were undertaking perhaps the last old-time crossing of a herd at Horsehead, the site which epitomized the essence of this river of peril, pitfall, and pestilence.

As they felt the power of their horses carry them up through the mud of the far bank, they were doing more than leaving the Pecos behind. They were leaving a way of life behind, for changes were astir, wrought by mechanization. For several years already, feed wagons and chuck wagons had been giving way to motorized vehicles, and now cattle trucks were primed to snatch away the last bastion of cowboying—cattle driving. Soon, the pickup truck, not the horse, would rule the Pecos, which itself faced a lingering death from dams, irrigation, sloughed banks, pollution, and salt cedars.

It had been a long ride for the cowboy of the Pecos, one that had carried him into the annals of not just history, but legend. For another decade or so, he would still have his moments—mere, fleeting ghosts of the old ways—but already the sunset was beckoning cowboy and river alike.

Note
1. Chon Villalba, taped interview with author, Fort Stockton, 9 February 1990.

BIBLIOGRAPHY

INTERVIEWS BY AUTHOR

Armentrout, Steve, Fort Stockton, Texas, 1 September 1989.

Baker, Louis, Coke County, Texas, 14 February 1990.

Blasingame, Tom, Armstrong County, Texas, 26 July 1989.

Boren, Walter, Post, Texas, 8 August 1990.

Coggins, Otis D., Alpine, Texas, 3 March 1990.

Davis, Ralph, Sterling City, Texas, 4 March 1989.

Durham, Will, Sterling County, Texas, 25 February 1989.

Eddins, L. B. "Bill," Kermit, Texas, 5 September 1989.

Fairweather, J. E., Midland, Texas, 1 March 1989.

Griffith, Lonnie, Big Spring, Texas, 30 March 1983.

Harris, Ethel Pitt, Albuquerque, New Mexico, 23 May 1985.

Hinton, Harwood, Midland, Texas, 9 July 1996.

Hubbs, Barney, Pecos, Texas, 19 March 1992.

Mankin, Green, Mills County, Texas, 14 September 1989.

Mayes, Hudson "Bud," Ozona, Texas, 22 February 1990 and 30 April 1991.

Midkiff, Tyson, Rankin, Texas, 9 August 1989, 11 December 1990, and 29 April 1991.

Owens, Claude, Fort Stockton, Texas, 2 March 1990.

Patterson, Paul, Crane County, Texas, 13 November 1989; Crane, Texas, 29 April 1991; Pecos, Texas, 1 July 1993.

Powers, Ted, San Angelo, Texas, 23 August 1989.

Proctor, Leonard, Midland, Texas, 2 March 1989.

Rankin, Billy, Rankin, Texas, 9 August 1989 and 29 April 1991.

Reding, Gid, Fort Stockton, Texas, 1 September 1989.

Smith, Gregory Scott, Fort Sumner, New Mexico, 17 February 1996.

Townsend, Bill, Odessa, Texas, 3 August 1995.

Villalba, Chon, Fort Stockton, Texas, 9 February 1990.

Witt, Jim, Loving, New Mexico, 17 July 1993 and 22 July 1995.

MISCELLANEOUS TAPED INTERVIEWS OR TRANSCRIPTS IN AUTHOR'S POSSESSION

Eddins, Carl M., place not known, 8 June 1968 (by Paul Patterson), Southwest Collection, Texas Tech University, Lubbock, Texas.

Hubbs, Barney, Pecos, Texas, 21 October 1991 (by Mike Cox).

Newland, Cliff, Upton County, Texas, 23 August 1964 (by Elmer Kelton).

Ussery, Huling, Carlsbad, New Mexico, 22 February 1982 (by Richard Mason), Southwest Collection, Texas Tech University, Lubbock).

INTERVIEW TRANSCRIPTS, NITA STEWART HALEY MEMORIAL LIBRARY, MIDLAND, TEXAS

Armstrong, Fount, Odessa, 2 February 1965 (by J. Evetts Haley).

Arnett, D. N., Colorado City, Texas, 18 October 1926 (by J. Evetts Haley).

Ballard, Charles, Luna, New Mexico, 9 June 1939 (by J. Evetts Haley and Hervey Chesley).

Barron, Mrs. J. H., Midland, date not known (by J. Evetts Haley).

Beal, H. D. "Nick," Gail, Texas, 11 September 1931 (by J. Evetts Haley).

Bell, Irbin H., El Paso, 18 March 1927 (by J. Evetts Haley).

Boyd, W. H., Sweetwater, 24 January 1932 (by J. Evetts Haley).

Calohan, Lod, Kansas City, Missouri, 1 January 1926 (by J. Evetts Haley).

Carr, W. J. D. "Bill," place not known, 1947 (by J. Evetts Haley).

Carter, Mrs. J. W., Dimmit, Texas, 31 October 1927 (by J. Evetts Haley).

Casey, Robert Adam, Picacho, New Mexico, 25 June 1937 (by J. Evetts Haley).

Cochran, Walter, Midland, Texas, date not known (by J. Evetts Haley).

Crosby, R. H., Kenna, New Mexico, 4 August 1937 (by J. Evetts Haley)

Dills, Lucius, Roswell, New Mexico, 5 August 1937 (by J. Evetts Haley).

Goodnight, Charles, Clarendon, Texas, 5 June 1925, 8 April 1927, and 12 September 1928 (by J. Evetts Haley).

Goodnight, Charles, site not recorded, 14 December 1928 (by J. Evetts Haley).

Graham, E. V., place and date not known (by J. Evetts Haley).

Holt, O. B., Sr., Midland, 3 January 1927 (by J. Evetts Haley).

Hayes, Mose, San Antonio, 3 March 1935 (by J. Evetts Haley).

Hill, H. M., Midland, Texas, 9 September 1931 (by J. Evetts Haley).

Hart, J. D., and Beverly, Bob, ranch near Lovington, New Mexico and Monument, New Mexico, 24 June 1937 (by J. Evetts Haley).

Holmsley, W. H., Midland, 17 October 1926 (by J. Evetts Haley).

Huffman, Junction, Texas, 30 November 1927 (by J. Evetts Haley).

Johnson, J. Arthur, Midland, Texas, 27 March 1946 (by J. Evetts Haley).

Johnson, Mrs. Woody, Pecos, 9 January 1927 (by J. Evetts Haley).

Jones, James P., Rocky Arroyo, New Mexico, 13–14 January 1927 (by J. Evetts Haley).

Knowles, H., place not known, 21 November 1936 (by J. Evetts Haley).

Liles, M. L. "Mike," Kenna, New Mexico, 4 August 1937 (by J. Evetts Haley).

Lloyd, Frank, Tularosa, New Mexico, 12 June 1939 (by J. Evetts Haley and Hervey Chesley).

McLendon, W. E., Clovis, New Mexico, 16 January 1927 (by J. Evetts Haley).

McNairy, D. H. "Bob," Mineral Wells, Texas, 22 January 1932 (by J. Evetts Haley).

Millwee, J. K., Lubbock, 3 July 1932, and 13 September 1932 (by J. Evetts Haley).

Nichols, John, Lampasas, 15 May 1927 (by J. Evetts Haley).

Owen, W. R., Carlsbad, New Mexico, 12 August 1926, 12 January 1927, 2 March 1933, and 24 June 1937 (by J. Evetts Haley).

Owens, George, Pecos, Texas, 10 January 1927 (by J. Evetts Haley).

Rainey, Tom, Willcox, Arizona, 1 March 1945 (by J. Evetts Haley and Hervey Chesley).

Roberson, G. W., Vega, Texas, 30 June 1926 (by J. Evetts Haley).

Rumans, John, Amarillo, 13 December 1928 (by J. Evetts Haley).

Wier, W., and Beverly, Bob, Monument, New Mexico, 22 June 1937 (by J. Evetts Haley).

Windham, A. T., Pecos, Texas, 10 January 1927 (by J. Evetts Haley).

MILITARY RECORDS

Fort Lancaster, Texas. Post returns, 1855–1861. National Archives, Washington, D.C.

Fort Stockton, Texas. Post returns, 1859–1861, 1867–1886. National Archives, Washington, D.C.

———. Letters and telegrams sent, letters and telegrams received, journal of marches, scouts, and expeditions, 1867–1886. (National Archives microfilm) Fort Stockton Public Library, Fort Stockton, Texas.

U.S. Department of War, Civil Works Map File, Q-154, Record Group 77, National Archives, Washington, D.C.

U.S. COURT OF CLAIMS

Indian Depredations Claim Number 5388, James Chisum, Administrator of Estate of John S. Chisum, versus the United States and Comanche and Mescalero Apache Indians, National Archives, Washington, D.C.

MAPS

(U.S. Geological Survey, 7.5-minute series, topographic, unless otherwise indicated)

Acme Quadrangle, New Mexico, 1962, rev. 1982.

Bonner Lake Quadrangle, New Mexico, 1968.

Carlsbad East, New Mexico, 1985.

Carlsbad West Quadrangle, New Mexico, 1985.

Conejo Creek East Quadrangle, New Mexico, 1967.

Cottonwood Draw Quadrangle, New Mexico, 1982.

Deering Place Quadrangle, New Mexico, 1967.

Eighteenmile Hill Quadrangle, New Mexico, 1982.

Eightmile Draw Quadrangle, New Mexico, 1982.

La Espia Peak Quadrangle, New Mexico, 1982.

Fort Sumner East Quadrangle, New Mexico, 1982.

Grandfalls Southwest Quadrangle, Texas, 1969.

Lake McMillan South Quadrangle, New Mexico, 1955.

Loving Quadrangle, New Mexico, 1985.

Malaga Quadrangle, New Mexico, 1985.

Melena Quadrangle, New Mexico, 1962, rev. 1982.
Mentone Quadrangle, Texas, 1961, rev. 1981.
Orla Quadrangle, Texas, 1:62,500, 1931, reprinted 1949.
Orla Northeast Quadrangle, Texas, 1968.
Orla Southeast Quadrangle, Texas, 1961.
Otis Quadrangle, New Mexico, 1985.
Pecos Quadrangle, Texas, 1:250,000, 1954, limited revision 1963.
Quito Draw Quadrangle, Texas, 1963, rev. 1981.
Red Bluff Quadrangle, Eddy County, New Mexico, 1985.
Rio Pecos Ranch Quadrangle, Texas, 1963, rev. 1981.
Seven Rivers Quadrangle, New Mexico, 1954.

BOOKS

Adams, Ramon F. *Western Words: A Dictionary of the American West*. Norman: University of Oklahoma Press, rev. edition, 1968.

Allen, Jules Verne, *Cowboy Lore*. San Antonio: The Naylor Company, 1943, 6th printing.

Armes, George A. *Ups and Downs of an Army Officer*. Washington: publisher not known, 1900.

Bartlett, John Russell. *Personal Narrative of Explorations and Incidents in Texas, New Mexico, California, Sonora and Chihuahua, 1850–1853, Vol. 1*. Chicago: The Rio Grande Press, Inc., 1965. Originally published, 1854.

Bell, Young. *Seventy Years in the Cow Business in Texas, New Mexico, Old Mexico, and Arizona*. Pecos: Elliott Printing Company, 4th edition, 1987.

Bieber, Ralph P., ed. *Exploring Southwestern Trails 1846–1854*. Glendale: Arthur H. Clark Company, 1938.

Biggers, Don H. *From Cattle Range to Cotton Patch*. Bandera, Texas: Frontier Times, reprint, 1944. Originally published, 1904.

Bolton, Herbert Eugene. *Spanish Exploration in the Southwest*. New York: Barnes and Noble, Inc., reprint, 1952.

Clarke, Mary Whatley. *John Simpson Chisum: Jinglebob King of the Pecos*. Austin: Eakin Press, 1984.

Conkling, Roscoe P., and Conkling, Margaret B. *The Butterfield Overland Mail, 1857–1869, Vol. 1*. Glendale: Arthur H. Clark Company, 1947.

Cook, Jim Lane, as told to Pearce, T. M. *Lane of the Llano*. Boston: Little, Brown & Company, 1936.

Cox, James. *Historical and Biographical Record of the Cattle Industry and the Cattlemen of Texas and Adjacent Territory*. St. Louis: Woodward and Tiernan Printing Company, 1895.

Daggett, Marsha Lea, ed. *Pecos County History*. Canyon: Pecos County Historical Commission, Staked Plains Press, 1984.

Dearen, Patrick. *The Big Drift*. Fort Worth: Texas Christian University Press, 2014.

———. *Bitter Waters: The Struggles of the Pecos River*. Norman: University of Oklahoma Press, 2016.

———. *Castle Gap and the Pecos Frontier*. Fort Worth: Texas Christian University Press, 1988.

———. *Crossing Rio Pecos*. Fort Worth: Texas Christian University Press, 1996.

———. *Devils River: Treacherous Twin to the Pecos, 1535-1900*. Fort Worth: Texas Christian University Press, 2011.

———. *Halff of Texas*. Austin: Eakin Press, 2000.

———. *Portraits of the Pecos Frontier, Revised Edition*. Lubbock: Texas Tech University Press, 1999.

Dobie, J. Frank. *A Vaquero of the Brush County*. New York: Grosset and Dunlap Publishers, reprint, n.d., originally published by Southwest Press, 1929.

———. *The Longhorns*. Boston: Little, Brown & Company, 1941, 16th printing.

Haley, J. Evetts. *Charles Goodnight: Cowman and Plainsman*. Norman: University of Oklahoma Press, 10th Printing, 1987.

———, ed. *The Diary of Michael Erskine*. Midland: The Nita Stewart Haley Memorial Library, 1979.

———. *Fort Concho and the Texas Frontier*. San Angelo: San Angelo Standard-Times, 1952.

———. *George W. Littlefield, Texan*. Norman: University of Oklahoma Press, 1943.

———. *Rough Times-Tough Fiber*. Canyon: Palo Duro Press, 1976.

The New Handbook of Texas. Six volumes. Austin: The Texas State Historical Association, 1996.

Hinkle, James F. *Early Days of a Cowboy on the Pecos*. Santa Fe: Stagecoach Press, reprint, 1965. Originally published, 1937.

A History of Crockett County. San Angelo: Crockett County Historical Society, Anchor Publishing Company, 1976.

Holmes, Kenneth L., ed. and compiler. *Covered Wagon Women: Diaries and Letters from the Western Trails 1840–1890, Vol. 9 1864–1868*. Spokane: Arthur H. Clark Company, 1990.

Hunter, J. Marvin, ed. and compiler. *The Trail Drivers of Texas*. Austin: University of Texas Press, reprint, 1985.

Klasner, Lily. *My Girlhood Among Outlaws*. Tucson: University of Arizona Press, 1972.

Lesley, Lewis Burt, ed. *Uncle Sam's Camels: The Journal of May Humphreys Stacey*. Cambridge: Harvard University Press, 1929.

Millard, F. S. *A Cowpuncher of the Pecos*. J. Marvin Hunter, n.d.

Myres, Sandra L., ed. *Ho for California! Women's Overland Diaries from the Huntington Library*. San Marino: Huntington Library, 1980.

Newcomb, W. W. Jr. *The Indians of Texas*. Austin: University of Texas Press, 1961.

Nolan, Frederick. *The Lincoln County War: A Documentary History*. Norman: University of Oklahoma Press, 1992.

Ormsby, Waterman L. *The Butterfield Overland Mail*. San Marino: Huntington Library, 1955.

Parsons, Chuck. *Clay Allison, Portrait of a Shootist*. Seagraves, Texas: Pioneer Book Publishers, 1983.

Raht, Carlysle Graham. *Reveries of a Fiddlefoot*. Odessa: The Rahtbooks Company, 1970.

Reports of Explorations and Surveys to Ascertain the Most Practicable and Economical Route for a Railroad from the Mississippi River to the Pacific Ocean, Vol. II, 33rd Cong., 2nd sess., House of Representatives Executive Document No. 91. Washington: 1855.

Reports of the Secretary of War with Reconnaissance of Routes from San Antonio to El Paso, 31st Cong., 1st sess., Senate Executive Document No. 64. Washington: 1850.

Richardson, Albert D. *Beyond the Mississippi*. Hartford, Conn.: American Publishing Company, 1867.

Taylor, Colonel Nathaniel Alston. *The Coming Empire or Two Thousand Miles in Texas on Horseback*. Dallas: Turner Company, reprint, 1936. Originally published, 1877.

The Texas Almanac for 1867. Galveston: The Galveston News.

Texas Almanac 1970–71. Dallas: A. H. Belo Corporation, 1969.

1990–1991 Texas Almanac. Dallas: The Dallas Morning News, 1989.

Wallace, Ernest, and Hoebel, E. Adamson. *The Comanches: Lords of the South Plains*. Norman: University of Oklahoma Press, 1986. Originally published, 1952.

Ward County 1887–1977. The Ward County Historical Commission, place and date not known.

Williams, Clayton. *Texas' Last Frontier: Fort Stockton and the Trans-Pecos, 1861–1895*. College Station: Texas A&M University Press, 1982.

Williams, O. W. *Pioneer Surveyor-Frontier Lawyer: The Personal Narrative of O. W. Williams, 1877–1902*. S. D. Myres, ed. El Paso: Texas Western College Press, 1966.

Wilson, John P. *Fort Sumner, New Mexico*. Santa Fe: Museum of New Mexico, 1974.

JOURNALS AND MAGAZINES

Baggett, W. R. "Early Day Irrigation Ditches On the Pecos." *Frontier Times* Vol. 19, No. 10 (July 1942): 364–366.

Cochran, W. C. "Walter C. Cochran's Memoirs of Early Day Cattlemen." Betty Orbeck, ed. *The Texas Permian Historical Annual* Vol. 1, No. 1 (August 1961): 36–42.

Cross, Cora Melton. "Tells of Indians and Cattle Thieves." *Frontier Times* Vol. 3, No. 2 (November 1925): 4–7, originally published in *Dallas Semi-Weekly News*, 21 May 1925.

Cureton, William E. "Westward I Go Free: The Memoirs of William E. Cureton." *Southwestern Historical Quarterly* Vol. 81, No. 2 (October 1977): 155–190.

Denney, Susan G. "Oral Recollections of the January 1918 Blizzard." *West Texas Historical Association Year Book* Vol. 65 (1989): 111-123.

Duke, Escal F., ed. "A Description of the Route from San Antonio to El Paso by Captain Edward S. Meyer." *West Texas Historical Association Year Book* 49 (1973): 128–141.

Ford, John S. "Letters and Documents, Opening Routes to El Paso, 1849." *Southwestern Historical Quarterly* 48, No. 3 (October 1944): 262–272.

Haley, J. Evetts, ed. "A Log of the Texas-California Cattle Trail, 1854." *Southwestern Historical Quarterly* 35, No. 3 (January 1932): 208–237.

Holden, W. C. "The Great Drouth of '86." *Frontier Times* Vol. 19, No. 10 (July 1942): 355–361.

Hunter, John Warren. "The Ill-fated Schnively Expedition." *Frontier Times* Vol. 2, No. 1 (October 1924): 18–19, originally published in *Hunter's Magazine*, 1911.

Kenner, Charles. "The Origins of the 'Goodnight' Trail Reconsidered." *Southwestern Historical Quarterly* 77, No. 3 (January 1974): 390–394.

Longfield, Kate. "Pioneer Woman Tells of a Perilous Trip." *Frontier Times* Vol. 14, No. 2 (November 1936): 56-57, originally published as "Three Days in 'Dobe Walls," *The Lampasas Record*, 3 September 1931.

Martin, Mabelle Eppard. "California Emigrant Roads through Texas." *Southwestern Historical Quarterly* 28, No. 4 (April 1925): 287–301.

Moses, Tad. "Some Texas Cattlemen and Their Operations." Pamphlet reprinted from *The Cattleman*, November and December 1947, and January and February 1948.

Murchison, Ivan, and Neighbours, K. F. "Ranching on the Pecos at the Turn of the Twentieth Century," *WTHA Year Book* Vol. 53 (1977): 127–136.

Myers, Lee. "Pope's Wells." *New Mexico Historical Review* 38, No. 4 (October 1963): 273–299.

Patterson, Paul. "A Forgotten Empire of the Pecos" (May 1943): 24–25.

"Record of Engagement with Hostile Indians in Texas, 1869–1882." *West Texas Historical Association Year Book* Vol. 9 (October 1933): 101–108.

Tankersley, Fayette. "Route Traversed by Southern Trail" (undated clipping from *Mertzon Weekly Star*). Haley Collection, Haley Library, Midland, Texas.

Taylor, T. U. "Olive and W. A. Peril." *Frontier Times* Vol. 53, No.4 (July 1979, reprint of 1939 article): 24–26, 42.

White, Grace Miller. "Oliver Loving, the First Trail Driver." *Frontier Times* Vol. 19, No. 7 (April 1942): 269–276.

Whitehurst, A. "Reminiscences of the Schnively Expedition of 1867." *Southwestern Historical Quarterly* Vol. 8, No. 3 (January 1905), 267–271.

Williams, Clayton. "The First Two Irrigation Projects on the Pecos River in Texas." *The Permian Historical Annual* 15 (December 1975): 2–6.

Williams, J. W. "A Statistical Study of the Drouth of 1886." *West Texas Historical Association Year Book* Vol. 21 (October 1945): 85–109.

LETTERS, FILES, AND MANUSCRIPTS

Beasley, Judge John, McCulloch County, to Gurley, General D. R., 10 July 1867, Throckmorton Papers, Texas State Library, Austin.

Bliss, Zenas R. "Reminiscences," five volumes. (Nita Stewart Haley Memorial Library, Midland, Texas).

Burnett, Ed. (J. Evetts Haley Collection, Nita Stewart Haley Memorial Library, Midland, Texas).

Burns, Rollie. "Reminiscence of 56 Years." (Nita Stewart Haley Memorial Library, Midland, Texas).

Carpenter, Marj. Letter to Patrick Dearen, 10 May 1996.

Cook, Jim. "Jim Cook's Dictation." (Nita Stewart Haley Memorial Library, Midland, Texas).

Goodnight, Charles. "The Cattle Trail and Its Effect on Finance and Civilization." (typescript, Nita Stewart Haley Memorial Library, Midland).

———. "Indians at Castle Canyon." (typescript statement, Charles Goodnight file, J. Evetts Haley Collection, Nita Stewart Haley Memorial Library, Midland).

———. "Recollections" (no volume number). (Charles Goodnight file, J. Evetts Haley Collection, Nita Stewart Haley Memorial Library, Midland).

———. "Recollections I." (Nita Stewart Haley Memorial Library, Midland).

———. "Recollections II." (Nita Stewart Haley Memorial Library, Midland).

Cochran, W. C. "A Trip to Montana in 1869." (Nita Stewart Haley Memorial Library, Midland, Texas).

Dow, Bob. "Daybreak All Over the World." (Nita Stewart Haley Memorial Library, Midland, Texas).

Dudley, Robert M. "Bob." Statement. (Mrs. Bob Duke file, J. Evetts Haley Collection, Nita Stewart Haley Memorial Library, Midland, Texas).

Harral, Edgar file. (Nita Stewart Haley Memorial Library, Midland, Texas).

Hart, J. D. (Nita Stewart Haley Memorial Library, Midland, Texas).

Hayter, Delmar. "The Crookedest River in the World: A Social and Economic Development of the Pecos River Valley from 1878 to 1950." (dissertation, Texas Tech University, Lubbock, Texas).

Henderson, Julius Drew. "The Life of an Oldtimer." (Special Collections, Library, University of Texas of the Permian Basin, Odessa, Texas.)

———. "Memories of an Old Cowboy" (Special Collections, Library, University of Texas of the Permian Basin, Odessa, Texas.)

Kellogg, Henry Pelham. "Pocket Journal Belonging to Henry Pelham Kellogg, Wheelock, Texas." (Nita Stewart Haley Memorial Library, Midland, Texas).

Loving, Oliver, to R. M. Garden, Weatherford, Texas, 22 May 1866. (Nita Stewart Haley Memorial Library, Midland).

Loy, M. H. Typescript dated 7 January 1930. (Nita Stewart Haley Memorial Library, Midland).

Newcomb, Samuel P. and Newcomb, Susan E. "Diary of Samuel P. Newcomb." (Nita Stewart Haley Memorial Library, Midland, Texas).

Nelson, O. H. "Judge O. H. Nelson, Pioneer: Breeder of High Grade Herefords." (Nita Stewart Haley Memorial Library, Midland, Texas).

Oden, Bill. "Cowboy Standards of 50 Years Ago." (typescript of an unidentified article in *Pecos Enterprise*, Nita Stewart Haley Memorial Library, Midland, Texas).

Oden, B. A. "Early Cowboy Days in New Mexico and Texas." (typescript, Nita Stewart Haley Memorial Library, Midland).

Pilgrim, Michael E., Archives I Reference Branch, Textual Reference Division, National Archives, Washington, D.C. to Patrick Dearen, Midland, Texas, 1 March 1996, in author's possession.

Rauk, James E., San Antonio, to Pease, Governor E. M., 17 August 1867, Pease Papers, Texas State Library, Austin.

NEWSPAPERS

The Colorado Tribune (Matagorda, Texas), 21 July 1854.

Dallas Morning News, 16 February 1896 and 8 June 1930.

The Fort Stockton Pioneer, 7 May, 23 July, and 17 September 1908.

Fort Worth Gazette, 16 January 1885.

The Galveston Journal, 26 May 1854.

Globe Livestock Journal (Dodge City, Kansas), 27 April and 25 May 1886.

Herald (San Antonio), 18 April, 20 and 26 of October, and 3, 10, 12, 17, 24, 26, and 27 November 1868.

The Highlander, 18 January 1973.

The Pecos Daily Times, 13 June 1911.

Pecos Enterprise (sometimes styled *The Enterprise* or *The Enterprise and Pecos Times*), 1916–1918, and 15 April 1932.

The Pecos Enterprise and Gusher, 27 July 1934.

The Pecos Independent and Enterprise, 16 November 1961 and 17 May 1962.

Rocky Mountain News (Denver, Colorado), 29 January 1886.

San Angelo Standard, 4 October 1884, 21 February and 9 May 1885; 24 April, 29 May, 12 June, 18 September, 2 October, and 16 October 1886; 16 April 1887; and 14 January and 28 April 1888.

San Antonio Daily Express, 19 July 1876, 25 May 1877, 13 January 1883.

The Staked Plain (Midland, Texas), 22 July 1886.

Texas Live Stock Journal, 10 January, 28 February, 28 March, and 5 December 1885; 8 May, 29 May and 10 July 1886.

Texas State Gazette, 21 April and 18 August 1855.

Times (Fort Morgan, Colorado), 15 January 1886.

Weekly Yellowstone Journal and Livestock Reporter (Miles City, Montana), 29 June, and 17 and 24 July 1886.

COLLECTIONS

J. Evetts Haley Collection, Nita Stewart Haley Memorial Library, Midland, Texas.

Clayton Wheat Williams Collection, Nita Stewart Haley Memorial Library, Midland.

DOCUMENTARY FILM

Dearen, Patrick, and Ely, Glen. With contributions by Cox, Mike. *Graveyard of the West: The Pecos River of Texas Where Myth Meets History*. Austin: Forest Glen TV Productions, Inc., 1993.

Index

About the Author

Patrick Dearen is the author of twenty-three books, including *The Last of the Old-Time Cowboys* and *Saddling Up Anyway* (both by Taylor Trade). Among his novels are a Spur Award finalist, *When Cowboys Die*, and the 2015 Spur Award–winning *The Big Drift*, which is set during the historic cattle migration of 1884. He lives in Midland, Texas. See patrickdearen.com for more information.